Scapegoating

A large cruise ship sinks after hitting some outcropping rocks near the shore. Who is to blame? In the face of negative events – accidents, corporate scandals, crises and bankruptcies – there are two organizational strategies for managing blame. The first is to take full responsibility for the event and to implement adequate corrective measures. The second is to create one or more scapegoats by transferring blame to some of the people directly involved in the event. In this way, the organization can appear blameless and avoid costly remedial interventions. Reappraising the *Costa Concordia* shipwreck and other well-known cases, Catino analyzes the processes and mechanisms behind creating the "organizational scapegoat". In doing so, Catino highlights the limits of explanations centered on guilt and individual solutions to organizational problems, and underlines the need for a different civic epistemology.

MAURIZIO CATINO is Professor of Sociology of Organizations in the Department of Sociology and Social Research at the University of Milan – Bicocca, Italy, and Visiting Scholar in the Department of Sociology at New York University. He is the author of *Organizational Myopia. Problems of Rationality and Foresight in Organizations* (Cambridge University Press, 2014), and *Mafia Organizations. The Visible Hand of Criminal Enterprise* (Cambridge University Press, 2019). He has also published in numerous journals, including *Social Networks, Organization Studies, European Journal of Sociology,* and *Crime and Justice.*

Scapegoating

How Organizations Assign Blame

MAURIZIO CATINO
University of Milano-Bicocca

CAMBRIDGE
UNIVERSITY PRESS

CAMBRIDGE
UNIVERSITY PRESS

Shaftesbury Road, Cambridge CB2 8EA, United Kingdom

One Liberty Plaza, 20th Floor, New York, NY 10006, USA

477 Williamstown Road, Port Melbourne, VIC 3207, Australia

314–321, 3rd Floor, Plot 3, Splendor Forum, Jasola District Centre,
New Delhi – 110025, India

103 Penang Road, #05–06/07, Visioncrest Commercial, Singapore 238467

Cambridge University Press is part of Cambridge University Press & Assessment,
a department of the University of Cambridge.

We share the University's mission to contribute to society through the pursuit of
education, learning and research at the highest international levels of excellence.

www.cambridge.org
Information on this title: www.cambridge.org/9781009297189

DOI: 10.1017/9781009297219

© Maurizio Catino 2023

Originally published in Italian as *Trovare il colpevole* ('the 'Original Work') by
Il Mulino © Maurizio Catino 2022

A catalogue record for this publication is available from the British Library.

*A Cataloging-in-Publication data record for this book is available from the
Library of Congress.*

ISBN 978-1-009-29718-9 Hardback
ISBN 978-1-009-29719-6 Paperback

Contents

Figures

Tables

Introduction

Suspicion and exasperation, unless they are restrained by reason and charity, possess the sad virtue of causing the unfortunate to be seized as criminals, upon the vainest pretext or the most rash assertion.

Alessandro Manzoni, *The Column of Infamy*, 1840

The search for a scapegoat is the easiest of all hunting expeditions.

Dwight D. Eisenhower, 1952

One of the largest cruise ships ever built sinks near the coast after hitting some underwater rocks. Several people die in the accident. Who is to blame? When coping with negative events, organizations can choose between two strategies: they can either take responsibility and implement (expensive) remedial actions or blame those who were directly involved in the fact – the scapegoats.

Organizations and institutions must learn from failures if they want to avoid repeating them. However, one of the main limits to organizational and institutional learning is addressing systemic problems of an organizational nature with solutions targeting the individual. This approach favors inertia and the creation of "organizational scapegoats". Pursuing scapegoats without changing the system only ensures that the actors will continue to behave as they did before, and no virtuous learning from the events that have occurred will take place in the organization.

The purpose of this book is to systematically understand how and why organizations create scapegoats. In doing so, the book outlines a general theory of scapegoating in organizations.

The term *scapegoat* means, in the ideal-typical formulation, a sort of sacrificial victim, an animate being (man or animal), or even an inanimate object, to which the evils and faults of the community are attributed – evils and faults which the community, through this process of transfer, is able to rid itself of. Another use of the term refers

1

to situations in which an innocent person is punished for wrongful or guilty actions committed by someone else. In this book I will consider a third, widespread type: the scapegoat in organizations. It is a tool of organizational rationality to divert all the blame toward a single individual, or a small group of individuals, who were involved in the event. I define the organizational scapegoat as the subject who pays for faults that *also* pertain to others. The scapegoat in organizations is not, therefore, a complete innocent who must take the blame for others – something that would be neither credible nor possible. The organizational scapegoat bears responsibility for the disputed event, but this responsibility is exaggerated by the accusers, who underestimate the context in which the event took place and the role and actions of other agents. In some cases the scapegoat, for convenience's sake, consents to assume this role; in others, this consent is not given.

The concept of scapegoat encompasses both a static (the type) and a dynamic dimension (the construction process). In this book, after analyzing the different forms and types of scapegoats, particular attention will be paid to the dynamic dimension: namely, we will focus on scapegoating, and will analyze the reasons and interests that lead groups of agents (the *blamemongers*) to construct the scapegoat. Methodologically, I argue that the definition of scapegoating is inseparable from its explanation. The fabrication of an organizational scapegoat has a characteristic development process. Typically, the initial stage begins with the manifestation of a negative event (e.g., a crisis, bankruptcy, accident, scandal); next, the organization faces the risk of legal sanctions and severe costs; and finally, there is a stage characterized by the identification of one or more people as scapegoats. This latter move leads to an outcome for the organization, which is generally a positive one, such as avoiding or reducing sanctions, costs, stigma and negative social evaluations.

The organizational scapegoat emerges in particular when organizations undergo a crisis. Corporate scandals, accidents and, more generally, organizational failures, undermine the image and reputation of organizations, generating organizational stigma, legal risks and economic consequences, in addition to the damage caused by the event. Faced with situations of this type, organizations can adopt two strategies to manage or divert guilt, in the sense of responsibility for an act that is viewed negatively. The first is to admit responsibility for the event and its consequences and implement measures for improvement and change: an organizational and institutional learning strategy. The second is to try to transfer responsibility to people immediately involved in the event – the *bad apples*. This can involve accusing the latter of negligence in the case of an accident, or of being *rogue employees* in the case of misconduct. This second strategy produces organizational inertia because by creating a scapegoat, the organization, and the ruling coalition in particular, will be safe: above all, they will not have to implement potentially costly remedial measures. Exemplary punishment of the scapegoat seems to be the solution identified by an organization to overcome a state of crisis. Blaming someone for what happened, or is happening, produces the feeling that the problem that caused the crisis has been solved.

The book focuses on scapegoating in organizations – the second strategy – but it also discusses the first strategy and its consequences for learning in Chapter 6. Scapegoating will be analyzed by examining a set of situations that favor this phenomenon (crises, scandals, accidents, and other types of organizational failures) and employing a perspective that considers the scapegoat as the outcome of a construction process by multiple agents, both internal and external to an organization. The indictment of individuals and their transformation into scapegoats becomes a useful expedient for delaying or avoiding structural changes, since public opinion is led to think that exemplary punishment of the person responsible for the error can serve as a deterrent in the future.

In the event of disasters characterized by the accidental or violent death of a large number of people, the creation of a political or social scapegoat seems inevitable: someone must be blamed. In such situations, the myth of the failure of the individual operator is particularly useful to deflect attention and blame from the leadership of the organization. It becomes relevant, therefore, to analyze the phenomenon of *blamestorming*,[1] which is the process aimed at investigating the reasons behind a failure and the allocation of blame. The problem of allocating blame is increasingly complex in contemporary societies – something that, according to Dingwall and Hillier (2016), could be a sign of a low level of social cohesion. The distribution of blame after negative events and organizational failures depends on the type

---

[1] The term *blamestorming* first appeared in the magazine *Wired* in 1997.

of interpretative frame: a different frame analysis produces a different candidate. Identifying a culprit in some way, a scapegoat, produces a sense of relief, a kind of catharsis that can help overcome the tragedy of the event (Douglas 1992).

While there are quite a number of anthropological and philosophical works on the subject of the scapegoat, there are few studies and little research on organizational sociology. The latter include the work of Bonazzi (1983a, 1983b), who was the first to tackle the issue from this perspective, followed by other scholars, including Boeker (1992) and Gangloff, Connelly and Shook (2016). Similarly, there is no great number of management studies concerned with analyzing processes aimed at transferring stigma to specific people to avoid damage to the organization's image (Warren 2007). Finally, research that analyzes the processes of collective, organizational, and inter-organizational construction of the scapegoat is even less common. This work intends, at least partly, to fill this gap.

The Theme and the Architecture of this Book

Two main questions drive the chapters in this book: Why and how do organizations create scapegoats? and, What are the limits of a purely individual response to systemic and organizational problems?

The first two chapters (1 and 2) concern the conceptual construction of the scapegoat in organizations as an instrument of organizational rationality, with the application of this construct to a few cases, and in particular to the *Costa Concordia* accident (Chapter 3). The two following chapters (4 and 5) deal with the problem of defining blame in organizations, and its sometimes perverse effects and related dilemmas (punishment/inertia vs learning/change). The concluding chapter (6) highlights the limits of dealing with collective problems through individual solutions and underlines the need for a different "civic epistemology" (Jasanoff 2005a) to account for organizational failures.

In more detail, Chapter 1 introduces the three different forms and types of use of the scapegoat concept: the archetypal figure/sacrificial victim; the innocent scapegoat; the organizational scapegoat.

Chapter 2 offers a detailed analysis of the characteristics of the scapegoat in organizations. In such contexts, it would not be credible for the scapegoats to be extraneous to the event that they are blamed for. It is therefore an individual, or a group of individuals, in some way involved in the event, who is blamed. They are an instrument of organizational rationality, strategically deployed by the organization to minimize legal consequences and economic damage. However, blaming a scapegoat also benefits the leaders of the organization because their personal reputation can be damaged by their association with a guilty organization.

The chapter presents some situations that can favor the creation of scapegoats: accidents, business scandals, organizational failures, crises, and policy fiascos. These events, particularly if amplified by the media, tend to generate scapegoats with the greatest frequency.

Chapter 3 is dedicated to the reconstruction of the case of the *Costa Concordia* accident, which occurred on January 13, 2012, off the west coast of Italy, near the island of Giglio, and presents an analysis of the scapegoating process that involved the ship's captain. Sailing very close to the coast, the *Costa Concordia* foundered on a rock. The impact tore open a gash in the ship, allowing in water which put the engines out of action. After traveling a short distance, the ship ran aground near the island, listing over onto its side. Out of over four thousand people on board, thirty-two died. The dominant view of this case from the judiciary, the media, and public opinion, was that the ship's captain was the main and, in fact, almost the only, figure responsible for the accident and for the inadequate management of the emergency. This book challenges the conventional interpretation of the accident, providing a revised history of the event and at the same time putting forward a different explanation.

The dominant reconstruction presents three limitations. First of all, the absence of an organizational perspective leads the event to be considered as an isolated accident, rather than the unexpected but predictable outcome of a risky practice such as that of the sail-by salute. It is as if the event came as a bolt from the blue, precipitated by the sudden madness of the captain: the same captain whose name had appeared in a commendatory post on the company's website on the very day of the event. It was, instead, not a matter simply of individual mistakes and failures, but rather a "predictable surprise", a heralded disaster with a long period of incubation. Events were, at the same time, favored by organizational criticalities and by the underestimation of the risks by controllers and regulators.

The second limitation of the dominant reconstruction consists in the prevalence of a conception based on the "short history" rather than on the "long history". The decision-making process in the three hours that preceded the disaster had a long incubation period, and needs to be looked at. It involves a "long history" that includes the progressive neutralization of several danger signals, such as the passage of a ship almost 300 meters long just a few dozen meters from the coast. These signals were seen as something to be rewarded and commended rather than as dangerous near misses. According to the various investigations (judicial, administrative, technical), however, as well as to expert reports, it seems that everything started at 18:27, just under three hours before the disaster, with the departure of the cruise ship from its last port of call.

Finally, the third limitation consists in the scapegoating of the captain of the ship by various collective agents. Certainly, the captain played a role, and an important one, in the accident, but the faults of others were also imposed upon him. During the emergency phase following the impact with the rock, mistakes were made and behavior inappropriate to the situation was displayed by the entire crew on the bridge. The organization was also responsible, for example, with regard to the selection and training of operators and to the provision of appropriate technology. For various organizational agents, a simplistic reading of the event irremediably stamped the captain with a stigma of immorality and made it possible to read the history of the accident in this light.

The morally negative portrait of the captain was instrumental in terms of increasing the credibility of accusations against him of disaster. Indeed, socially stigmatized people, as is known, are those most likely to become the scapegoats for a more widespread responsibility (Bartollas, Miller and Dinitz 1974). Processes of blame in organizations tend to redefine complex problems of a sociotechnical nature in terms of individual morality – thus, judgment regarding facts is replaced with judgment regarding people.

Chapter 4 illustrates some typical steps in the process of identifying organizational scapegoats and discusses the complex relationship between individual and organizational contribution in the etiology of critical events and organizational failures. In part, this involves the analysis of two emblematic cases: the torture of detainees that took place at Abu Ghraib prison and the scandal known as "Dieselgate". These two cases show that scapegoating is an organizational strategy that can be implemented by both private, for-profit organizations as well as non-profit, governmental ones. These strategies can be used to cope with different crises ranging from (involuntary) incidents to (deliberate) violations of laws and moral norms.

Chapter 5 compares two different investigative logics that follow on from organizational failures: the accusatory approach, based on the person, and the system approach, aimed at organizational learning. It concludes by illustrating possible undesired effects of the accusatory approach through discussion of the widespread practice of defensive medicine.

To conclude, Chapter 6 discusses the limits of a purely accusatory approach in dealing with complex events such as the various types of organizational failure (except, of course, in cases of malicious intent and gross negligence) and its contribution, even if involuntary, to scapegoating. The accusatory approach renders organizational and institutional learning processes problematic, putting an end to complex events with the mere sanctioning of "bad apples".

To sum up, then, the book proposes a theoretical and methodological frame for the analysis of intra- and inter-organizational scapegoating, integrating the micro (individual) level with the meso (organizational) and macro (organizational field) levels. At the same time, the limits of a purely punitive approach are discussed (except, it is worth repeating, in cases of malicious intent and gross negligence) and the need to find alternatives to criminal investigation (alone) in order to explain, and find solutions to, complex social problems in organizations.

This book is part of a research path that I embarked upon toward the end of the 1980s, dedicated to the study of accidents and failures in organizations beyond the perspective of human error or technological failure (Catino 2003, 2005, 2006a, 2010a, 2010b). Parallel to the study of the factors explaining the organizational etiology of such events, I began to conduct research into post-accident consequences, in particular investigatory logics, the perverse effects of the blame culture, and the problems of organizational learning (Catino 2006b, 2008, 2009a, 2009b, 2011; Catino and Patriotta 2013). Scapegoating seemed to me a decisive subject to move forward within this interpretative framework.

1 | Forms and Types of Scapegoat

1.1 An Overview

The scapegoat performs an instrumental function for ends that do not pertain to the individual who plays the role, but to other subjects. Its instrumental function therefore dictates its origin. While, as Girard (1999) states, exercising an indisputable role in our world, both on an individual and collective level, the phenomena relating to scapegoating are not much studied as such, especially within organizations.

The concept of the scapegoat is frequently used to cover a wide class of phenomena. Inaccurate use of the term can lead to situations of semantic ambiguity regarding its meaning and with respect to its empirical referent. This "conceptual stretching" (Sartori 2011) fosters a multiplicity of empirical referents for the term, with the risk that the usefulness of the concept is lost.

Analyzing cases of scapegoating in contexts that are also very different from one another, and on the basis of an inductive process, it is possible to group this empirical variety into three types:[1] the *archetypal scapegoat*, the *innocent scapegoat* and the *organizational scapegoat*.[2]

1.2 The Archetypal Scapegoat

The archetypal scapegoat can be defined as the subject who must take on the sins of the community in order to atone for them. The community chooses this individual (although, in the past, it could also be

---

[1] The purpose of a classification like the one proposed here is to organize types in order to show similarities and differences by identifying the underlying system of properties and also by identifying types not yet studied that are generated by the same system (Berger and Zelditch 1968, 447).

[2] The concept of the scapegoat has been analyzed by several disciplines, including psychoanalysis. Given the scope of this book, this perspective will not be discussed here. For more information see Perera (1986) and Lopez (2008).

an animal) as a sacrificial victim, who is then in some way driven out. His removal makes it possible to overcome the crisis and to purify the community. The sacrifice is carried out through a ritual within the community; in many cases, it takes place through a number of phases. The predominant agent is an individual – an innocent figure who has no causally direct relationship with the event for which he is sacrificed.

This ideal type of scapegoat has several elements in common with the role of the victim in the great Jewish ceremonies mentioned in the Bible (Leviticus 16, 21–22) and of the victims of similar rites that existed in archaic societies known as "rites of expulsion".[3] A goat was the ritual victim during ceremonies such as Yom Kippur, with which the Jews asked forgiveness for their sins.[4] Two goats were taken during this type of ritual,[5] one dedicated to the Lord and one to Azāzel, an evil spirit hostile to Yahweh, who the ancient Jews and Canaanites thought inhabited the barren desert, a place where Yahweh did not exercise his powers of fecundation.

While the first goat was sacrificed to Yahweh, the high priest placed his hands on the head of the second goat, the scapegoat, which was thus symbolically burdened with all the sins committed by the Jews – everything, in other words, that could exacerbate relations between the members of the community (Girard 1972 [1979], 1982 [1989], 1999). The animal was then driven out into the desert in honor of Azāzel: through this removal, it was believed that the sins were expelled and the community was therefore free of them. The goat served to transfer evil from one part to the other, with Azāzel representing this "other" side in opposition to Yahweh and his people. The desert, meanwhile, where the second goat was exiled, stood in contrast to the fertile fields of mankind.[6]

---

[3] These rites derive from a primitive Semitic custom, where a goat was taken into the desert and sacrificed in order to remove the sins symbolically transferred to it.

[4] As well as in the Bible, the rite is also present in the Talmud (folios 66–67). The term "scapegoat" originates from the translation (*caper emissarius*) that St. Jerome made of the Hebrew word Azāzel in the passage in Leviticus relating to the "day of atonement" (Kippur).

[5] The English translation, or rather the invention of the term "scapegoat", dates back to 1530, when William Tyndale invented the word, combining *goat* with *escape*, the "goat that escape", to indicate the goat sacrificed for Azāzel. In this way, the second goat in the atonement ritual became the *scapegoat*.

[6] This "transmission of evil" was known about and practiced by several civilizations. For example, the Babylonian–Assyrian civilization, the Egyptians, the Kaffirs (the Bantu of the south-eastern provinces of the South African Republic), and others (Pestalozza 1930).

Beginning in the eighteenth century, some anthropologists began to highlight similarities between the rite described in Leviticus and other rituals practiced by certain societies in various parts of the world. James Frazer was one of the first to study atonement processes as a common religious category and practice in several ancient cultures. In *The Golden Bough* (1915), Frazer showed how the goal of the atonement process was to remove all the evils that afflicted a specific community in one fell swoop, transferring them to inanimate objects, animals, or humans. This could happen in different ways. For example, wrote Frazer, the inhabitants of the Leti Poa and Lakor islands in the Indian archipelago built a small boat, loaded it with food and consigned it to the sea, thus removing diseases and other ills from the village.[7] Other rites involved the sacrifice of animals, in the belief that they embodied evil influences.

In some cases, the scapegoat was represented by a human being. In one area of New Zealand, an atonement ceremony was created in which the sins of the tribe were transferred to a single element: a man with a fern stem tied to his body jumped into the river and released the stem, sending it into the current so that it carried its freight of tribal sin down to the sea. In other cases, the ritual of atonement involved human sacrifice, the victims, wrote Frazer, imbued with the troubles that threatened others. In Onitsha, on the Niger, for example, it was customary to sacrifice two people every year to wipe out the sins from the community. The various rites, both violent and non-violent, practiced by the different communities, tended to become periodic. What united them was the aim of eliminating the evils that afflicted a people with the expulsion of malign spirits through a scapegoat, or other animal or material vessels (Frazer 1915 [2009]).[8]

---

[7] Frazer's concept of the scapegoat is heavily criticized by Girard (1987), who considers it confusing and simplistic.

[8] Burkert (1979) identifies a typical model for the scapegoat ritual, practiced by numerous cultures and based on a common sequence of actions. Although the occasions that trigger it are different (such as a famine or plague), what they have in common is a situation of anxiety. First, a selection is made – sometimes an individual regarded in some way as repulsive, sometimes an animal. Then there are the rites of communication, with the offering of food and decorative items, followed by the solemn rites of contact and separation in order to establish a polar opposition between those who are safe on one side, and the passive victim on the other. The scapegoat is then cast out beyond the confines of the community's territory, the final effect of the procedure being salvation from evil and anxiety, which disappear together with the condemned and expelled victim.

Atonement rites also took place in ancient Greece and Rome, and could sometimes be very bloody. Every year in Athens, in the month of May, during the festival of Thargelia in honor of the god Apollo, two people regarded as being somewhat repulsive in appearance were chosen and expelled from the city (Bremmer 1983).[9] The rite was a widespread one, similar in many respects to that of the scapegoat, and aimed at obtaining purification through the removal of a figure called *pharmakós* (the Greek φαρμακός can be translated as "the accursed one"). Through this rite, the community poured out its aggression onto an outcast, his deformity marking him out as a symbol of evil. Robert Parker (1983) pointed out that the *pharmakós* had to be accused of some crime, unlike the blameless scapegoat of Leviticus. Obviously, the unlucky *pharmakós* had no real guilt, other than that of representing every form of possible misfortune in the eyes of others. By sending this person away, the city freed itself of a being freighted with the sins and curses of the whole community. In this way, the *pharmakós* represented both the outcast to be expelled and the savior who allowed the community to continue to live in peace and safety, warding off pestilence, drought, and famine. His sacrifice, states Girard (1985), constituted a social restorative, the *pharmakós* thus transformed into *phàrmakon* – the expiatory victim becoming a social medicine. Similar rites, practiced by different cultures that had no contact with each other, are, according to Frazer, a clear indication of the universal existence of sacrificial representation. This, however, does not clarify the psychological or unconscious causes that brought this kind of representation about.

A fundamental contribution to the study of this phenomenon is the work of René Girard (1972 [1979], 1982 [1989], 1999) and his investigation into the persecutory mechanism. This mechanism is an integral part of the sacrifice: a victim is chosen at random without having anything to do with the event that has occurred. The contextual condition that characterizes the formation of the scapegoat is a state of crisis caused by famines, epidemics, floods, or religious and political conflict. Normal institutions are weakened and replaced by the mob, which exerts decisive pressure on the former. Since the mob, says Girard, tends toward persecution, and often cannot act on the real causes of a problem (such as the natural causes of famine or pestilence), it seeks other possible

---

[9] Some scholars believe that the two unfortunates were killed, others that they were only cast out (Bremmer 1983, 315).

causes to sate its hunger for violence, in order to purge the community of the impure elements that corrupt it: people who have committed particular kinds of crime, ethnic or religious groups, foreigners, or individuals with particular physical and/or mental characteristics. The further a figure is distanced from what the community regards as normal, the greater the possibility of becoming a target of persecution. Oedipus was the first example of a human scapegoat (Girard 1974). He is the ideal type: he has committed horrendous crimes (patricide and incest), has physical defects (a limp), and is a foreigner.[10] The more signs of victimhood there are, the greater the likelihood of becoming a scapegoat. By expelling Oedipus as a *pharmakós*, as a scapegoat, the city will once again find purification and salvation (Vernant 1972).

According to Girard, all cultures and all religions are built around a foundational lynching – mass violence turned against a scapegoat. The scapegoat is, therefore, a universal theme and its effects, states Girard (1972 [1979]), are more deeply rooted in the human condition than we are willing to admit. The ritual sacrifice of the scapegoat, he goes on to say, is a necessary condition for society to shift from the uncontrolled violence of primitive barbarism to the controlled violence of civilization. Paying for the sins of the whole community, the scapegoat creates the conditions for social pacification and the advent of a stabilizing hierarchy.[11] Along similar lines, Kenneth Burke (1941) argues that the creation of the scapegoat is a liberating mechanism from socially generated tensions and states of anxiety: a part that assumes the burden

---

[10] As Girard (1974) writes, the search for Oedipus as a scapegoat is triggered by the oracle when he says that there is a murderer in the community and that removing this figure will bring an end to the plague. The sacrifice of Oedipus puts an end to the pestilence, thus restoring the unity of the community. According to Girard, however, Oedipus does not appear as an innocent destroyed by the blind passion of the masses. This victim is regarded as a real criminal, as the only culprit in a community now liberated from its violence. Oedipus is a scapegoat, Girard continues, in the fullest sense, because he is never designated as such (1974, 843). A second figure that Girard describes as an emblematic type of permanent scapegoat, as an example of an expiatory victim, is Job (Girard 1985). The life of the mythical hero Oedipus shares many similarities with that of Job, so that, behind the two texts that describe them, a glimpse is allowed of one and the same phenomenon: the transformation of the popular idol into a scapegoat.

[11] Girard's scapegoat theory can be collocated within more general "mimetic theory", according to which most human behavior is based on imitation. The imitation of desires leads to conflict, and when a build-up of conflict threatens to destroy all the parties involved, a scapegoat is employed to restore balance.

of the whole (406–408).[12] This is a mechanism that is still current, and not one limited to pre-technological societies: no individual, group or nation is immune from the tendency to look for someone to blame for their troubles.[13]

Although no longer ritualized, the scapegoat mechanism continues to exist, generally in an attenuated form. Since the use of violence is subject to strict prohibitions, resentment and anger cannot be vented on what is considered, even if erroneously, the direct cause. A replacement is therefore initiated with victims who are the modern equivalent of the sacrificial victims of the past. Even if it no longer leads to physical, but to psychological violence (Gemmill 1989; Girard 1999),[14] sacrificial substitution is still a widespread phenomenon needed for the (temporary) reconciliation of the group (Casanova 2014).

To summarize, the archetypal scapegoat serves as someone to blame for the sins, the faults, the misfortune of a community, to take all that evil onto themselves and away from others. It is a concept that persists and changes throughout the centuries. The expression then took on a figurative sense to indicate a subject, or a social group, singled out in order to be accused of a specific fault and then removed in order to atone for it, based on the belief that, by punishing and removing that person or group, the problem will disappear.[15] However, the archetypal scapegoat does not account for a series of other phenomena

---

[12] To bolster our weak self-esteem, says Burke (1969), we seek someone to blame for our moral corruption and social inadequacy.

[13] According to Burke (1941), there are three main ways to designate a scapegoat: *fatalistic*, through prophecies and signs from heaven; *poetic justice*, when the sacrificial victim is considered too pure for this world; and *legalistic*, when the victim somehow deserves what happens because they have transgressed moral or legal justice.

[14] Peter Thiel, a student of Girard, developed some of his teacher's entrepreneurial ideas in the book *Zero to One* (2014). He argues, for example, that Facebook is in fact an embodiment of two principles of Girard's thought: mimetic imitation and the sacrifice of the scapegoat.

[15] The scapegoat theme has been the subject of several novels and films. An interesting theory on the relationship between the detective story and the scapegoat was put forward by Guido Vitiello (2008), through analyzing the works of writers such as Agatha Christie, Northorp Frye, Nicholas Blake, Brigid Brophy, and Michel Butor. Vitiello considers the detective novel as a game, the aim of which is to expel from a community the figure who, committing an act of violence, has destroyed communal peace and disseminated discord (19). A detective story must have a culprit, so it is necessary for the blame to be placed on only one character, who in this way assumes the burden of responsibility.

attributable to this concept, albeit characterized in a different way such as the *innocent scapegoat* and the *organizational scapegoat*, which will be analyzed in the following sections.

1.3 The Innocent Scapegoat

A second type of scapegoat is the innocent scapegoat, a person upon whom wrongdoing has been displaced. Unlike the archetypal figure, the innocent scapegoat is not punished for general "sins" of a community, but for specific facts and events, with respect to which he is completely extraneous. The innocent scapegoat is therefore sacrificed for reasons connected to the collective interest, in response to problems of social insecurity, to satisfy aggression, or to transfer certain states of unrest to specific subjects. The innocent scapegoat is regarded as the cause of these conditions of unease.[16]

The originating context is society itself; this type of scapegoat can be constructed both from below (by mob rule), and from above (by organizational, institutional, or political control). The predominant agent is an individual or a specific social group (immigrants, a foreign country, or some other type of group). In addition to being innocent of the disputed facts, having played no role at all in the events, the scapegoat refuses to accept the role of victim, in part because he cannot derive any benefit from it. In this case, the ritual dimension that characterizes the archetypal figure is lacking; the scapegoat is not defined as such ex ante, but is turned into one based both on the specific circumstances and on the individual and social characteristics that in some way make him a potential candidate.

---

[16] A variant of this type of scapegoat is the so-called "criminal stereotype" (Chapman 1968), introduced in the 1960s by so-called critical criminology. According to this Marxist and classist line of thought regarding criminal deviance, a tendency existed on the part of the judicial system to prosecute only crimes committed by the lower classes, by proletarians lacking in resources and education. The same antisocial behavior, if perpetrated by someone belonging to the middle or upper classes, is instead immune from punishment. In this way, criminals belonging to the lower classes become scapegoats, a social and legal artifact functional to the preservation of the established order. The offender, in this view, was a person selected to fill the role of scapegoat, thus providing an expedient perspective on the criminal problem.

In *The Joke and Its Relation to the Unconscious*, Sigmund Freud (1905 [2003]) tells a very interesting story about scapegoating and its usefulness. In a Hungarian village, a girl was killed. Investigations identify the blacksmith as the killer. The elders of the village form a tribunal and condemn him to death: he will be hanged in the main square. But the evening before the execution, the *bürgomeister* realizes that the murderer is also the only blacksmith in the community, that there is no replacement readily available, and that if the sentence is carried out, the village will quickly be bereft of tools and equipment. On the other hand, the village does have two tailors, only one of whom is really necessary for the requirements of the population. Therefore, he duly chooses one of the tailors to be hanged the next day instead of the more useful blacksmith. The village continues to be well-supplied with keys and knives and, at the same time, thanks to the sacrificed substitute, has satisfied its need for justice. The mechanism is clear: it is not important who the real culprit is, but who it is most convenient to blame.

As already mentioned, the construction of this type of scapegoat can take place from either below or above. From below, through mob rule, scapegoats emerge in situations of collective dissatisfaction that provoke strong hostility toward individuals held responsible for a condition perceived as negative (Smelser 1962). From above, on the other hand, scapegoats are designated when the construction of the scapegoat is the result of a power group's political strategy. The distinction is only analytical, since in reality the two phenomena can overlap, as with the persecution and extermination of Jews under Nazism.

Plagues and diseases have long been associated with the creation of scapegoats. Thucydides, Jean Froissart and Guillaume de Machaut described the fears, anxieties, and suspicions that emerged during a pandemic. The expression *pestilentia manufacta* – the "intentionally spread pestilence" – was first introduced by the Latin philosopher Seneca in *De Ira*[17] and there are also references to it in the ancient and medieval world. In the seventeenth century, the theory that the plague was caused by human intervention was deeply rooted in culture, in medical, theological, and political treatises (Preto 1987). This theory persisted, albeit in an attenuated form, throughout the eighteenth century. Very few doctors doubted the existence of intentional

---

[17] "Et pestilentiam manu factam" (*De Ira*, Book II, 9.3).

"plague-spreaders", figures that appeared for the first time centuries before, even if initially they were accused of only infecting animals. The first evidence of "plague spreading" dates back to 1530, in Casale Monferrato. As Preto (1987) states, the sixteenth and seventeenth centuries were characterized by a theological, medical, and academic culture according to which the plague was created by man for economic and political purposes, or by the Devil, through pacts with plague-spreading humans. It is important to underline, continues Preto, that these beliefs were not developed by the ignorant and superstitious, but by learned "men of science", such as doctors and theologians, who transmitted them to the lower classes.

In this belief system, every unknown evil was frequently attributed to others, with the search for a scapegoat: the "evil" could not be generated by those who suffered it, but had to have an external origin. The origin must therefore lie in a particular social group. Examples are the extermination of lepers accused of spreading the plague, or of Jews accused of all kinds of wickedness – poisoning wells, practicing ritual murder, spreading infection (for example in the pogroms that accompanied the Black Death in Germany and Catalonia).[18] Ginzburg observes that "the tendency towards marginalization affected precisely these groups because their condition was ambiguous, liminal" (2017, 17). Their suspicious extraneousness designated them as perfect scapegoats in times of crisis (Delumeau 2011). In the Middle Ages, says Frugoni (2020), the violence taken out on the body (such as suffering aimed at purifying oneself from sin and exorcising evil) was transferred to an external target, finding an ideal scapegoat in the Jews.

---

[18] Guillaume de Machaut argues that the Israelites poisoned wells even before the plague appeared. It is clear that the plague broke out in a climate of anti-Semitism (Delumeau 2011). An original hypothesis on why Jews became the scapegoats for the spread of the "black plague", something that had been happening since 1346, was formulated by Martin J. Blaser. Blaser believes that Jews were largely spared from contagion, compared to other groups, because wheat was taken away from their homes at the time of Passover, thereby discouraging the presence of rats, which spread the disease. The plague had in fact peaked in spring, around Easter. Therefore, the fact of not having been affected by the plague, as others were, raised the suspicion that they were in fact the spreaders (Donald G. McNeil Jr., "Finding a Scapegoat When Epidemics Strike", *The New York Times*, August 31, 2009).

In Hugo Bettauer's novel, *The City Without Jews* (1922 [1929]), rumor begins to circulate that if the Austrians have become impoverished, it is the fault of the Jews, if they remain unemployed, it is the fault of the Jews, if the peace treaties have brought humiliation upon them, it is the fault of the Jews, and so on.[19] Anti-Semitism seemed to offer a clear and convenient explanation for any problem, social tension, or fear deriving from economic and social change brought about by the processes of modernization and industrialization.

Similarly, Alessandro Manzoni in his *The Column of Infamy* (1840 [1964]) recounts the construction of authentic scapegoats. In 1630, in Milan, Gian Giacomo Mora and Guglielmo Piazza were unjustly accused of spreading the plague: after being tortured for a long period of time, they were condemned by a court, mutilated, broken on the wheel, and executed.

At first, the idea spread among the people that the plague had its origin in a sin that had unleashed divine wrath. Subsequently, an attempt was made to identify scapegoats to which the collective guilt might be transferred: foreigners envious of Milanese power, travelers, individuals who were marginal to, or in general not well integrated into, the community (Canosa 1985). It was believed that some of these people smeared the walls of the main streets, houses, and churches with pestiferous substances. According to some there was no doubt that this kind of smearing took place, but there was no certainty with regard to the motive – hypotheses ranged from a student jape to political conspiracy (Nicolini 1937).[20]

Instructions began to be printed inviting the population to report the plague-spreaders. In addition to these reports, there were attempts

---

[19] Although a novel, Bettauer's work describes well the political and social climate of Vienna at the time – times he himself would later fall victim to, killed in March 1925 by a young supporter of the Nazis. An interesting theory regarding Israel and Europe was put forward by Niram Ferretti (2019), who said that, in a post-war European scenario of suppression and negation of the grave responsibilities of several countries in relation to fascism and Nazism, Israel became a convenient scapegoat. Accused of all kinds of wickedness and of behavior absurdly similar to that of the Nazis, Israel could no longer make any moral demands on European countries, thus relieving the latter of the guilt inherited during the dark years (Ferretti 2019, 15–16; Joffe 2004).

[20] It should be remembered that at that time many scientists, such as the talented physicist Ludovico Settala and the doctor Alessandro Tadino, also believed in a "manufactured plague" and in plague-spreaders (Clini 1967).

to lynch strangers, who were pointed out as spreaders by the mob and saved by soldiers. As well as strangers, even simple passers-by were denounced for conduct considered suspicious. Complaints increased, as did collective panic and delirium. At some point, Spanish and public bodies had to do something to pacify the mob, to show that culprits were being sought out and severely punished. The plague evolved from a health problem into a social problem, and it was therefore necessary to find scapegoats to assume responsibility for the contagion, otherwise the mob might turn their anger against the public bodies themselves.[21]

It was in this context that the trial began which culminated in the torture and execution of Gian Giacomo Mora and Guglielmo Piazza. Pietro Verri (1804 [2006]) was the first to recount the event, believing that it was caused by ignorance of the causes of the plague.[22] In Manzoni's view, however, it was judicial error that brought about the scapegoating. It was not a question of ignorance of the nature of the plague, but rather the result of "perverse passions", as well as the readiness of the magistrates to seek out guilty parties. Procedural rules, therefore, were violated by the judges, who, had they instead done their duty, would not have been able to condemn the two unfortunate men. The fear aroused by an unknown natural phenomenon such as the plague made the figure of the spreader "politically necessary" (Cordero 1985). Their sacrifice served to allay the anguish of a contagion that no one at the time knew how to combat.[23]

---

[21] For a better understanding of the social context of that period, in addition to Manzoni, see the accounts by Giuseppe Ripamonti (1641 [2009]) in *De peste quae fuit anno 1630* libri V/Desumpti ex Annalibus Urbis, apud Malatestas, Mediolani (published in Giuseppe Ripamonti, *La peste di Milano del 1630*, Milan, Mediolanensia, edited by C. Repossi, 2009). On this topic and on the trial of the spreaders, see also Clini 1967 and Farinelli and Paccagnini 1988.

[22] The history of the Column of Infamy had already appeared in *Considerazioni sul commercio dello Stato di Milano*, completed in 1763.

[23] Cordero (1985) accuses Manzoni of not having understood the logic of the penal system and of the rules he criticizes, of persecuting "the judges with an inquisitive rage beside which the methods used on Mora and Piazza pale in color" (303) – Cordero considered the two executed men to be "food for the gallows". There is an anti-Manzonian hatred in these criticisms, almost as if the writer himself were a defendant in the trial. Nicolini and Cordero's conclusions were, in turn, strongly criticized by various scholars,

The consensus among scholars of different disciplines is almost unanimous regarding the fact that Mora and Piazza, as well as other unlucky figures, were completely innocent scapegoats. However, there were also authoritative scholars, who accused Manzoni of Enlightenment anti-historicism (Croce 1916) and of having conducted archival research in a hasty manner, operating more as a moralist than as a historian (Nicolini 1937). The judges, say Manzoni's accusers, acted in impeccable accordance with the laws and context of the time (Nicolini 1937; Cordero 1985, 2007). The two suspects were not, according to Cordero, entirely innocent. The judges, therefore, did not transgress the rules that they themselves knew well: on the contrary, they respected the case law in force at the time, even more so than in many other contemporary cases. They made no significant errors, and even acted "with great exemplarity", employing scrupulous fairness and analytical diligence (Cordero 2007).

However, it should be noted that the judges upheld their belief in a manufactured plague when the defendants before them were ordinary citizens, but not when they were faced with a Spanish nobleman who was accused of being an architect and even leader of a conspiracy (Clini 1967). Two forms of justice and one political trial, therefore. In addition, there were several people, though not many, who did not believe in a manufactured plague, and these included important figures of the times such as the historian Giuseppe Ripamonti and Cardinal Federico Borromeo (Preto 1987).[24]

The innocent scapegoat is the type of scapegoat referred to in novels, broadcasts, and newspaper articles when they tell the story of victims of unjust violence or discrimination, especially when these victims are accused or punished for both the "sins" of others and more general tensions, conflicts, and problems. In this way, the scapegoat makes

including Leonardo Sciascia ("Nota", in *Storia della Colonna Infame*, 1981 (pp. 171–190), a reworking of a 1973 piece) and Mino Martinazzoli (*Per una requisitoria manzoniana*, 2020); then as an introductory essay to *Storia della Colonna Infame*, Periplo, 1997; finally republished in Alessandro Manzoni, *La peste a Milano. Storia della Colonna Infame. I Promessi Sposi* (chapters 31, 32, 34), commentary by Mino Martinazzoli, Collana Orso blu, Brescia, Scholè, 2020).

[24] On this see Leonardo Sciascia, when he states that "times were not so dark and an intelligent and honest man, especially one exercising the office of judge, could and should have shared, if not the conviction of Ripamonti, at least that of Borromeo" (Sciascia 1981, 180).

it possible for persecutors to evade problems that seem intractable.[25] Some crime policies (e.g., "Law and order", "War on drugs", "Zero tolerance"), rather than aiming at the resolution of deviance, seem designed to produce a sense of security, clearly identifying the enemies to be regarded as scapegoats (Christie 1986; Feeley and Simon 1992; Luban 1993; Simon 2007; Forman 2012).

In more recent times, the Dreyfus affair (Locatelli 1930; Revel 1936) in France, between the late nineteenth and early twentieth centuries, or the case of Gino Girolimoni in Rome in 1927 (Sanvitale and Palmegiani 2011), are illuminating examples of the persecutory mechanism.[26]

In 1894, in a climate of intense nationalism and increasing racism, the Alsatian Jewish army officer Alfred Dreyfus was accused of espionage and treason for having transmitted secret military information to Germany. Dreyfus was completely innocent – as became clear later, the real traitor was another officer, Major Ferdinand Walsin Esterhazy. Evidence of the betrayal consisted of a document found in the waste bin in an office in the German embassy in Paris. This squared, cream-colored sheet, which would go down in history with the term *bordereau* (a delivery note or list), contained information

---

[25] Analyzing some cases of wrongful conviction connected to the relationship between law and science, such as the link between vaccines and autism, the 2009 earthquake in L'Aquila, the Xylella bacterium, the story of the virologist Ilaria Capua and others, Luca Simonetti (2018, 2020) finds many similarities in the construction of scapegoating between these legal affairs and that of *The Column of Infamy*. These similarities also extend, in some cases, to the form of the procedural documents.

[26] Between 1924 and 1927, seven girls were the victims of a series of kidnappings, rapes, and murders that took place in Rome. The newspapers, feeding on popular anguish and at the same time nourishing it, urged that the killer be found. In May 1927, Gino Girolimoni, an accident mediator and photographer, was arrested. The press emphasized the features of the typical degenerate, with very strange eyes, and an oblique, false, elusive gaze: elements that were stigmatic signs of a scapegoat. The poorly conducted investigations did not lead anywhere and Girolimoni was therefore released from prison, though news of this was not given in the papers – Mussolini, indeed, had ordered that neither Girolimoni nor other cases of violence of this type should be publicized. On the basis of a great deal of evidence, Police Commissioner Giuseppe Dosi believed that he had identified the real culprit: an English Protestant pastor. He failed, however, to furnish sufficient proof, and the pastor left Italy, never to return. Despite his innocence, the name Girolimoni has long remained in everyday slang to denote an individual involved in acts of pedophilia and perversion.

regarding the artillery and deployment of French troops. Given the confidential information contained therein, it could only have been provided by an officer of the French General Staff. First of all, twelve people with potential knowledge of this information were identified, including Alfred Dreyfus – who, as a Jew, was already regarded with suspicion. On the basis of handwriting studies, by no means unanimous in judgment, it was concluded that the traitor was Dreyfus.

Doubt gave way to certainty and he was taken into custody on October 15, 1894. Dreyfus was hastily condemned by military court, publicly cashiered, and deported into permanent exile on Devil's Island, in French Guiana. Two elements determined the sentence: statements by Major Hubert-Joseph Henry, an intelligence officer, and a secret document sent to the court by the Minister of War, General Mercier. Dreyfus's defense was unable to disprove the allegations, citing only lack of evidence as a defensive strategy.

After the conviction, Major Georges Picquart found evidence that the real traitor was Major Esterhazy. He was not believed, however, and was posted to a war zone in Africa. Meanwhile, a fierce struggle took place between two opposing factions. On the one hand there were the "Dreyfusards", most notably Emile Zola, who on January 13, 1898 published an article entitled "J'accuse" in which he claimed that Dreyfus had been condemned in the absence of evidence only because he was an Israelite. On the other hand, there were the "anti-Dreyfusards", which included a large number of anti-Semites.[27] The following year, Dreyfus's main accuser, Major Henry, was arrested on suspicion of being the author of the *bordereau*, but the next day he committed suicide in custody. The manner of his suicide, however, was considered by many to be rather anomalous. Following new legal developments, a retrial was allowed and in 1899 Major Esterhazy confessed that he had written the document unjustly attributed to Dreyfus, in obedience

---

[27] French writer Maurice Barrès, a leading figure in French nationalism, said: "I really don't need anyone to come and explain why Dreyfus should have committed a betrayal. That Dreyfus is capable of treason I deduce from his race!" (in Marrus, 1990, 105; Coen, 1994, 133). Thomas Mann dealt with the Dreyfus case in his book *Betrachtungen eines Unpolitischen* ("Reflections of a Non-political Man", 1918), interpreting the affair as a clash between two opposing sides: one, the political front aimed at safeguarding fundamental values such as homeland, military honor, French institutions and, when it intervened against Dreyfus, the Catholic Church; the other, a heterogeneous set of people united by the desire for truth and justice.

to orders from his superiors. During the retrial, the military court came under extreme pressure from the General Staff and, despite the evidence, Dreyfus was again convicted of treason, albeit with extenuating circumstances and a judgment that was not unanimous. As Silvestri wrote (2012, 13), the innocent Dreyfus found himself blocked on every side: the army had no wish to review the decisions taken and face a loss of authority, Parliament did not want to clarify matters and risk a loss of electoral consensus, citizens did not want to question the correctness of a verdict issued by official figures and renounce a Jewish scapegoat.

However, the incredible decision to uphold the conviction influenced the election to the national parliament, which brought a liberal-radical majority to power. The new president accepted the plea of forgiveness and Alfred Dreyfus was finally free. The wrongful conviction itself was only quashed in 1906 and Dreyfus was readmitted into the army: in a climate of profound tension and division, however, the new judicial verdict was not accepted by all the French people. Two years later, in fact, Dreyfus was wounded in an attack.

It was a complex series of events: the innocent Dreyfus was seen as a scapegoat to be sacrificed in a climate of nationalist frustration for the military defeats of 1870, with the loss of the provinces of Alsace and Lorraine during the Franco-Prussian war, and of growing anti-Semitism in large sections of French public opinion, at all levels. The Jew, even if French, was regarded as a foreign body to the nation. In some way, the "suicide" of Henry, the author of the falsified *bordereau*, served to deflect any threat to the political-military power group that had directed the spy trial against Dreyfus.

In the Dreyfus case we find some typical elements of scapegoating. First of all, the hypothesis that gave rise to the charge was not wholly without foundation: Captain Dreyfus was one of the few officers (although certainly not the only one) to be aware of the information contained in the *bordereau* delivered to the Germans, and his writing resembled the writing in the document. In addition, given his Jewishness, the suspect belonged to a minority group. The judges, rather than seeking the truth, had tried to establish the defendant's guilt by any means possible, in a situation where evidence was dubious if not actually absent. False and secret documents had taken the place of real evidence (Vergès 2011).

It should be noted that the cases cited cannot be considered only as cases of wrongful conviction, contrary to the claims that are sometimes made. For there to be error, there must be no intentionality, since if there is intentionality, it is a matter of violation. In the cases analyzed so far, the construction of the guilty figure is an intentional act, either with artificial evidence or with convictions handed out even in the face of evidence in favor of the convicted person. Thus, the second type of scapegoat described here is not that of an innocent figure who falls victim to judicial error, but rather an innocent who is intentionally convicted in the place of someone else due to certain specific interests and motivations, and whose conviction is believed by a large number of people to be a fair one.

Going back to the theme of pestilence, even in the twentieth and twenty-first centuries belief in plague-spreaders and manufactured plagues is still present. In southern Italy, the cholera epidemic of 1910–1911 set an angry mob against administrators, doctors, and even King Vittorio Emanuele III, accused of spreading the disease with a "powder". A few years later, the flu that was known as "Spanish" was attributed by various people to those elsewhere and given a name that placed the responsibility for its outbreak on another country.

With solid research and a host of examples, Preto (1987) has documented how, from 1630 until the Spanish flu, the belief that alleged plague-spreaders made use of powders, unctuous materials, or other substances to transmit disease was widespread and deeply rooted in Italy. In many cases the "manufactured plague" was attributed to a foreign power, a religious sect, or a specific social class, who used the plague-spreaders as simple hirelings in order to circulate contagion.

With the spread of the disease, there also began the hunt for the scapegoat, the person or people held responsible for what had happened. Popular fear followed on from belief in the plague-spreaders, and this in turn was followed by violence against, and massacres of, individuals considered to be the perpetrators and propagators of the epidemic: foreigners, heretics, vagabonds – even the doctors and pharmacists who treated the infected. Witches, too, were suitable scapegoats for all adversities: singled out as heretics and apostates, they were guilty of treason against God, and as servants of the devil they were part of a conspiracy aimed at subverting Christian society and ethics, the hierarchical structure established by the Lord. They were therefore accused of undermining the social order, giving rise to real "hunts", driven by judicial fury, being organized to track them down (Levack 2016).[28] According to Lynn Thorndike (1936), the witch was the scapegoat for many of the ills of the waning medieval society and thus was mainly the victim of psychological and sociological pressures than of religious dogma.

In some cases, belief in a manufactured plague became the inspiration for class struggle, with the poorer classes accusing the wealthy of spreading the plague in order to wipe them out, while the wealthy protected themselves from the disease through exclusive treatments.

1.4 The Organizational Scapegoat

The first two types of scapegoat are fully extraneous to the negative events for which they bear responsibility. Therefore, they are innocent. Instead, the third type, the organizational scapegoat, is involved to some extent in the disputed event for which he bears responsibility. Nevertheless, his responsibility is exaggerated by the accusers, who underestimate or ignore the context in which the event took place, and the role and actions of other agents.

I define the organizational scapegoat as the subject who pays for faults that *also* pertain to others. While in the two previous types the scapegoat is innocent in relation to the accusations of bringing about negative events and situations, in organizations he is somehow involved in the genesis and dynamics of the event for which he is deemed guilty. The distinctive trait of the organizational scapegoat is that while he is responsible, to a certain extent, for the negative event, he assumes more than his fair share of the guilt. If for Girard (1987, 88) and Douglas (1995, 55) the scapegoat is arbitrarily selected and has no real link with the event, in the type analyzed here a link does indeed exist. The main agent is an individual or a group of individuals *that are somehow involved* in the event at the origin of the construction of the scapegoat.

---

[28] Peter Leeson and Jacob Russ (2018) analyzed 43,000 witchcraft trials held between 1300 and 1850 in twenty-one European countries. The ingenious thesis of the two scholars is that there originally existed competition between the Catholic and Protestant churches for the religious "market share" in the various disputed areas of Christianity. The two churches fought over who could offer the most protection. Where greater competition existed between the churches, witch hunts were more frequent. Once the market shares between the two churches were established, such hunts gradually dwindled in number, until they finally disappeared from Europe completely.

The organizational scapegoat is secularized with respect to the archetypal image: it loses the religious, spiritual, and mythical dimension of sacrifice to assume a functional role in the politics and interests of the organization (Bonazzi 1983a). The scapegoat is no longer a ritual, but a model of social behavior; no longer a way to defend a community but rather a way to protect one or more people and organizations (Douglas 1995; Campbell 2013). While the archetypal and the innocent scapegoats are the product of unaware social processes, as individuals do not realize the inadequate, casual, or lack of, reasoning behind their selection of a subject, scapegoating in organizations does not occur in an unconscious way (Girard 1987), nor it is an unintended side effect (Stuchlik 2021). Rather, it is the conscious result of *intentional* or *emerging* strategies: in the first case, the result of deliberate choices aimed at its definition; in the second, the result of the convergence of behaviors by various agents.

The relevant element that characterizes this third type of scapegoat, and distinguishes it from the previous examples, is the organizational dimension: in other words, it emerges within organized contexts and in relation to them. This is also due to the fact that organizations are a pre-eminent if not dominant feature of modern society: a society of organizations, founded on organizations (Presthus 1962; Perrow 1991). Organizations were obviously also present in ancient civilizations, in Chinese, Greek, Indian, and other societies, but it is only with modern society and in the aftermath of the Industrial Revolution that organizations have progressively become the most relevant and ubiquitous collective actor in the social system. Virtually all collective action takes place in and through organizational contexts.

James Coleman (1982; 1990) has highlighted how, in modern societies, person–person and person–organization relationships are paralleled, even surpassed in some cases, by organization–organization relationships. An important indicator of this change concerns the role of law and the courts. For example, in the US Federal Courts in 1985–1991, most lawsuits involved disputes over business contracts between two or more companies. These lawsuits were more common than those involving a person against a company.[29] In the context of social

---

[29] Coleman (1982); see also Milo Geyelin, "Suits by Firms Exceed Those by Individuals", *Wall Street Journal*, December 3, 1993, B1. Coleman also highlights a significant shift in media attention, increasingly more concerned

theory, says Coleman, with no conception "of the corporate actor *as* actor, having the same status in social theory as natural persons in their capacities as actors, the theory is crippled, and blind to a large part of the action that takes place in modern society" (1982, 31–32).[30]

The organizational scapegoat does not replace the archetypal and innocent types described above but adds to them. The emergence of the corporate actor as a central subject in contemporary social systems leads to the relocation and redefinition of the scapegoat phenomenon in a different context and with a different operating mechanism. Some scholars (e.g., Coombs 2007; Gangloff et al. 2016; Djabi and Sitte de Longueval 2020; Roulet and Pichler 2020) analyzed scapegoating as an organizational discursive strategy aimed at shifting responsibility (and penalties) for negative events. They pointed out that, because the attribution of blame is a discursive process and situations are ambiguous, organizations can win the audiences and influence the outcome by choosing a scapegoat and arguing for his exclusive responsibility. While these studies greatly improved our understanding of blame attribution and scapegoating in organizations, less attention has been paid to its characteristics, organizational mechanisms, and actors' power and interests (Eagle and Newton 1981; Bonazzi 1983a, 1983b; Boeker 1992; Daudigeos, Pasquier and Valiorgue 2014; Danniau and Meynckens-Fourez 2015; Uhalde 2016).

The scapegoat in organizations is a tool of organizational rationality that aims to remove or contain any legal consequences and economic damage for the organization. A series of agents, the *blamemongers* (Dingwall and Hillier 2016, 9), try to blame negative organizational events on the scapegoat for their own advantage. The outcome of blamemongers' strategies is not predetermined, rather actors – including the scapegoat – can proactively influence the attribution of responsibility and blame. They can catalyze and strengthen scapegoating or channel

with corporate actors at the expense of people. For example, the *New York Times* reduced the proportion of attention paid to people on its front page from 40 percent in 1876 to about 20 percent in 1972, while in the same period, also on the front page, it significantly increased its attention to corporate actors (Coleman 1982, 12–13).

[30] Coleman prefers to use the concept of corporate actor, rather than organization, in order to emphasize the dimension *of the action* of a subject whose behavior is aimed at achieving ends (1982, 33). With this concept, he refers to large impersonal subjects, such as companies, trade unions, voluntary associations, and even the state (153).

and prevent it, leading to either the scapegoat's isolation, expulsion, cohabitation, or assimilation (Djabi and Sitte de Longueval 2020).

At other times, the role of scapegoat in organizations is formalized. Because of its position within the organization, the scapegoat is a *lightning rod* that is surely involved in the event of organizational failures, even if his contribution was not decisive in relation to the events. For example, with regard to accidents, the safety managers at the top of the organization are frequently brought into the picture regardless of the role they actually played in the etiology of the event. In other cases, the role of the scapegoat is not formalized and emerges from the specific contingencies of the event. In other words, it cannot be deduced ex ante, but only ex post.

The fabrication of the organizational scapegoat is favored by the logic of criminal law – something we will look at in more detail later. This logic, based on the "short history", reduces the genesis and dynamics of a complex event to the behavior of one or more individual agents. Responsibility for the negative conduct triggering the event is therefore attributed to subjects, who will have to pay the consequences. Through this sacrifice (conviction, sometimes accompanied by being pilloried in the media), the organization involved is able to reduce and adjust its own guilt.

However, this can mean that people are not only punished in a way that is sometimes excessive compared to the role they actually played, but also that the real causes of a problem (and sometimes the real culprits) are concealed.

It is worth pointing out that an individual, with an eye to future earnings, can also accept the position of scapegoat (Acceptance vs Nonacceptance, see Table 1.1). For example, in corporate crime events, a person somehow involved in the situation, in exchange for substantial gain and/or a better corporate position, could agree to assume unwarranted blame in order to protect the leadership and other figures from perilous judicial investigations.

Scapegoating within an organization involves the identification by the dominant coalition of the person or group of people who will be able to fill that particular role (Bonazzi 1983a). The processes of symbolic blaming following accidents (unintentional) and misconduct (intentional) are advantageous for the various parties involved as they mask criticalities present in the organization which may in fact have substantially contributed to the genesis and dynamics of the event.

Forms and Types of Scapegoat

Table 1.1 *Scapegoats: types and defining properties*

	The archetypal scapegoat	The innocent scapegoat	The organizational scapegoat
Subject and significance	A person who takes upon themselves the sins of the community in order to atone for them	An innocent person who is punished for what a guilty person has done	A person who is punished not only for their own faults but also for the faults of others
Function	Atonement for the sins of the community	To be punished for the faults of others	Instrument of organizational rationality
Originating context	Community, both from below (mob rule) and from above	Society, both from below (mob rule) and from above	Intra- and inter-organizational, mainly from above
Predominating agent	Individual	Individual, social groups	Individual, groups of individuals
Role in relation to events	Not involved, extraneous to the facts	Not involved, extraneous to the facts	In some way involved
Formalization of the role	Present	Absent	Present or emerging
Organizational context	Not relevant	Not relevant	Decisive
Acceptance/ Non-acceptance	Non-acceptance	Non-acceptance	Non-acceptance; sometimes also acceptance (out of self-interest)

The sociology of disasters and accidents in organizations can also provide a useful field of study of the processes of symbolic blame-giving and scapegoating. Scapegoating has been detected in numerous cases of accidents and disasters: for example, after a fire (Veltford and Lee 1943); a plane crash (Bucher 1957); an explosion

(Drabeck and Quarantelli 1967; Drabeck 1968); a winter storm (Neal and Perry 1980); in the management of a toxic waste site (Levine 1982); and in cases of air pollution and health problems (Neal 1984), etc. Faced with a disaster, the actors who are potentially involved try to establish a distance between their role and their responsibility and what happened, in order to place the undesirable outcome in a light that is more favorable to them (McGraw 1991, 1137). Drabek and Quarantelli (1967) consider the identification of scapegoats following a disaster as a rational self-defense strategy on the part of figures who could be legally accused of bearing responsibility for the event themselves. It is therefore a matter of management strategy (Warren 2007).

Setting blame at an individual level is, on the one hand, a way to hide organizational flaws; on the other, it can exonerate the organization from costly organizational changes that are potentially threatening to the existing power structures. In this way, scapegoating "shifts fault for complex social challenges from in-groups to out-groups" (Crocker 2021, 1947). According to Kennedy, "The essence of scapegoating is the attempt to identify the sources of social problems as external to the group" (2000, 833). For instance, when an accident occurs, the desire to accuse someone is intense, and this can favor the creation of a scapegoat – a process that focuses mainly on the existing and most visible evidence while ignoring what is less conspicuous (Kahneman 2011, 85).

Alexander (2005, 30) notes that in Western societies there is a growing tendency to equate disaster with notions of recrimination, scapegoating, neglect, and guilt. These are ideas with strong moral connotations. In this process, societies try to neutralize the fear of disaster through anger and guilt. The prosecution and indictment of individual agents becomes a useful expedient that makes it possible to delay or avoid structural change, as public opinion is led to believe that the exemplary punishment of the "guilty" individual can serve as a deterrent in the future (Bonazzi 1983a). But there is no relationship between the severity of individual punishment and organizational change, particularly if the event was generated unintentionally.

In some cases, the scapegoat may not be an individual or a group of individuals: it might also be, for example, a system of rules deemed wrong or excessively bureaucratic, which impedes the efficient functioning of the organization and can give rise to problems (Perrow 2014). In this case the rules become the scapegoat for a whole series of organizational problems that are difficult to anticipate and analyze.

The scapegoat in organizations is the figure who pays the price in place of someone else. Importantly, he must be a credible figure for the part, otherwise the desired result will not be obtained. To be credible, he cannot be wholly extraneous to the situation, rather he must have played a role in the genesis and dynamics of the event which gave rise to the negative consequences. The search for an organizational scapegoat is not an irrational act – quite the opposite. If the scapegoat is to take the blame for others, the culprit identified must be a reasonable choice, someone who could conceivably be responsible for what happened.

According to Bonazzi (1983a), the satisfactory criterion for distinguishing a scapegoat from an effective manager relates to the degree of congruence between the set of resources entrusted to the person and the set of objectives that he must pursue. If the resources are inadequate from a qualitative and quantitative point of view with respect to the assigned objectives, then a scapegoat situation arises. It could be objected that the person, aware of this inadequacy, should have reported this criticality and, in the absence of change, resign. But this is not always entirely true or possible, both due to the fact that ex ante there is not often a clear awareness of this inadequacy of resources (something that is often explicit ex post), and to the individual's possible lack of power within the organization.

If the power group's scapegoating exercise does not produce the expected results, it is possible that the group will decide to sacrifice one or more members located in distant and marginal positions, who will become additional scapegoats. In this way, the creation of a scapegoat is configured as the price to be paid by a power group in order to overcome a state of crisis and minimize the negative consequences. It is a harm reduction strategy, which does not affect the ruling coalition but which must meet certain conditions to be credible. The scapegoat candidate must hold a position that is somehow functionally connected with the negative event, and there must be a certain proportionality between the hierarchical role and the severity of the accident. The ideal nature of this strategy is that the scapegoat is found "at the intersection point between the lowest (furthest) hierarchical level from the top of the homogeneous power group and the minimum sufficient degree of social credibility" (Bonazzi 1983a, 44). This strategy is supported by the fact that the public does not reject scapegoats per se, it only rejects those perceived as being outside the area of power. It is as if to say that the conditions for deception exist, as long as it is done well.

Bonazzi (1983a), for example, writes that the public may know that the person to be punished is in reality only a scapegoat, but can accept the sacrifice as a symbolic compensation for what happened. The public, therefore,

> while in principle demanding justice that is real and complete, is satisfied in concrete transactions with power if someone perceived as objectively participating in the power group is punished. For example, if only one individual out of five responsible for a decision that turns out to be the cause of an accident is punished, the responsibility he actually bears is 20%; but he will at the same time be seen as a scapegoat, since his sacrifice makes it possible to cover the remaining 80% of guilt that remains unpunished. (Bonazzi 1993a, 53)

However, the conditions under which such solutions can actually prove satisfactory require more detailed investigation.

In conclusion, the phenomenon of scapegoat construction in organizations, also defined as corporate scapegoating, is an instrumental model of behavior designed to distort the correct attribution of responsibility (Wilson 1993). It is also a pattern of *intentional* behavior, deployed by certain actors as a defensive mechanism to avoid blame by shifting it to someone else. However, it is also true that, when things go wrong, people try to avoid blame by shifting it toward organizations (Crant and Bateman 1993). In this regard, Bailey identifies an interesting mechanism, the opposite of the one previously described, defined as *individual scapetribing*. This refers to "individuals pointing the finger of blame at organizations (or groups, institutions, and systems) as means of excusing, or ascribing responsibility for, their personally enacted behaviors" (Bailey 1997, 47). In scapetribing, an individual (or a group of individuals) falsely blames a corporate body or, more informally, a larger group of people, for their own actions. The term "scapetribing" implies the sacrifice of the whole "tribe" through the attempt to blame, with no particular precision, the whole group for certain outcomes. In this, scapetribing is similar to the sacrifice symbolized by the scapegoat, although it operates in the opposite direction. It can be a type of reaction to an organization's attempt to create a scapegoat. It is particularly frequent in cases of accidents and disasters, when guilt is traced to the top management of organizations and institutions because they bear formal managerial responsibility.

Finally, to understand the processes that lead to organizational scapegoating, we should first identify the main agents involved and the role that they play. We can distinguish three kinds of agents involved. First, the *promoters* who triggered the scapegoating. Second, the *beneficiaries*, those who benefited from identifying a scapegoat by avoiding their own involvement. Third the *helpers*, those who, without being directly involved in the event and in the trial, favored the construction of the scapegoat.

2 | The Scapegoat as an Instrument of Organizational Rationality

2.1 Blame Avoidance and Lightning Rods

Blame attribution is a social process (Palmer 2014) that starts when agents such as journalists, prosecutors, or society in general, report that an important negative event has occurred, and that someone must take responsibility for it (Brändström 2016, 118). At this stage, external audiences analyze and evaluate the behavior of the accused individual or organization (Palmer 2013; Mohliver 2019; Radoynovska and King 2019; Roulet 2020) and their judgment, often negative, entails costs for the organization (Coombs and Holladay 2006). Nevertheless, in case of ambiguous situations, the accused organization can successfully shift the blame because external actors can only infer about who is responsible (Allport 1954 [1979]; Crocker et al. 1991; Faulkner 2011; Johansen, Aggerholm, and Frandsen 2012; Jacquart and Antonakis 2015; Butler, Serra, and Spagnolo 2020). Roulet and Pichler (2020, 3) call "blame game" this "collective and discursive phenomenon of social actors instrumentally positioning themselves to protect themselves and deflect blame".

One important field for the study of blame games, especially organizational scapegoating, is politics. Policy-makers usually employ different *blame avoidance* strategies to gain and maintain consensus and avoid the attribution of blame, responsibility in case of wrongdoing (Weaver 1986; Hood et al. 2009), and sanctions. A first set of strategies (*agency strategies*) involves avoiding blame by limiting responsibility through the attribution of formal proxies (Hood 2002) – for example, by appointing an organizational manager for a specific, potentially risky, activity. A second set of strategies (*policy strategies*) involves designing policies that obscure the causal relationship between the policy-maker and the result of his decisions (Weaver 1986; Pierson 1994) – for example, by limiting the traceability of an unpopular but necessary political decision. Finally, a third set of strategies (*presentational strategies*) involves framing the events that occurred by trying to manipulate public and media perception (McGraw 1990; Brändström and Kuipers 2003; Hood et al. 2009).[1] Communication is crucial to manage accusations of wrongdoing and avoid major legal, economic, and reputational costs (Coombs 2007; Bolino et al. 2008; Bundy and Pfarrer 2015; Bundy et al. 2017).

Transferring blame plays an important role in the dynamics of a company's micro-politics, and serves, for example, to provide a justification for complaints or mask inadequacies. Furthermore, together with the development of networks of allies, it appears to be one of the significant requirements for a person's career in a company (Jackall 1988).

The blame avoidance strategy has been used in particular by several American presidents (Ellis 1994; Preston 2011). To say that a president should think about how to avoid being blamed for events resulting from his actions means to say that the president must always think about what will happen *when* (not if) things go wrong (Ellis 1994). Politicians are motivated more by the desire to avoid blame for unpopular actions than by the willingness to claim credit for popular ones. This is consistent with the *prospect theory* of Kahneman and Tversky (1979), and derives from the "negativity bias" of voters – their tendency, in other words, to be more sensitive to actual or potential losses than to gains. Incentives to avoid blame induce politicians to adopt a range of political strategies, including: limiting the agenda – so, not considering potentially costly choices; "passing the hot potato" – forcing *others* to make politically costly decisions; and "jumping on the bandwagon" – supporting more popular political alternatives. Politicians therefore make different decisions than they would were they primarily interested in pursuing good policy or maximizing opportunities to claim credit. Blame avoidance strategies are combined with the creation of a scapegoat, internal or external to the organizational context, in order to divert blame toward others.

---

[1] McGraw (1991) identifies five forms of management relating to the blame process of an event: (1) arguing that it was something impossible to predict; (2) placing the blame on the group previously in control, since the incident is a consequence of their actions; (3) attributing responsibility to the context, indicating a situation involving insufficient resources despite good intentions; (4) adopting the *blame us all* method, indefinitely extending blame to everyone, creating a horizontal dispersion of responsibility and preventing anyone specific from being blamed; (5) adopting the *blame them up/down there* method, placing blame on a superior or a subordinate.

If things do go wrong, occupying certain organizational roles makes it more likely for people to be identified as relevant actors, even though they have not contributed significantly to the genesis and dynamics of the negative events. This gives rise to the lightning rod role.

An example of this refers to events dating back to the *Tangentopoli* (or "Bribesville") period in Italy, a term that has been used since 1992 to define a widespread system of political corruption. It was opposed by a series of investigations called *Mani Pulite*, "Operation Clean hands", principally conducted by the public prosecutor's office in Milan. The investigations brought to light a system of corruption extending to multiple levels. Politicians from almost all government parties were charged with crimes such as corruption, stolen goods, extortion, conspiracy, violation of the law regarding public funding, and other crimes. Party treasurers, who illegally received and managed money without necessarily accruing any personal advantage, became the "lightning rods". They inevitably ended up figuring significantly in the investigations precisely because they were the receivers of the money. One exemplary "lightning rod" case involved Severino Citaristi, the administrative secretary of the Christian Democrat Party, who became one of the symbols of *Mani Pulite* (Carra 1999). Starting from May 1, 1992, Citaristi received 74 notices of motion from nine different prosecutors for violation of the law regarding public financing of parties and other crimes. Things could hardly be otherwise, given that he received the money, even though he did not benefit directly from this.

A particularly interesting example of a successful lightning rod strategy is the Habache affair, which took place in France between January and February 1992.[2] Georges Habache was a Palestinian leader of the Palestine Liberation Organization, one of the founders of the Popular Front for the Liberation of Palestine and a wanted terrorist. Habache had asked to have surgical treatment in France. The President of the French Red Cross acted as mediator and contacted the Secretary General of the Foreign Ministry who, after informing

---

[2] See the investigation report on the case: "Gérard Larcher (rapporteur), Rapport de la commission d'enquête chargée de recueillir tous les éléments d'information sur les conditions dans lesquelles il a été décidé d'admettre sur le territoire français M. Georges HABACHE, dirigeant du Front populaire de libération de la Palestine (F.P.L.P.), Paris, Sénat, June 18, 1992, 275", www .senat.fr/rap/r91-424/r91-4241.pdf.

the Chief of the Cabinet Staff of the Ministry of the Interior, gave the authorization. The Red Cross also requested that Habache not be legally prosecuted in France during his hospital stay. The Ministry of the Interior verified that there were no criminal prosecutions against him in France and agreed.

As soon as Habache flew into Paris, reporters took notice and stirred up a scandal. Both the Minister of Foreign Affairs and the Minister of the Interior stated that they had only become aware of Habache's arrival after his departure from Tunis, or even after his hospitalization. The opposition parties accused the government of complicity with the terrorist and demanded the resignation of the Foreign Minister. Instead, the resignations of certain lightning rods were handed in, such as the Secretary General and Chief of Staff of the Ministry of Foreign Affairs and the Chief of Staff of the Ministry of the Interior. At the request of the board of directors, the president of the French Red Cross also resigned. The Parliamentary Commission of Inquiry found clear communication problems between the various state departments and a certain "laxity" in the action of the ministries involved. However, the management of the Habache affair was classified as an error and no high-level politician was forced to resign. The lightning rods in this case were sufficient.

The concept of the lightning rod as a blame avoidance strategy has also been developed in political science, in the analysis of various scandals that have affected some American presidents. In this regard, Preston writes that "a time-honored blame-avoidance strategy is to find an individual or organization reluctant or unable to defend itself to serve as lightning rod or scapegoat" (2011, 89). The concept of lightning rods is based on the assumption that the behavior of political leaders is determined by how the general public perceives and attributes responsibility (Ellis 1994). Blame, therefore, is not automatically attributed on the basis of objective events, but is instead assigned after filtering events through a perceptual schema.

Just as, according to Machiavelli (1513 [2015]), a prince must delegate unpleasant tasks to others, so presidents must try to shift blame on to subordinates. To understand the popularity of a president, it is essential to analyze the process through which he transfers blame to others. In this regard, the consultants who make up his group of closest collaborators are perfectly placed to become lightning rods to deflect criticism (Ellis 1994). Greenstein (1982) argues that President

Eisenhower's success stemmed from the fact that he kept away from the daily controversies of his administration by resorting to a series of lightning rods – consultants who "lent their face" to controversial political issues. In this way, he could shift the blame for negative or disappointing results onto his collaborators. He was certainly not the only one to resort to this strategy. The use of officials, consultants, secretaries of state, and even vice presidents as lightning rods to accept blame and voter criticism has been a strategy followed by many American presidents (Ellis 1994). It didn't always work, however. In the Watergate scandal, the progressive creation of scapegoats, closer and closer to President Nixon's center of power, did not prevent the latter from being punished in person (Bonazzi 1983a).

Employing a lightning rod is more than just a way to conceal failure. According to Ellis (1994), it is a way to close down an investigation, to wrap a cloak of self-justification around yourself, ignoring the harmful consequences of inept behavior. While this may be good for a political leader, it is certainly not good for the citizens. The use of lightning rods by American presidents renders an already irresponsible system even more irresponsible.

Organizations, as well as individuals, can also play the role of lightning rods. Some are better candidates than others. The CIA, for example, "has always been a convenient lightning rod for the White House because its general and foot soldiers are disinclined to come out to defend themselves" (Drumheller 2006, 2). As a result, it has functioned as a scapegoat for various foreign policy disasters. The intelligence community appears to be a convenient scapegoat for political decisions that go wrong. Furthermore, it provides political leaders with another possible blame avoidance tactic to use with lightning rods: the classic defense that "If my subordinate had really disagreed with my position/policies, they could have said something or objected, but they didn't" (Preston 2011, 92). This strategy of blame avoidance and the creation of lightning rods/scapegoats was followed by President Bush in the second Iraq war (Preston 2011).

Regulatory agencies also tend to play the role of lightning rods in the event of a disaster. Indeed, according to Hutter and Lloyd-Bostock (2017) they sometimes seem to have been created precisely in order to relieve politicians and governors of difficult decisions: if these are attributed to regulators, then they will be held responsible when crisis situations occur.

Returning to the theme of blame avoidance, it might be useful to recap the distinction between risk and danger introduced by Niklas Luhmann (1991). A risk situation exists when damage is seen as a consequence of a decision and therefore attributed to it. A dangerous situation exists when damage is believed to be due to external factors and is attributed to the environment. The distinction is relevant in order to understand the meaning of certain complex political decisions. Luhmann cites the case of some military exercises conducted with the use of missiles in Sweden. For the occasion, it was considered politically appropriate to evacuate a large number of Lapps by helicopter. Nevertheless, since the affected area was vast and sparsely inhabited, the probability of a helicopter accident was much higher than the likelihood someone would be hit by a stray fragment of missile. But the first case was a question of political risk, the second, of danger.

Dilemmas of this type arise in particular situations, such as military actions in which drones are used to eliminate dangerous terrorists, with the risk of harming innocent victims. In the film *Eye in the Sky* (2015), director Gavin Hood presents a complex and realistic decision-making process. A drone locates a den of jihadists on the outskirts of Nairobi, a hideout for two very dangerous fugitives and other extremists who are preparing a kamikaze attack with explosive vests. A missile could stop them immediately. The risk is that innocent victims might be involved, in particular a young girl. What should be done? The decision-making process involves three organizations and three different powers: the military is impatient, focused on the goal of eliminating the danger, and paying less attention to the collateral consequences of decisions. Politicians are more uncertain, concerned as they are about the consequences of the eventual death of the child – not so much out of compassion as for the negative effects on their image. The lawyers, meanwhile, are intent on the legitimacy or otherwise of a risky action of this type, anxious not to violate established procedures (the "rules of engagement").

The dilemma of political responsibility emerges clearly just a few minutes before the decision to launch the missile. At that moment, as one of the terrorists is English, the British Foreign Minister has the last word with regard to authorizing the attack. Since a parliamentary consultant opposes the launch of the missile, the minister asks him a rhetorical question: who will have to go on television to say that the terrorists were not stopped in order to avoid collateral damage and that as a result dozens of people died because of the suicide bombers? The parliamentary consultant replies: "Yes, I would save the child and take the risk … Politically I would prefer to blame Al-Shabaab for the death of eighty people who were out shopping, rather than have to justify an armed attack by our army in which an innocent child was killed".

Following a certain rational line of thought, it would certainly be more useful to eliminate the two terrorists and suicide bombers even with the – limited – loss of innocent victims (in this specific case, only one). The suicide bombers would certainly be responsible for many more victims. However, the political cost for that single victim would risk undermining the result achieved, diverting blame on to the political decision maker.

2.2 Scapegoats and Criminal Investigations

Criminal investigations sometimes play an important role in scapegoating, in particular in certain cases of corporate scandal and misconduct. In this regard, William Laufer (2002, 2008) distinguishes two types of strategy on the part of public prosecutors. A first strategy, called "forward whistle-blowing" involves guaranteeing reduced sentences, or even exclusion from sanctions, to those who hold middle-level roles in an organization, in exchange for information about crimes committed by their superiors. Prosecutors tend to employ this specific strategy in periods when controls regarding the conditions of legitimate business conduct are especially intense – in other words, when business scandals shake public opinion in relation to business ethics.

At other times, a second strategy called "reverse whistle-blowing" seems to prevail. In contrast to the first, public prosecutors obtain the cooperation of high-ranking company figures, who provide information about subordinates or intermediate-level managers in exchange for leniency for the company and perhaps even exclusion from criminal prosecution. This may happen, for example, when a senior manager provides evidence of a subordinate's guilt in response to an internal investigation carried out by the regulatory authorities, a criminal prosecution by the public prosecutors themselves, or a threat of criminal prosecution.

Reverse whistle-blowing, according to Laufer, occurs when company managers agree to collaborate with public prosecutors and accuse intermediate-level employees of offenses. In this way, senior figures remain protected and at the same time further investigations into the company are made less likely. Large corporations, says John Coffee, might view middle managers as fungible items that can be sacrificed as a convenient scapegoat and easily replaced (1981, 126). The identification of a deviant employee as a scapegoat seems an optimal solution for both parties: the company and its management team remove the risk of serious criminal prosecutions and high economic costs, while the attorney achieves an effective result by arresting or prosecuting a perpetrator relatively quickly.

By analyzing what actually happens when criminal charges are brought against a large company in the United States, Garrett (2014) shows the complex world of deals "behind the scenes". Punning on the famous "Too big to fail" phrase describing American banks bailed out by the Federal Reserve, Garrett called his book, *Too Big to Jail*, referring to companies considered so valuable to the economy that public prosecutors might not hold them accountable for their corporate crimes. Garrett presents data from over a decade of federal cases, showing an increase in the size and importance of Federal Court cases against corporations.[3] These include companies such as AIG, Bristol Myers Squibb, BP, Google, HealthSouth, J.P. Morgan, KPMG, Merrill Lynch, Monsanto, and Pfizer.

However, the quantitative increase in judicial proceedings was followed by a different approach by the public prosecutors based on deferred prosecution agreements. This is an alternative practice to criminal proceedings, negotiational in nature and consisting of an agreement between the investigating authority and the company under investigation. This agreement involves a process based more or less on the concept that the prosecutors will leave the company out of the investigation "just this once", in exchange for the company's promise not to repeat the disputed behavior and to implement measures of remedy and change. These agreements contain typical elements of plea bargaining and probation, but differ from the latter in terms of the absence of a conviction and the pre-trial nature of the process. With these negotiation activities, the public prosecutors allow the company to avoid a conviction, instead imposing fines and working to reshape

---

[3] Garrett has built an original database with over 250 cases of agreements between public prosecutors and companies in ten years, starting from 2001.

the corporate governance, including the introduction of independent observers to the board of directors. In this way, the public prosecutors try to prevent the company from suffering the collateral consequences of a conviction. For instance, in the case of KPMG, under investigation for embezzlement, a conviction could have produced negative consequences for the prevention of company frauds, among other things. This was something that had happened a few years earlier with Arthur Andersen. Thus, the prosecutors proved the case in a way that avoided weakening the auditing sector.

The rise in corporate fines, Garrett notes, shows how public prosecutors are seeking to rehabilitate companies by changing the way they are run. Prosecutors help companies to put in place systems to detect and prevent economic crime among their employees and, generally, to foster a culture of ethics and integrity within the company. A new and ambitious approach to governance, in other words, in which public prosecutors help reshape the policies and culture of institutions as a whole.

The spread of this type of deferred prosecution agreement has, over time, led to greater control over their use. But Garrett revealed how these "behind the scenes" deals transform corporate crimes into a cost item for doing business. The fact that it is enough to pay to avoid serious personal conviction could favor moral hazard, rather than limit the spread of the phenomenon. In this regard, Uhlmann[4] argues that this type of agreement should be granted only to those who commit violations for the first time, and to a less than significant extent. If not, they should be prosecuted.

As Brent Fisse and John Braithwaite observed: "Corporations, if left to their own devices, will try to deflect responsibility to a select group of sacrificial personnel, often at a lower level than the actual source of skullduggery" (1993, 182–183). The organizational scapegoat (Wilson 1993) therefore becomes a defensive strategy that shifts blame from the organization toward a more vulnerable target, thus avoiding having to implement remedial measures or costly structural change. One solution to avoid these lowball agreements that produce a scapegoat is to mitigate the benefits for the company that employs these solutions, thus blocking cooperation between the prosecutor and the company management.

In some situations, the identification of a person as a scapegoat in an organization could be based on consent, in exchange for some form

---

[4] D.M. Uhlmann, "Prosecution deferred, justice denied", *The New York Times*, December 13, 2013.

of gain. A company employee, who would in any case be involved in legal proceedings, could be induced to declare themselves the only culprit in exchange for a reward to be collected once the sanction period has elapsed. A consensual scapegoat, in other words (Fisse and Braithwaite 1993).

2.2.1 Model Agent vs Model Organization

Faced with cataclysmic events, as well as accidents and disasters, a cause is always sought – a human cause. Even when it is a matter of events of natural origin, it is necessary to seek out the culprit. Sometimes the judiciary contributes to the blame process, in particular when it uses the category of "model agent". The model agent is an ideal agent who behaves in the best possible way in a given situation because he is "able to hypothesize, within reasonable limits, the most serious consequences of a phenomenon, even a recurring one".[5] This is an elusive and rather problematic concept, with a tone that tends toward the optative and deontological rather than the descriptive.

An example in this regard is presented by the procedural events that followed the disaster caused by the flooding of a stream in Genoa, in Italy, on November 4, 2011. The flooding was caused by a self-regenerating storm, a very rare, unpredictable event that occurs only once every few centuries. Three young girls and three adults drowned. The mayor of the city, the safety councilor and some officials were sentenced to modest sentences, accused of not having ordered the closure of schools, of not having warned the principals not to let the pupils out, of not having been able to deal with the situation during the emergency and of having corroborated false reports that backdated the time of the flood and other false statements.

In this way, responsibility for the results of the most intense rain that had ever occurred in this area,[6] together with a territory racked by decades of deforestation and uncontrolled urban development, was placed on a handful of people. An interesting re-analysis of the case and of the trial in particular (Coletti 2020) effectively revealed a

---

[5] As decided by the Italian Court of Cassation, Cass. Pen. Sez. IV of April 12, 2019 n. 22214, 176.
[6] In just a few hours the rainfall was equivalent to what would normally occur over six months.

number of critical issues both in the investigation phase and in the trial itself. In particular, the mayor was cast in a guilty light from the outset, with disparaging, unsolicited, and unnecessary statements betraying the biased attitudes of the first and second instance magistrates.[7] It seemed almost as if the intention was to mix judgment regarding the facts with moral judgment regarding the person.

Above all, the idea of the predictability of an unpredictable event is rightly criticized. In this case it is the flooding of a runnel that had never flooded in previous decades and that day overflowed due to a very rare event – something that had not occurred for centuries. In addition to predictability, the idea of a "model agent" – which the magistrate's judgment is based on – is also discussed.

According to Coletti, the defendants were accused of not having done what they should have done in the abstract, without taking into account what it would have been humanly possible to do in an hour, in the given situation. Their role as guarantors required, in fact, that they be model agents. The Supreme Court of Cassation considered the flooding of the Rio Fereggiano to be an inevitable event, the consequences of which should have been avoidable.[8] Between 11:56 and 12:50, according to the magistrates, there would have been time for the accused to intervene, if well-prepared and prudent, to contain the damage caused by the flooding. Therefore, in the Supreme Court's view the fault was that adequate intervention measures had not been prepared in the event of danger, to be activated at the time of the disaster.

The mayor and the other defendants were convicted for what they *should* have done in an hour, as the role required (model agent), and not for what they humanly *could* have done. This leads on to the concepts of prevention and prediction, which are regarded as distinct but in reality are closely connected. It is logically possible to carry out

---

[7] Tribunal of Genoa, First Section, Sentence no. 6302/2016 of 11/28/2016; Genoa Court of Appeal, Second Criminal Section, Sentence no. 1100 of 23/03/2018; Supreme Court, Criminal Section, Fourth Section, Sentence no. 22214, of 12/04/2019.

[8] According to the magistrates, municipal police cars should have been moving around the city, equipped with megaphones to alert the population, as well as vehicles with tape and barriers to carry out road closures, ready to focus on the areas that were seen to be the most critical. In the hour before the stream flooded, there should also have been constant contact between the police and the fire brigade, as well as with school management and public transport companies. In reality, however, according to the magistrates, nothing was done.

prevention only if there is a previous idea of prediction. Prevention therefore implies an idea of prediction, an idea of a possible future, of a possible scenario. Starting from the 1990s in Italy, observes Coletti (2020), the term "prevention" has undergone semantic emptying, bringing it increasingly to coincide with the term "prediction", with the judiciary defining what these two terms actually mean.

The verdict on this case raises many doubts about the category of model agent, which seems to function as a stepping stone to the scapegoat. For there to be a model agent, two conditions must be met. On the one hand, there must be a reference model – a clear and achievable protocol of activities to be carried out that the operator can actually follow. On the other, there must be a model organization within which the operator is able to act: an organization, that is, that functions in the best possible way – otherwise, the model agent will not be able to act in the optimal way required. In other words, a model agent is only possible in a model organization. In the absence of clear procedures and an exemplary organization, the risk is that the model agent is only a scapegoat, with a slippage from personal responsibility to strict liability linked to the role covered.

2.3 Mechanisms of Stigmatization and Blame

Mary Douglas (1992) stated that indictment and acquittal processes strengthen the organization model and are actually an integral part of it. In order to analyze the processes of the blaming and construction of scapegoats, it is necessary to identify the different social actors involved in various capacities, both individual and organizational. Also, the field of interests and values within which the process of identifying responsibility takes place must be reconstructed. The mass media and the judiciary play a particular role in this, as we shall see.

Scapegoat construction processes in organizations are closely intertwined with stigmatization processes, even though the literature on the subject has treated the two elements separately. Stigma refers "to an attribute that is deeply discrediting" (Goffman 1963, 3). It can assume different forms depending on whether it concerns (1) physical appearance (for example, bodily anomalies); (2) demographic data (for example, ethnicity, religion, or even a specific industrial sector); and (3) character (for example, weakness of will, being dominated by unnatural passions, dishonesty, etc.).

Stigma can be related to organizations as well as to people. Devers et al. (2009) define it as "a label that evokes a collective stakeholder group-specific perception that an organization possesses a fundamental, deep-seated flaw that deindividuates and discredits the organization" (Devers et al. 2009, 155). Once emerged, stigma can transfer and spread "by association" to other organizations, even if they are not involved in the misconduct. Nevertheless, organizations – both the offending and the uninvolved ones – can adopt a range of strategies to manage and cope with stigma (Elsbach 1994; Hudson and Okhuysen 2009; Carberry and King 2012; Vergne 2012; Helms and Patterson 2014), and they can even succeed in removing it (see Zhang et al. 2021 for a review of stigmatization).

Stigma by association can originate from negatively valued organizational characteristics such as a specific corporate form or a country of origin (Naumovska and Lavie 2021). In other cases, it originates from a labeling process which associates an uninvolved organization with misconduct because of some characteristics it shares with the offending organization. Once defined with negative attributes, the organization is discriminated against (Diestre and Santaló 2020) and it may also suffer from negative stock market returns (e.g., Gleason, Jenkins, and Johnson 2008; Paruchuri and Misangyi 2015).

Organizational stigma can also originate at the sector level when the labeling process connects an organization to the broader sector to which it belongs, and which for some reason is negatively evaluated (Ashforth and Humphrey 1995, 1997; Jonsson, Greve, and Fujiwara-Greve 2009; Mishina and Devers 2011; Vergne 2012). For instance, Roulet (2015) found that actors can stigmatize an organization through stigmatization of the underlying institutional logics of the sector the organization is part of.

Stigma can also emerge from single, exceptional, negative events that involve the organization (Hudson 2008) such as accidents, crisis, and policy fiascos.[9] Since organizational stigma can have devastating

---

[9] Warren distinguishes stigma from blame, even if the two aspects can coexist, as in several cases of corporate scandal. While stigma "captures the discrediting *effects* of the blame that the organization or the employee experiences, those who are not blamed for the scandal's events may still experience a demographic stigma" (2007, 479). It is for precisely this reason that it is important for some organizations to identify a scapegoat that is the bearer of both guilt and stigma – the scapegoat.

effects on their business, companies must try to minimize this risk, if possible, by transferring it to a figure, internal or external, to be punished. Therefore, it can become very important for organizations to try to separate the individuals who generated the event from the organization for which they work, even if this organization has in some way pre-established the conditions that gave rise to the event. Organizations therefore develop stigma-management strategies to protect reputation, identity, and business, minimizing legal risks for management. In this regard, Sutton and Callahan (1987) identify some strategies that companies adopt in order to minimize the damage resulting from these events, in particular in cases of bankruptcy.[10] However, not all avenues can be followed: if the blame for a bankruptcy can be partly traced to variables external to an organization, such as economic trends, it is not as easy to deny responsibility, given that these events are usually the result of errors and misdeeds (Marcus and Goodman 1991, 284). Blaming the environment is not always an optimal strategy for companies suffering from poor financial performance (Siegel and Brockner 2005).

However, these studies do not take into account that it can be very useful for a company to recognize failures and misdeeds, while placing the responsibility for these on a particular organizational unit or the failure of a specific worker. Warren (2006), for example, studies the case of an organization that quietly tolerates the use of deceptive advertising practices by its marketing team. Should these practices be discovered, the organization could shift the blame to the team by claiming that they had acted without its approval. Boeker's (1992) research on scapegoats highlights how companies with powerful CEOs and poor financial performance are more likely to replace executives who report to the CEO, rather than the CEO himself.

Van Rooij and Fine (2018) investigate three cases of wrongdoing: the massive oil spill involving British Petroleum's Deepwater Horizon platform in 2010; the Volkswagen fraud to pass car pollution tests discovered in 2015; and the scheme, unearthed in 2016, organized at the Wells Fargo bank, which had opened millions of accounts

---

[10] The stigma-management phases identified by Sutton and Callahan (1987) include: (1) concealing the financial circumstances, (2) defining the situation for the audience, (3) denying responsibility, (4) accepting responsibility, and (5) withdrawing from the audience.

without customer authorization, then imposed charges for a series of unsolicited services. In all three cases, the firms implemented a *blame deflection* strategy, offloading blame on to subordinates. In the British Petroleum case, this included workers who had died in the accident and who had for some time been reporting poor safety conditions. As a strategy, blame deflection is not only unfair – it also promotes and reinforces normalization of deviance (Vaughan 2016).

2.3.1 Change: Scapegoats and Signals

One of the simplest ways to deal with an organization's negative results and failures is to change the management. This signals a willingness to change to the outside world. A similar phenomenon also occurs in the world of football, with the dismissal of the team manager after a series of disappointing results. There are three hypotheses as to why this happens. The first considers the manager as solely responsible for a team's results. His sacking and the arrival of a new manager will therefore have a positive effect on the team's performance, with new tactical schemes aimed at eliminating the mistakes of his predecessor. In the second hypothesis, substitution will lead to the continuation of negative performances, the arrival of the new manager causing confusion in company relations, leading to negative results. In the third hypothesis, closer to the scapegoat idea, the change is attributed to reasons that have little or nothing to do with the team's actual results: the replacement of the manager will appease fans and mitigate pressure from the media, even if it has no actual influence on the team's overall results.

Jan Van Ours and Martin Van Tuijl (2016) studied the motivations for, and consequences of, changing the manager in professional football teams in the Netherlands over fourteen successive seasons. The manager's seasonal change depended on the results of the matches and the difference between actual results and expectations, measured using data from bookmakers. Research results showed that, after the replacement of the manager, the teams performed better. However, performance was also better for a control group where there were no substitutions. The authors therefore conclude that replacing managers per se does not improve team performance.

Moving on to other types of organizations, changing the management of an organization in case it is involved in misconduct may be considered an important act. Surprisingly, however, there is little empirical evidence confirming the alleged benefit of executive turnover as a result of wrongdoing. Gangloff et al. (2016) analyze the reactions of investors to CEO turnover following false financial statements, distinguishing two types of actions: the creation of a scapegoat, when the replacement is provided by a subject inside the organization, and signaling, when substitution takes place with an external subject.

Substitution with an internal subject serves to appease the external demand for change, without, however, bringing about strategic discontinuity (Boeker 1992); it is more of a ritual to appease shareholders (Gamson and Scotch 1964; Rowe et al. 2005). Replacement with an external subject, on the other hand, could be seen as bringing in a "guard-dog". The scapegoat solution (internal substitution) can be seen as a signal to investors, although it is a relatively neutral signal. In this way, the message conveyed externally is based on the idea that the company is not willing to admit the presence of systemic problems and that it intends to maintain previously established practices. However, this is unlikely to really bring benefits to the company. Implementing strategic change, however, is a powerful signal. To be credible to outside observers, a signal must be expensive and irreversible (Connelly et al. 2011). Replacing the CEO with an outsider as a result of financial misrepresentation meets such criteria.

2.4 Situations and Events that Favor the Creation of a Scapegoat

It is necessary to think of the organizational scapegoat as a ceremonial process (Gamson and Scotch 1964) that begins with the manifestation of a negative event (e.g., a crisis, bankruptcy, accident, scandal), continues with the identification of one or more people as scapegoats, and ends with the production of a result for the organization – generally a positive one, such as avoiding or reducing sanctions, costs, stigma and negative social evaluations (Roulet 2020) (see Figure 2.1).[11] Scapegoats thus act as an instrument of organizational rationality, as a remedy in the event that other possibilities have not been either successful or feasible. Therefore, when a crisis threatens the established

---

[11] "Negative social evaluations" is a term to depict any assessment of an actor that has a negative valence (Roulet 2020, 10). However, under certain boundary conditions, negative evaluations could be beneficial (155).

Figure 2.1 Genesis of the organizational scapegoat

order, the organization may choose, stigmatize, persecute, and sacrifice a scapegoat to restore the previous order (Girard 1982 [1989]; Bonazzi 1983a, 1983b; Boeker 1992; Casanova 2014; Daudigeos et al. 2014; Djabi and Sitte de Longueval 2020). Other possibilities include the idea of bad luck; a forced overall silence; the depersonalization of the scapegoat and the shifting of blame on to procedures, technologies or something similar; and covering up the investigation (Bonazzi 1983a, 72).

Scapegoating is an organizational strategy that can advance both organizational and individual interests. On the one side, scapegoats allow the organization to avoid any legal consequences, major economic costs, and reputational damage. On the other side, since association with a tainted organization is damaging, scapegoating also benefits the managers of the organization (Wiesenfeld, Wurthmann, and Hambrick 2008; Pozner and Harris 2016). As I will discuss in the case of the *Costa Concordia* there was a convergence of different interests towards scapegoating the captain of the ship. Finally, sometimes the scapegoat himself benefits from his role because, in return for bearing the blame, he will receive substantial rewards from the organization.

When other possibilities fail, the scapegoat strategy becomes a solution. The most recurring situations that favor its genesis are given below.

2.4.1 Crisis, Disaster, and Policy Fiascos

Crisis situations represent a particularly important field for analyzing the creation of the scapegoat – the price to pay for the ruling coalition to overcome the crisis unscathed or with the least possible damage (Boin, McConnell, and 't Hart 2008; Boin et al. 2017). Crises are defined by 't Hart (1993) as episodic interruptions of familiar patterns that legitimize the pre-existing political order. The future of political leadership depends on how the crisis is framed, managed, and resolved. Crises and disasters, like policy fiascos, become politicized rather quickly, and this leads to two possible outcomes. The first is *accountability*, where the leadership takes responsibility for what happened and what was done before, during, and after the crisis. The second is *learning*, through the evaluation and redesign of institutions, policies, and practices with a view to their improvement (Rose and Davies 1994). While the accountability process of a crisis or disaster looks mainly at the past, at what happened, and is aimed at judging the behavior of the actors in the situation, the learning process is instead aimed at the future, at improving structures and organizations.

Crisis and disaster learning processes are aimed at identifying remedial measures that could and should prevent similar events from happening again. While some organizations are "bad learners" (Stern 1997), others, such as high-reliability organizations (Weick and Sutcliffe 2015), are able to develop learning processes from errors. We will return later, in Chapter 5, to the distinction between the two processes of accountability and learning.

Moving on to the concept of policy fiasco, Bovens and 't Hart define it as "a negative event that is perceived by a socially and politically significant group of people in the community to be at least partially caused by avoidable and blameworthy failures of public policymakers" (1996, 15). Unlike accidents or disasters, policy fiascos are not immediately recognizable phenomena, but require interpretation (Bovens et al. 1999): this, in turn, in some way involves the attribution of responsibility and blame for what happened. Assessments of the failures or successes of a given public policy tend to be quite variable, as it is a question of giving a judgment with regard to specific events that have occurred.

Policy fiasco may concern a "program failure" or a "political failure" (Bovens et al. 1999, 123). In the former, failure relates to the technical dimension of policy-making and organizational behavior. It occurs when a political decision, plan, or strategy fails to achieve the desired impact on a certain target of the population, or produces unintended consequences. With political failure, however, policy fiasco concerns the way in which policy is perceived by public opinion and the political arena and not its social consequences. The distinction between political and program failure is important in order to understand the behavior of political elites and how they try to defend themselves from the attribution of blame and responsibility for their failures.

To better understand the dynamics of these events, it may be useful to briefly describe the different phases that characterize the analysis (Bovens and 't Hart 1996). The first phase, called "assessing events", concerns a certain combination of events that exceed the normal zone of public tolerance and are regarded as undesirable by the public. They are perceived as damaging to the public interest – such as the flooding of a river, for example. The second step involves "identifying agents". These negative events are perceived as the result of actions or omissions by public officials or agencies appointed to deal with them. Their origin is, therefore, not considered as deriving from impersonal forces. For example, in the case of a flood, the emphasis is not on the particular weather conditions, such as the unusual amount of rainfall, but rather on the erosion of the river banks and the absence of adequate river dams, both seen as man-made. The third phase, "explaining behavior", considers the actions or omissions to be the result of avoidable failures by the people or organizations responsible for dealing with such events. The absence of preventive measures and actions that could have contained the flooding are attributed to the weakness of the political leadership in coping, for example, with the rejection of local environmentalists in relation to the construction of river dams. Finally, the last phase is that of "evaluating behavior".

On the one hand, there is consensus that those responsible for the event should be punished. On the other, there is no consensus as to who exactly should be punished and for what. In the case of the flood, some may hold environmentalists guilty for hindering the creation of remedial measures (such as river dams) aimed at conserving the environment. Others may see local authorities as primarily guilty for allowing the construction of housing and industrial plants in unsafe areas. Still others may blame the government for failing to adequately protect the public interest.

Once a certain event is interpreted as a fiasco, questions about responsibility immediately arise: who should be held accountable for the negative event? Who should be sanctioned? Who should compensate the victims? (Bovens et al. 1999, 126). In response to attacks, those held to be responsible can employ different defensive tactics during the various phases of the genesis of the event. For example, in the "assessing events" phase: denying the incident, accusing the accused, or giving positive interpretations (claiming that compensation has been paid for the damage); in the "identifying agents" phase: reframing the event as a success, or questioning causality; in the phase relating to "explaining behavior": blaming those who speak out about the event, arguing that, by increasing its visibility, further damage is caused, in addition to that of the event itself, or devaluing the work of the investigators as unqualified, politically influenced, etc.; in the "evaluating behavior" phase: finding justifications for their action or inaction, or apologizing for what happened and declaring themselves ready to pay damages. In this last phase, a further possible tactic is to identify a scapegoat in order to shift blame from the organizational or political upper levels to subordinates. To this end, the latter are presented as the main culprits and then sanctioned with suspension, resignation or dismissal in order to satisfy the public's need to see punishment inflicted and be presented with a scapegoat.

Even in cases like these, complex events with a multi-causal nature and a "long history" can be simplistically interpreted as only being due to the action or omission of one person or more. This gives rise to processes of politicization and blame-placing in public arenas that can result in the identification of scapegoats for the affair, with no remedial measures therefore being put into place for the future.

2.4.2 Accidents

The term "accident" refers to an unexpected, unwilled, unwanted, and undesirable event that has consequences for the life, and physical and mental integrity of human beings and/or economic consequences. It should not be confused with an attack or an act of sabotage, in which the damage is explicitly desired or sought by the perpetrator or perpetrators. When accidents occur in complex sociotechnical systems such as air and rail transport, the chemical industry, nuclear plants, telecommunications systems, the medical system, and so forth, they can have catastrophic consequences (Reason 1997). Those accidents, which can be defined as "organizational accidents", are the type of events that tend to generate scapegoats.[12] As Luhmann states (1991), one of the

---

[12] As dangers increase, accompanied by political inertia, says Beck (1986), a risk society becomes a scapegoat society. The situation is reversed, however: it is not the dangers that create general social unrest, but rather those who denounce them.

possible reactions to an accident by an organization involves identifying a sacrificial victim. Indeed, for a long time, the cause of accidents in organizations was identified as lying in technology failure, in errors by operators. What these explanations have in common is the attribution of all responsibility for the accident not to the organization and its operating practices, but to the most convenient scapegoat: human error.

Nevertheless, organizational accidents have multiple causes. In his seminal book, *Man-made Disasters*, Barry Turner (1978, Turner and Pidgeon 1997) introduced the idea that disasters are the result of social and organizational processes – in particular, of latent factors in the organizational system. As demonstrated later by the organizational theory of accidents in organizations, the greater the number of organizational criticalities and design defects, with consequent flaws in the control systems, the more likely it is that a human action decision will cause an accident (Reason 1997; Perrow 1999; Catino 2006a; Vaughan 2016). These critical factors are the preconditions of the erroneous individual action that violates safety conditions. In other words, if accidents and near misses are generated, in most cases, by human error or violation, those errors and violations are socially constructed by complex organizational processes and structures. The term "organizational error" identifies situations predisposed to error regardless of the person who acts: although the actor might change, the situation itself does not.

Following the Three Mile Island nuclear accident (1973), the collision of two planes during take-off in Tenerife (1977), and other organizational accidents (Catino 2006a), the conception of the etiology of events of this type has progressively changed. They are no longer considered as uncontrollable events, but as risks that were not properly managed, as a failure of risk management. Accidents are regarded as sociotechnical events in which social, administrative and managerial factors play an important role. If it is true that a human error triggers the accident, it is equally true that this error is organizationally constructed (Vaughan 2016) and can be amplified by the sociotechnical context in which it occurs.

2.4.3 Scandals

Scandals are publicized transgressions that run counter to established norms (Piazza and Jourdan 2018). They can affect individuals (Alexander 1988; Thompson 2000; Adut 2005) and entire organizations (Jensen 2006; Keenan 2011; Piazza and Jourdan 2018). In this book, I will refer to scandals in organizations. These can seriously damage organizations that are found guilty and even threaten their existence, as demonstrated by the Enron case (Jensen 2006). In particular, scandals can cause both legal (Pontikes, Negro, and Rao 2010) and economic (Jensen 2006; Piazza and Jourdan 2018; Jonsson et al. 2009) damage, and can have a significant impact on the dynamics of competition and the criteria of legitimacy of an entire economic sector (Barnett and King 2008; Parachuri and Misangyi 2015; Piazza and Jourdan 2018); they can even influence the country of origin of the organization involved (Weeber 2008).

Scandals can damage the reputation of organizations, generating stigmatization with lasting negative effects on trust (Owens 2011) and legitimacy (Fine 1997). In addition to the organization involved, other organizations also risk suffering the negative consequences of a scandal, which is a phenomenon capable of rapid expansion. Indeed, it can infect other organizations regardless of any real responsibility, even through simple association (Jonsson et al. 2009; Pontikes, Negro, and Rao 2010; Parachuri and Misangyi 2015). Scandals, therefore, expose organizations deemed guilty of transgression to serious consequences. However, they can adopt a variety of strategies to deflect guilt and the associated damage. Attribution of blame following a scandal does not, in fact, occur automatically, but is the result of a process of social interaction (Bucher 1957; Weiner 1986). Likewise, organizations can influence the severity of the consequences. For example, the stigmatization of organizations involved in a scandal is not inevitable, but is the result of a collective process of *labeling*.

There are three strategies organizations can adopt to avoid blame and its consequences (Weaver 1986).[13] The first, *denial*, involves denying the event they are accused of or contesting the negative interpretation given (Marcus and Goodman 1991; Lamin and Zaheer 2012; Benoit 2015). A second strategy is *focus shifting* – in other words, shifting attention (media, public opinion, stakeholders) from organizational criticalities toward socially desirable aspects and actions, such as the financing of

---

[13] Politological studies have observed that policy-makers adopt different strategies aimed at blame avoidance (Weaver 1986), in other words, to avoid unpopular decisions and policy errors being transformed into electoral retribution (Boin et al. 2010). The study of the scandal in political action is particularly interesting, giving rise to a specific field of study called *scandalogy* (Markovits and Silverstein 1988).

social programs or the adoption of corporate practices to protect the environment (Zavyalova et al. 2012). The third strategy, *blame shifting*, involves identifying and indicating a culprit, shifting responsibility away from the organization and, at the same time, reaffirming adherence to collective values (Lamin and Zaheer 2012, 54). Organizations can thus shift blame on to exogenous or endogenous factors or actors.

With the former, the organization attributes blame to elements it claims are beyond its control, since they are part of the environment in which it operates. For example, the organization can divert blame to another organization (Blaney, Benoit, and Brazeal 2002; Jensen 2006), the environment, increased competition, or to market difficulties (Sutton and Callahan 1987).

With the second category, blame can be attributed to endogenous elements. For example, organizations may decide to point the accusing finger at the previous leadership group (Sutton and Callahan 1987, 427–428). However, when the alleged culprit is still part of the organization, organizations can distance themselves from the actions that caused the event by firing the person involved (Elsbach and Sutton 1992; Brinson and Benoit 1999), closing production units (Devers et al. 2009), changing the management (Marcus and Goodman 1991; Boeker 1992), or replacing the CEO (Arthaud-Day et al. 2006; Desai, Hogan, and Wilkins 2006; Collins, Reitenga, and Sanchez 2008). The culprit identified is not necessarily the main person responsible for the event, but can function as a scapegoat. For example, when a CEO has too much power to be easily removed, it is the managers who work closely with the CEO who will be punished (Boeker 1992). In other cases, the CEO is made the scapegoat (Gangloff et al. 2016). This is evident when, following wrongdoing, the CEO is replaced by a member of the top management team, a person involved in the company's previous management, rather than by an external figure. Scapegoating, therefore, is another blame-shifting technique available to an organization in order to manage a scandal.

3 | *Corporate Scapegoating: The* Costa Concordia *Accident*

3.1 Prologue

This chapter looks at the case of the *Costa Concordia* accident that occurred in 2012, when the cruise ship collided with a reef near the island of Giglio, off the coast of Tuscany, in Italy. The aim of the analysis is twofold: on the one hand, to demonstrate that it was a "predictable surprise" – a foreseeable disaster, in other words, that had a long incubation period, an organizational accident and not just a human error (Section 3.4.4); and, on the other, to demonstrate the scapegoating process in relation to the figure of Francesco Schettino, the ship's captain (Sections 3.5.1 and 3.5.2).

The analysis will consider the work carried out by public prosecutors and courts through three degrees of judgment and other official investigations and public statements. We will also pay attention to the role played by various organizations, including the Costa Crociere cruise company, the Port Captaincies, local authorities, the media, and other agents. This will, in my opinion, bring out the light and shadow of the case, its numerous inconsistencies and many critical aspects. The investigation of the attorney's office will be re-analyzed, as well as the role of the mass media, and the trial in its various phases, as a case of "historiographical experiment" (Ferrajoli 2000). Much of the "evidence" provided will come in for questioning, highlighting the limits of the investigation which neglected the organizational dimension of the incident. It will be argued that the focus of investigations on the "short history" (which started only three hours before the incident) precluded a more adequate understanding and explanation of the event.

From a judicial point of view, the story of this accident ended on May 12, 2017, with the verdict of the Supreme Court of Cassation that sentenced Captain Schettino to sixteen years' detention. Reduced sentences were given to certain people involved in the event to various extents. It should be noted that I do not intend here in any way to question the good intentions, good faith, or competence and adherence to ethical standards of the various agents and those who collaborated with them. The facts analyzed must be read in the light of this general consideration. Final sentences must be respected, even when a person might not agree with them – as long, of course, as there exists the right to criticize them, with equal respect. The critical observations set out here, therefore, are not aimed at individuals, but at the mechanisms and logics of organizational functioning that may have characterized some actions and decisions which could be considered dubious. It is in fact the right of every citizen, as well as of those who carry out research in the academic field, to highlight criticalities in laws and their application and in the functioning of certain organizations, with the intention of identifying learning, logics, and improvement strategies.

3.2 Analytical Strategy, Methods, and Data Gathering

No reliable and well-developed methodology exists to explain complex organizational events (Rasmussen 1990; Snook 2000; Yin 2018) including scapegoating, which is a phenomenon difficult to access and often denied (Girard 1982 [1989]; Desmond and Kavanagh 2003).

The research on the *Costa Concordia* disaster was based on the study of a single case (Eisenhardt 1989; Eisenhardt and Graebner 2007; Yin 2018), through a longitudinal organizational analysis. In order to explain the actions and decisions taken on the night of the accident, it is necessary to analyze the event in a context and in a longitudinal dimension that is broader in scope than a criminal investigation, integrating history, ethnography, and organizations (Van Maanen 2011; Grey 2012; Vaughan 2016; Vaughan 2021). In other words, the decisions taken that night are the result of decisions and actions that have accumulated over time.

To reinforce the analysis, I have carried out four types of triangulation (Denzin 1978; Patton 1987): (1) triangulation of data, with multiple sources of data on the same theme (in particular on the dynamics of the accident and on the practice of sail-by salutes); (2) triangulation of investigations, with the analyses of various investigators and analysts, such as judges, expert witnesses of the different parties involved in the trial, and experts; (3) theoretical triangulation, with the use of different theoretical and methodological perspectives to interpret the same data set; and (4) methodological triangulation, with the use of different sources such as interviews, written documents, audio, and video. I was not, therefore, a participating observer within the organization, but an external observer who retrospectively reconstructs organizational structures, decisions, and processes based to a significant degree on documents and interviews. In particular, I have used the following sources:[1]

(1) Investigations. I have analyzed over eight thousand pages of documents. These include:
   (a) Proceedings and documents of criminal prosecution against Captain Francesco Schettino, relating to the preliminary investigation phase (the first judicial interrogation and special evidence pretrial hearing), first instance judgment, appeal proceedings, and Court of Cassation appeals; audio recordings of certain stages of the trial hearings, and transcriptions and summaries of the hearings.
   (b) The administrative investigation carried out by the Coast Guard based on the Italian Navigation Code and aimed at determining the causes of and possible responsibility for the accident.
   (c) The "Report on the Safety Technical Investigation" created by the Ministry of Infrastructure and Transport and aimed at identifying the causes of, and circumstances that led to, the accident, from a purely technical perspective, in order to improve maritime safety.
(2) Written documents. Publications and books on the subject; technical reports; analysis of nautical charts and routes; navigation laws and regulations; parliamentary and official documents; memoirs of ship captains.
(3) Audiovisual materials. I analyzed the videos of the Automated Identification System (AIS) of the sail-by salute that led to the disaster (January 13, 2012) and of the previous salute carried out in August 2011, again near the island of Giglio, the black box (Voyage Data Recorder), and some interceptions with people involved in the event. I also collected numerous photos and videos that testify to the practice of sail-by salutes in places other than that of the accident.

---

[1] See the complete list in the sources at the end of the book.

(4) Interviews. I conducted interviews, often more than once, in person, by telephone, by email, and by videoconference with certain privileged witnesses. The main subjects interviewed were: the captain of the *Costa Concordia*, lawyers, journalists, engineers, security experts, and inhabitants of the island of Giglio and neighboring places.

(5) Mass media. I analyzed the media coverage of the event over time by the main local, national, and international newspapers and news broadcasts. In particular, I conducted a systematic analysis of the approximately three hundred articles published on the subject by the daily newspapers *La Repubblica* and *Corriere della Sera*, from the day following the accident (January 14, 2012) until the ruling of the Supreme Court of Cassation (2017); of the press summary regarding the accident and the practice of tourist navigation and sail-by salutes; of investigative TV programs and news broadcasts; and interviews with, and video testimonies of, the captain and the main agents involved in the event.

Empirical analysis has privileged the longitudinal–historical dimension, not so much because it was an event that happened a few years ago, but rather because, in order to explain the event, it was essential to reconstruct the "long history" of its incubation period. I retrospectively reconstructed the event, integrating the micro (individual), meso (organizational) and macro (organizational field) levels, according to a longitudinal perspective. Particular attention was paid to the strategies implemented by the various agents, especially with regard to the media–judicial circuit following the event.

3.3 The Accident: The Short History

3.3.1 The Event and the Facts

The *Costa Concordia* disaster occurred on January 13, 2012 at 21:45 when the ship collided with a group of rocks known as *le Scole*, a few dozen meters from the island of Giglio, off the coast of Tuscany.

The *Costa Concordia* was one of the world's largest cruise ships: 289.59 meters long, with a beam of 35.50 meters, 61.50 meters high above the surface of the water, a draft of 8.29 meters at full load and a net tonnage of 87,196 tons. In her 2,101 cabins she could hold up to 4,890 people, including passengers (1,500 cabins) and crew (601 cabins). She could reach a speed of 23.2 knots, and was equipped with all the most modern technological instruments.[2] Built in 2004, the ship was owned by Costa Crociere, a shipping company of the Carnival Corporation & plc group. The ship was equipped with a Safety Management System (SMS), a set of company policies and procedures aimed at mitigating the risks associated with specific operational factors.

The *Costa Concordia* left on January 7, 2012 for a cruise in the Mediterranean which, after departure from the port of Savona (Italy), included six stops: Toulon (replacing Marseille due to adverse weather conditions), Barcelona, Palma de Mallorca, Cagliari, Palermo, Civitavecchia, then back again to Savona.

On Friday January 13, the *Costa Concordia* sailed from the port of Civitavecchia for the port of Savona, the last leg of her journey. On board there were 4,229 people: 3,206 passengers and 1,023 crew members. The route communicated to the maritime authority included the fact that it would pass close to the island of Giglio.[3] At 18:27, after routine checks, Captain Schettino asked the cartographer to plan a route that would allow tourist navigation near the island of Giglio, passing half a mile to the east of the *le Scole* rock formation.[4] This maneuver would make it possible to carry out a so-called "sail-by salute" – passing close to the coast in order to make a "salute" in honor of the family of the ship's restaurant manager, a native of Giglio, who was currently on duty on board, and of a former captain, now retired, who resided on the island. The event had originally been planned for the previous cruise, but had been postponed due to bad weather. The course change was loaded onto the Radar-Integrated Electronic Cartography System, which provided two "waypoints" describing the ship's change of direction in order to approach the coast: these were 0.5 miles from the Giglio coast, while the normally scheduled distance was about 4–5 miles. The captain approved the new route and,

[2] Global Positioning System (GPS), Electronic Chart Display and Information System (ECDIS), Automatic Radar Plotting Aid (ARPA), AIS, etc.

[3] The description of the facts is based on the data recorded by the VDR, as reported in the Technical Report (RT) of the consultants appointed by the GIP (judge for preliminary investigations) of the Tribunal of Grosseto (11/09/2012) and in the first instance judgment (Tribunal of Grosseto, February 11, 2015).

[4] 1 mile = 1,852 meters; 0.5 miles = 926 meters.

looking at the approach points, indicated a point further south of the shoals to the cartographer, expressing the wish to pass south of the waypoints, but without making any changes to the planned route. In the late afternoon, the captain also contacted the restaurant manager by phone to invite him to the bridge at about 21:30; in this way he would have a better view of the ship's passage near the island.

At 18:57 the *Costa Concordia* left Civitavecchia and headed toward Savona. At about the same time, the ARES message was sent to the Port Captaincy of Livorno;[5] this conveyed the information that the ship would pass between the island of Elba and the Tuscan coast. The change of route was not indicated in the message. At about 19:15, the captain, who until then had been in charge of navigation, left this task to the first officer and, before leaving the bridge, ordered the second watch officer to call him when they were 5 miles from Giglio. After a few minutes, the rudder steering changed from "manual" to "track pilot" in "course" mode, which allowed the ship to follow the route set by the watch officer. The ship continued in this way until about 19:45, when it switched to integrated navigation mode, which allowed the ship to execute a pre-set voyage plan.

At 20:01, the changeover took place between the outgoing officer and incoming first officer, who was informed of the change of route and the order to notify the captain 5 miles from the first waypoint. On the bridge there were five watchkeepers from 20:00 to 24:00: the second officer, who was supporting the first officer in view of the scheduled change at Savona, the third officer, the helmsman and a cadet officer. At 20:18, the first officer called the chief guard in the engine room to tell him to decrease speed to 15.5 knots.[6] This was to delay the start of the approach to the island by about a quarter of an hour, scheduled for 21:45. At about the same time, the restaurant manager telephoned his mother on Giglio to announce that the ship would pass close to the coast in order to "salute" the island on that particular day as well. At 21:04, the ship left the route that had been originally planned to follow the course set by the cartographer. Shortly after, the first officer called the captain, who had just finished dinner, and told him that

---

[5] Automated Search and Rescue System. This is a message that must be sent to the Port Captaincies in order to provide updated information regarding a ship's movements in order to facilitate assistance and rescue operations in the event of danger.

[6] 1 knot = 1.852 kilometers/hour, so about 28 kilometers/hour.

they were 6 miles from the first waypoint (21:19:09). At 21:34:38, 2.54 miles from the rocks of *le Scole* and just 11 minutes from impact, the captain came onto the bridge. The restaurant manager and the ship's hotel director were already there, waiting to see the salute to the island as the ship sailed past. Other non-official figures were also present on the bridge. Radar number 2 was then set to a 3-mile scale, making it easier to spot any nearby obstacles. The captain ordered the switch to manual navigation (21:35:01). However, since the helmsman moved to his place at the helm, from this moment the position of lookout remained uncovered. A minute later, despite the fact that he had not yet taken charge of the maneuver, the captain asked for a CPA (Closest Point of Approach): this set a safety circle of 0.5 miles on the radar to identify obstacles in the area of reference. The ship deviated from the route planned by the cartographer shortly before departure (21:36:49). Meanwhile, the captain started a telephone conversation with Mario Terenzio Palombo, a former Costa Crociere captain and well known in maritime circles (21:37:54). Schettino informed him that the ship was deviating from its course to pass close to the island. Palombo replied that he was not there that evening. The captain asked him if there was water at 0.3–0.4 nautical miles, referring to the depth of the seabed, and Palombo confirmed this. At 21:38:59 the ship was already off course but, receiving no communication or warning, the captain continued to believe that it was on the route he had indicated at the start and that everything was going as it should, or at least in the way that he had planned.

At that point, the captain assumed command of the ship, uttering the phrase "I take the conn" (21:39:17). During the trial, Schettino said that the first officer "passed a boiling pot into his hands without saying that it was hot". He then ordered the speed to be increased to 16 knots (21:39:31), a speed that the Grosseto Court would consider high, given the dangerous nature of the maneuver. The captain then ordered the helmsman to follow a new course and to make the approach "slowly, easy" – in other words, with low rudder angles,[7] to prevent the ship from veering due to the high speed (21:40:02). In transmitting the order to the helmsman regarding the route, the captain was misunderstood. The first officer intervened, in turn reporting an incorrect figure. Since both subordinates had misunderstood,

---

[7] Rudder angle relative to the keel of the boat.

the captain repeated the correct course. For the moment, no one was aware of any danger, no member of the bridge watch staff signaled to the captain and watch officer any doubts about what was happening. This is clear evidence of low situational awareness on the part of all the command staff on the bridge.

Two minutes before impact, the first officer pointed out to the captain that the ship was proceeding at 15.9 knots, but Schettino did not respond (21:43:30). The first officer, however, made no attempt to give the captain a further warning. Schettino therefore ordered a correction of the maneuver, but the helmsman for the second time failed to understand the order (21:43:45). For this reason, both captain and first officer repeated the correct order together. Following this, the captain immediately stated: "Otherwise we go on the rocks". At that moment, the ship was 0.25 miles (450 meters) away from the reef.

On the bridge, a general silence fell across the officers who should have been in charge of navigating the ship. The captain suddenly noticed the foaming sea outside, breaking against the bow of the ship, indicating that the vessel was heading into dangerously shallow waters. He launched an evasive emergency maneuver aimed at circumventing the obstacle, ordering to tack 10° to starboard (21:44:14), then 20° to starboard and then full to starboard, so that each successive order cancelled the previous one – this, in order to prevent the rudders from pausing in intermediate positions, which would have reduced the effectiveness of the tactic.[8] Having cleared the bow from the shallow water, the captain received confirmation from the helmsman that the two rudders had actually reached the position of the tiller whole to starboard. He ordered the tiller to the center (21:44:37) and, following the same criterion by which each subsequent order canceled the previous one, ordered 10° to port (21:44:44) then 20° to port (21:44:46) and then full to port at 21:45:05.

---

[8] It should be noted that the description of the last hectic moments before the collision seems to differ in terms of the point of view of interpretation – certainly not of the facts – from that of the courts. For the latter, it was a succession of improvised maneuvers that were incompatible with the situation, with a sequence of commands where each new order canceled the previous one before it reached the expected result, due to the inertia of the ship. However, the analysis carried out here, which also makes use of the VDR, does not seem to confirm this interpretation by the courts.

Only with the opening of the black box did it emerge that the helmsman, placed behind the captain, executed the orders he was given in a way that was actually diametrically opposite, putting the rudders to the position of 20° to starboard and not 20° to port as Schettino had requested.[9] The second officer, positioned behind the helmsman, reported no anomalies and did not warn the captain, let alone the helmsman, of the error. And it was a crucial error: in the final phase, it prevented the stern of the ship from halting in its approach toward the rocks, thus leading to the gash in the last part of its hull.[10] This was a controversial point in the inquiry and we will come back to it later.

The helmsman realized his error only 13 seconds later and finally turned the rudder to port, but by then it was too late. In reality the ship continued to move toward the rocks and at a speed of 14.2 knots the left flank of the ship collided with the outcrop, tearing a gash of about 36 meters (21:45:07). The water that poured in brought the engines to a stop, blacked out the electrical system and made the ship unmanageable.

At this point the emergency phase began. The rudder became inoperable due to the flooding of the engine room. About 15 minutes after impact, damage assessment was being carried out to understand whether or not the ship should be abandoned. The stability of the ship was compromised, but the crew was unaware of this. Realizing at this point that the ship was going to sink, the captain decided to evacuate the vessel, which came to a halt a few dozen meters from the coast of Giglio, keeling over on to one side. The rescue operations ended a few hours later, at 05:45 the following day. Most of the passengers and crew had been rescued but thirty-two people had died after 24:00 and

---

[9] The black box data concerning the movement of the rudders was acquired in the proceedings and unequivocally shows the helmsman's error. It clearly emerges that the rudders were moving smoothly and with no delay, with the exception of the error made by the helmsman in the final part of the maneuver which prevented him from completely circumventing the obstacle.

[10] The maneuver performed by the captain was recognized by court experts at the pretrial hearing as the only possible way to avoid an obstacle that suddenly appears in front of and in the path of a ship. Incomprehensibly, as emerges from the procedural documents, for the simulations the court experts used a ship of about forty years before as reference – one with two propellers and a single central rudder and not a ship like the *Costa Concordia*, with two rudders in line with the lines of thrust of the propellers, a configuration that makes far more advanced maneuvers possible.

sixty-four people had been seriously injured. Most of the victims were killed as they moved from the port to the starboard side of the ship, having been forced to abandon some of the port-side lifeboats that they had originally sought safety on.

According to the verdict of the court, during the emergency phase the captain went on to commit further procedural violations. Specifically, he delayed the order for the passengers to abandon ship, and demonstrated behavior inappropriate to the situation, until he himself abandoned the ship before the last passenger had safely left the vessel. As will be seen, this is a version that seems reductive and simplistic at the very least.

3.3.2 Criminal Convictions

The *Costa Concordia* accident gave rise to two separate criminal trials for the six people sent to trial. While five people opted for, and obtained, plea bargaining, which took place behind closed doors and without a great deal of media concern, the first instance judgment in relation to the captain was a completely different phenomenon. Lasting a year and a half and consisting of seventy-one hearings, it featured an intense level of attention from the media, both national and international. It was held not in a courtroom but in a cinema, in order to accommodate all the participants and the more than two hundred civil parties involved, consumer associations, and other subjects.

The Court of Grosseto held Captain Schettino to be the main person responsible for the sinking of the cruise ship and the death of thirty-two people, and for this reason he was sentenced to sixteen years' detention. He was declared to be responsible for a long series of violations and errors and accused of recklessness, negligence, and incompetence and of violating laws, regulations, order, and discipline. He was accused in particular of having brought about the disaster by taking the ship close to the mainland in a wholly inappropriate way, and then, following the collision, of having badly organized the rescue operations and of having abandoned the ship before the safety of all the passengers had been ensured.[11] Other figures were sentenced with

[11] More specifically, the captain was held responsible by the court for a series of violations, such as: having changed the planned route with inadequate instrumentation (nautical charts); not having communicated this change either

minor charges: two officers (1 year, 11 months and 1 year, 6 months of detention); the helmsman (1 year, 8 months); the hotel director, present on the bridge at the time of the disaster (2 years, 6 months); and the head of the Costa Crociere crisis unit (2 years, 10 months), for his part in the management of the post-impact emergency.

Some lawyers representing the civil parties considered these sentences to be unfair, given that they did not take into account the role of various subjects in the etiology of the event. In particular, the shipping company Costa Crociere S.p.a., to save costs, had not adequately prepared and trained the crew for emergencies. Aspects relating to the inadequacy of the safety systems present on the ship and their malfunction were also highlighted, as was the practice of so-called "sail-by salutes", which were carried out strictly for commercial and promotional purposes. All these elements played a part in bringing about the shipwreck.

3.4 The Accident Revisited: The Long History, the Three Phases, and the Organizational Factors

In his last book, *The Drowned and the Saved* (1986), Primo Levi questioned the problem of simplification in the understanding of certain dramatic historical and social events. On the one hand, simplification is necessary in order to unravel the infinite and indefinite tangle of the surrounding world; on the other, it is problematic as an effective explanation of these events.

This is what frequently happens with organizational accidents and with wrongdoing in organizations, when the preference is usually to

to the maritime authorities or to the company; having allowed unauthorized persons to be present on the bridge; having arrived late to the bridge with regard to the maneuver that had to be carried out; giving orders to the first officer and the crew on the bridge without having first taken effective command of the ship; not having strengthened the visual lookout, given the conditions of visibility and the maneuver he was about to carry out; having used his cell phone during the approach; having decided to sail closer to the island without adequately assessing the risks; having attempted the maneuver at an excessive speed (16 knots); not having promptly communicated the emergency to the Port Captaincy Office; having given the order to abandon ship late (at 22:54); not having managed the emergency phase according to the procedures provided (for example by forming a crisis unit on board, etc.); having abandoned the ship before all the people on board were rescued.

focus mainly, if not exclusively, on the agents involved in frontline operations. The "short history", based on a single event with a limited time span, is looked at, while an in-depth longitudinal analysis of the "long history" is avoided. But, "time matters" (Abbot 2001). The historian Thucydides, 2,400 years ago, (Tucidide 1979) traced the origin of the Peloponnesian war to the desire of the Athenians, led by Pericles, to assert their hegemony over the Greeks. The triggering event for the conflict, the *casus belli*, was the intervention of Athens in the internal affairs of certain cities (Corcira, now Corfu, and Potidea) and, above all, the Athenian trade block of Megara, which was seen as seriously damaging to a city in the Peloponnesian League. Sparta considered all this an unacceptable threat, accused Athens of having violated the peace established in 446 BC, and declared war. The long history, in other words, determined the short history.

It is often very clear where certain events, such as misconduct and accidents, come to an end, but it is not always so clear exactly where they start. Analyses that are limited in terms of time and the subjects involved do, however, tend to be more frequent. This "short sight"[12] in the analysis of historical and social events is also supported by certain mental processes that lead our minds to favor short causal chains over longer ones. Furthermore, more complex and longitudinal analyses are certainly not encouraged by criminal law, which essentially seeks individual responsibility and therefore favors investigations centered on people, and often only on those directly involved in the event. Finally, interests at stake and power relations can further encourage more limited investigations, ones that do not affect pre-existing power structures, thus leaving the role of organizational factors in the background.

In contrast to reductive perspectives of this kind, the literature on accidents in organizations (Reason 1997; Turner and Pidgeon 1997; Perrow 1999; Catino 2006a, 2010a; Vaughan 2016), and on corporate misconduct and wrongdoing (Vaughan 1999; Palmer 2012; Palmer, Smith-Crowe, and Greenwood 2016; Van Erp 2018) has gone beyond the role of the human factor alone, and the figure of the rogue employee as a cause of error, by highlighting the contribution of organizational factors in the genesis and dynamics of events. It is not possible to understand individual behavior without taking into account the organizational and environmental context in which such behavior takes shape.

---

[12] Dante, *The Divine Comedy*, Heaven, canto XIX (trans.: Clive James).

Furthermore, the inter-organizational level must be considered. Many studies on failure and deviance in organizations tend to imply a prevailing focus on the single organization, as if it could exist independently of the external forces and constraints that create relationships, processes, and structures within it (Glasberg and Skidmore 1998, 426). It therefore becomes essential to analyze the organizational network and the forms of regulation present in the organizational field (Vaughan 2016). In this way it is possible to overcome a conception limited only to amoral individual behavior and/or deviant organization (Lee and Ermann 1999). Each organization is part of a field that is "organizational" (DiMaggio and Powell 1983; Powell and DiMaggio 1991) and legal (Edelman and Stryker 2005), and this helps define and limit its courses of action. An "organizational field" is the set of organizations that operate within a recognized area of institutional life.[13]

In the case of the *Costa Concordia*, the organizational field consists of the organizations responsible for regulating and controlling the activity of maritime transport and traffic.[14] The most relevant subjects at this level are the Port Captaincies, peripheral offices coordinated by the General Command, which are entrusted with the safety of navigation. The activities they carry out include the exercise of disciplinary power over maritime personnel, the supervision of the operation of shipping lines, and the control of general security in ports and their adjacent areas, on ships in port and during navigation in territorial seas.

In light of the theoretical evidence, a longitudinal[15] and systemic approach is required in the analysis of an organizational accident. This is exactly the opposite of what happened with the *Costa Concordia* case,

---

[13] For example: key suppliers, consumers, regulatory agencies, and other organizations that produce similar products and services (DiMaggio and Powell 1983, 148).

[14] First of all, the producers of standards: at the national level, the Ministry of Infrastructure and Transport; at the community level, the European Parliament and Council; and, at the international level, the International Maritime Organization (IMO) and the International Association of Marine Aids to Navigation and Lighthouse Authorities (IALA). Then there are the regulators and controllers, the General Command of the Corps of the Port Captaincies-Coast Guard, on which the individual Port Captaincies, the Maritime Directorates and other minor offices depend.

[15] On the importance of the historical dimension in organizational studies, see Zald 1990. For an example of research that takes this dimension into account, see Selznick 1949 and Fligstein 1987, 1990.

where the magistrate's questioning of experts mainly concerned the short history, from 18:27, when the sail-by salute was planned, to the end of the emergency, a little more than 11 hours later. The timeline requested from the experts started at 19:00, when the ship sailed from the port of Civitavecchia (Court of Grosseto 2012c, 17). Of the fifty questions asked, only fifteen concerned technical aspects (suitability of safety systems, compliance of the ship's design with current legislation, adequacy of maintenance, construction defects, etc.). Not one, however, seemed designed to go more deeply into the risk, in general, of the practice of the sail-by salute. From the public prosecutor's office, there immediately emerged a very specific focus of attention on what was important and, above all, on what was not relevant (Court of Grosseto, 2012c, 10–14).

The answers of the experts to the questions from the attorney's office are divided into four categories concerning: (1) the planning of the route and the availability of the correct instrumentation; (2) the manner in which the accident occurred; (3) the causal link with other factors; and (4) emergency signals and operations. If we exclude some critical issues that have to do with the structure of the ship and the training of personnel in emergency situations, in this evaluation there is not much regarding previous events – the accident's incubation period. In each case, the technical and organizational criticalities were analyzed in an isolated and non-systemic way. No adequate investigation was carried out, as we will see later, to verify the *interactions* between the criticalities detected in determining a certain course of events. The analysis of critical issues, however, should always be conducted in relation to the interactions between them. The accident can be divided into three phases (see Figure 3.1).

The *first* phase, in terms of the long history, dates back to October 1, 1993, with the beginning of the practice of sail-by salutes. The *second* phase begins at 18:27 on January 13, 2012, with the ship sailing from its last port and the planning of the route, and ends at 21:45, with the vessel foundering on the rocks. The *third* phase, crisis management, begins immediately after the impact with the rocks and ends at 05.45 the following day, approximately eight hours after the collision, with the rescue of most of the passengers (the length is 11 hours and 18 minutes in total, from the change of route at 18:27 until the end of the emergency). For a number of reasons, which we will look at closely, both the judicial investigation and media attention focused only on the "short history" – in other words, on the second and third

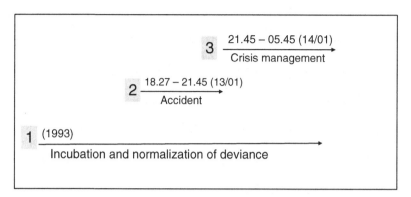

Figure 3.1 The three phases of the *Costa Concordia* accident

phases. Using this reductive and imprecise version of the events, a veil has been drawn over the long history, which is crucial to an understanding of why a ship almost 290 meters in length was passing just a few dozen meters from the coast. Can an arc of around eleven hours really explain an event of this kind? It is this first phase, then, the long history, that will be the main object of analysis here.

From the point of view of analysis strategy, I have reconstructed phases two and three mainly on the basis of judicial documents and repeated interviews with privileged witnesses. Phase one, dealing with the normalization of deviance deriving from the practice of sail-by salutes, has instead been reconstructed through historical and journalistic sources and evidence, and interviews.[16] There follows a detailed study of the three phases.

3.4.1 Phase One: A Predictable Surprise

Chance does nothing that has not been prepared beforehand.

Alexis De Tocqueville, *Souvenirs* (1848–1849 [2000])

The first phase was wholly undervalued – indeed, virtually ignored – during the criminal proceedings. It began on October 1, 1993, when the practice of the sail-by salute – in the sense of sailing close-in to the

---

[16] On the analysis of micro-history and on the evidential paradigm for the analysis of events, see Ginzburg (1989).

coast – came into being, with Captain Mario Terenzio Palombo at the helm of the *Costa Romantica*. As he himself writes in his memoirs:

In the evening around 10 pm I had the opportunity to pass in front of the port of the island of Giglio and, with a significant reduction in speed, illuminate the whole ship as, passing very close to the coast, I saluted my island with three long whistles. It was the first time that such a large ship, the flagship of the Costa fleet and the Italian fleet, had passed so close in order to salute the inhabitants who, attracted by the lights and whistles, immediately rushed on to the quay. (Palombo 2008, 149)

There are several other examples of this kind of maneuver in Palombo's book. For instance, on Sunday October 3, 1993, he is about 300 meters from the Ligurian coast, and later, referring to the retirement home in Camogli, he writes: "I felt I could have touched it with my hand" (150). On other occasions he mentions navigating through Venice in front of Piazza San Marco and, on July 25, 1996, passing near the island of Giglio with the *Costa Victoria*.

Contrary to what emerged from the sentencing and the media reconstruction, therefore, the accident was hardly a bolt from the blue, but rather a "predictable surprise" (Bazerman and Watkins 2004) – a wholly undesired consequence of the risky and repeated practice of the sail-by salute. A predictable surprise is "an event or a set of events that take an individual or a group by surprise, despite prior awareness of all the information necessary to anticipate the events and their consequences" (Bazerman and Watkins 2004, 1). It is up to the leadership, entrepreneurial, organizational, and/or political, to identify and avoid such surprises, precisely because they are predictable.

A great deal of evidence shows that the sail-by salute that led to the disaster was not an isolated case but common individual and organizational behavior repeated over time. It was habitual, not exceptional. The accident that followed was therefore not an unexpected bombshell but an event with a long incubation period, featuring the repetition over time of the same behavior by other captains and ships in a variety of places, with no precise rules to guide its execution. The sail by-salute was not only not seen as a potential source of danger, it was even encouraged by the company and promoted in some of its brochures. The behavior of captains practicing the sail-by salute was therefore not considered deviant but actually conformed to the rules in use.

The importance of individual responsibility should not obscure the fact that groups and organizations can have a very significant influence on individual behavior (Asch 1952). Pressure to conform to group and social norms is quite common (Asch 1952; Moscovici 1985). Furthermore, in an organization, there are social and economic pressures to conform to the views of others, particularly those of one's superior (Prendergast 1993). In some work environments, such pressure can influence the tendency to adopt irresponsible and unethical behavior (Bailey and Alexander 1993).

The Sail-By Salute

To understand how a practice such as that of the sail-by salute became common in tourist navigation, a longitudinal analysis is needed to shed light on how it began and how it became embedded within the navigation system and turned into something almost routine.

The term "sail-by salute" is a maritime expression used to indicate a salute given toward the mainland, making use of illuminated signals and whistling from the ship's siren. This is reciprocated from terra firma, with aural signals also employed in the past. Over time, the sail-by salute became a variant maneuver in tourist navigation. In essence, it was a variation of the route with respect to the ship's predetermined course, involving an approach toward the mainland. The salute then developed into an even closer move, with the ship passing nearer to the mainland coast or the coast of an island.

Originally, the term indicated a safety maneuver. In certain stretches of sea typically traversed by strong winds, it is safer for ships to pass close to the coast (Gaeta 2012, 46–47). Later, the practice of the sail-by salute became more widespread with a different purpose, functioning as a tribute from those at sea to those who lived in coastal resorts. It was a custom the captain shared with the crew, a form of "rite". For example, in the 1950s and 1960s, some captains sent a salute to relatives and friends in this way, albeit not at such close quarters. At that time, ships that passed through the waters of the Sorrento peninsula in Campania (Italy) approached the coast to greet the shipowner Achille Lauro, who, from the terrace of his estate, responded to the greeting by waving a white handkerchief. However, ships were smaller in those days, and passing in close proximity to the shore was easier. The tradition was then handed down to modern cruise ships, which were much larger in size.

The same goes for Giglio's inhabitants. On the evening of the accident, in fact, the following message appeared on Facebook, posted by a member of the restaurant manager's family: "The Costa Crociere's *Concordia* will soon be passing nearby. A big hi to my brother, who will finally disembark in Savona to enjoy a little vacation". A user asks what time the ship will go by and the answer is: "At 21:30, as usual" as if to underline that the event was a typical occurrence and that it was very popular. Numerous confirmations of this came out of the interviews made with the resident population on the island and from an analysis of the local press that advertised these events.

Knowledge of the salute was, then, widespread, including within the company itself, which encouraged the practice for commercial and marketing purposes, both for the passengers already on board and potential future customers. An aporia emerges from Captain Schettino's testimony: on the one hand, he was criticized for not having notified the company and the authorities of the ship's deviation from its course; on the other hand, he was publicly praised by the company for making a similar sail-by salute on August 30, 2010, in front of the island of Procida. On the very same day as the disaster, on the company's website, the following post appeared (and was later deleted):

On August 30, 2010, before arriving in Naples at around 13:00, the *Costa Concordia* paid homage to the island of Procida with a salute and brief stop in the bay of Corricella, all thanks to Captain Francesco Schettino from Meta di Sorrento. An emotional moment not only for the island's inhabitants but also for the numerous tourists present who, from motorboats, fishing boats and boats of all kinds, welcomed the huge, imposing ship with applause, banners, music, trumpets and vuvuzelas. The arrival of the vessel was announced with 10 mortar rounds to which the *Costa Concordia* responded with her ritual greeting of 3 siren whistles. Surely a joyful new experience for everyone, including the passengers on the *Costa Concordia*, ready on the external decks with cameras and video cameras to immortalize that unique moment, celebrating and saluting with flags and handkerchiefs. As the ship's first officer – a native of Procida himself – declared, "It was a real celebration, a gesture of affection and a tribute to the maritime tradition that the folk of Procida and Sorrento have imbedded in their DNA".[17]

---

[17] "When Costa thanked Schettino for his sail-by salute to Procida", *Corriere della Sera/Corriere del Mezzogiorno*, January 18, 2012.

During the day, therefore, Captain Schettino was deserving of fulsome praise on the company's website; by nightfall, he had turned into a figure both incompetent and immoral. Something, here, does not add up. The fact that the post was deleted so swiftly from the site also arouses a certain suspicion.

The *Costa Concordia* also carried out a close-in sail-by salute to the island of Giglio on August 14, 2011, a few months before the accident, but with a different captain on the bridge. Comparing the routes followed by the same ship on August 14, 2011 and on January 13, 2012, it can be seen that they almost coincide. However, the circumstances that led to the salute were different: while on January 13, 2012 it was a "courtesy", on August 14 the previous year it seems to have been programmed by the company for advertising purposes. The purpose may have been different and, in both cases, questionable, but this obviously does not change the nature or the danger of the maneuver. For the prosecutors, however, this aspect seemed to be a relevant one. A paradox emerges from Schettino's first judicial interrogation: the sail-by salute, an extremely risky maneuver in itself, if done for commercial purposes, seems to be tolerated; if done for other, noncommercial, purposes however, it is to be stigmatized and punished (Court of Grosseto 2012, 67).

The sail-by salute of August 14, 2011 was announced on July 23 by Captain Palombo on the website of the newspaper *Giglio News*. The message, which Palombo had written himself, shows that sail-by salutes were well received not only by the inhabitants, but also by the island authorities. In particular, he thanks the mayor for "the marked sensitivity shown towards our seafaring tradition" (Court of Grosseto 2012a, 5). In this regard, the email communication of thanks (published on the *Giglio News* website) sent by Giglio's then mayor is especially interesting, as is the reply. The thanks were sent to the captain of the *Costa Concordia* at that time, Massimo Calisto Garbarino, and Garbarino in turn sent his response to the whole community of Giglio. The mayor wrote:

Dear Captain,
    Following the incredible show last night, when the *Concordia's* immense presence passed in front of the port of Giglio, I could not fail to send you a message of satisfaction on behalf of our entire community, including the very welcome tourist guests, honored by this important event. Thanks to the intercession of my dear friend Mario Palombo, one of Costa Crociere's

historic captains, we witnessed a show unique of its kind, one that has become an indispensable tradition of which I am extremely proud. For this reason, I would like to send my personal thanks to you and to your crew, begging you to extend our gratitude also to the Costa Crociere company, which for years has in this way been honoring an island that is one of the most beautiful in the whole national panorama. I sincerely hope that one day you will be our guest here in this area, naturally by agreement with Mario, an irreplaceable and authoritative supporter of the island. Yours sincerely.

To which Captain Garbarino replied:

Mr. Mayor, good evening,
   I apologize for the delay in replying to your very welcome letter. This is the second time now that I have passed with the Costa Concordia in front of the island of Giglio in the month of August. It was a wonderful experience three years ago, and it was just as thrilling this year. Last night, passing in front of the port, I was able to notice the thousands of camera flashes, and also visible were the numerous tourists who witnessed the salute, thanks in part to the announcement you placed in *Giglio News*. The salute was also advertised on board our ship, and many guests on the outer decks enjoyed this special event. Yours is a wonderful island, just the kind I like, small, and which I was able to "visit" from above thanks to internet technology. It is a little paradise that I hope to visit sometime in the next few years, and I am sure that I will fall in love with it, thanks also to the stories of our mutual friend Mario. It was a beautiful event, and I hope it will become a tradition for us on board as well. Wishing all the best and prosperity to your community, I take this opportunity to send you my best regards.

This sail-by salute, too, had not been authorized and had also involved passing just a few meters from the rocks.[18] However, neither Costa Crociere nor the maritime controllers (the Port Captaincies) had indicated any problems. Events of this type, therefore, could be repeated. In fact, on the Internet there are many videos of close-in salutes made in previous years near other islands, such as Stromboli, Ischia, and

---

[18] In a press conference, the CEO of Costa Crociere stated that Captain Garbarino's sail-by salute had been authorized by the *Autorità Marittima Locale* (Local Maritime Authority) and the company, and that the ship had passed at least 500 meters from the coast. Both statements were untrue. The first was denied by the maritime office of Porto Santo Stefano and the island of Giglio, which claimed not to have authorized any sail-by salute; the second by the images of *Lloyd's List Intelligence*.

Procida and other coasts. Those close-in salutes were made not only by Costa Crociere ships, but also by those of other companies, such as MSC *Splendida* near Sorrento and another MSC ship in the Strait of Messina. There are a great number of testimonies that demonstrate that the sail-by salute was a well-known practice that was tolerated and even encouraged.

Faced with evidence of this type, those involved tended to underplay the whole thing. The CEO of Costa Crociere at that time said:

The term "sail-by salute" indicates a search for more protected routes in situations characterized by adverse climatic conditions and, therefore, in the present case, it is used improperly. I would consider it more correct to speak instead of tourist navigation, which constitutes a form of cruise product offered by all the companies and which is carried out with specific purposes and following specific protocols. It is in fact decided by the ship's command, carefully assessing weather conditions, traffic conditions and all other circumstances of the situation. Approaching the coast is not in itself prohibited and is indeed an ordinary operation, if one thinks, for example, of entering port, but it all depends on the way in which it is carried out. In the case that occurred on January 13, 2012, there was no authorization from the Company.[19]

It seems almost as if the CEO had never heard of the practice before. However, the president of the *Registro Italiano Navale* (RINA – the Italian Naval Registry), claimed a few days after the accident that Costa Crociere knew all about sail-by salutes.[20] In a rather similar way to the company, the Admiral Commander-in-Chief of the Corps of the Port Captaincies stated that:

I would like to note that it is not forbidden to sail near the coast line, as long as the safety of the unit, of the people transported therein and of the other units that are in that area is always and constantly safeguarded. In relation to the so-called sail-by salute, it is necessary to specify that this term does not refer to a particular maneuver, scheduled or prohibited according to the case, but refers to a seafaring tradition – one that, contrary to what is reported by some media, is not so well-established and frequent – which involves taking a rather close course parallel to the

---

[19] Senate of the Republic, 8th Permanent Commission, Hearing of the Costa Crociere CEO, session of January 25, 2012.
[20] RINA rejected the statements of its president, who then modified his statements and resigned.

coast line in order to allow the so-called salute of the ship, but always in safety. The tradition, as far as we have been able to ascertain in detail, is not only Italian but common to other countries as well and there is no preclusion at national or international level … In recent days, it has often been asked if the Port Captaincies were aware or not of the so-called practice of sail-by salutes. Well, it is still necessary to specify that we cannot speak of tolerance on the part of the Maritime Authority in this regard, since it is, as I said, not a particular seafaring maneuver, but essentially an approach, in conditions of safety, along the coast, which can be carried out by the units without any specific preclusion, except that dictated by absolute compliance with the safety rules of navigation, required and variable according to the type of unit conducted, the places in which it is navigated and, more generally, compliance with the principles of prudence, relying on the experience and professionalism of the captain. (Senate of the Republic, 2012, 5–6; also represented in the Public Prosecutor's Office, Court of Grosseto 2013b, 178–179).

It is stated, therefore, that it is possible to sail close to the coast, even with ships hundreds of meters long and with thousands of people on board, as long as safety is guaranteed. How safety is to be guaranteed, however, is in no way made clear. Logically, the only way to guarantee safety would be to navigate at a suitable speed, maintaining a safe distance from rocks and other obstacles. But the risk is that the adequacy of the distance and congruity of the speed, in the absence of objective and predetermined parameters, can only be ascertained ex post, in the event that an accident occurs, with the easy logic of hindsight. In Schettino's first judicial interrogation, for example, the public prosecutor noted the excessive speed set for the approach of January 13, 2012, compared to the legal limits (Court of Grosseto 2012, 73). In reality, as we have seen, the practice of the sail-by salute has no clear formal regulation. How, then, to evaluate the right speed ex ante?

The Admiral-in-Chief also argues that sail-by salutes are not widespread, despite empirical evidence to the contrary, and that his organization shows no tolerance toward them. However, he does not refer to any restrictive order issued by the Port Captaincies, to at least reduce the practice in potentially dangerous areas, and leaves matters of safety to the professionalism of the operators, with no rules or checks.

The Grosseto attorney's office, which investigated the accident, also seemed to underestimate this practice, accepting the truth of this reconstruction and producing no investigative insights. Mainly on the basis of statements from the company CEO and those of the admiral cited above, it was concluded that those who reported any form of danger in the meantime did so in a completely inaccurate way and for polemical purposes (Public Prosecutor's Office, Court of Grosseto 2013b, 158, 178 and following). It was therefore in the interests of the company, which had actually encouraged the practice for the commercial purposes mentioned above, and the controllers, who clearly had no control over the practice, to give it the appearance of a vestigial and infrequent maneuver and, in any case, one that was carried out following the required safety regulations. The prosecutors, however, accepted the declarations of these subjects without ascertaining what the precise margins to be respected were in order to guarantee safety, let alone actually checking the veracity of the statements.

The attorney's office, meanwhile, argued that:

Tourist navigation is logically therefore carried out – only and exclusively – during daylight hours, in climatic conditions that make it possible to enjoy the experience from the uncovered areas of the ship and with ample publicity for the scheduled event. (Public Prosecutor's Office, Court of Grosseto 2013b, 186)

However, no evidence or documentation was produced for this statement and it was not submitted to any verification – it was simply reproposed from subjects who had every interest in minimizing the use of the practice of the sail-by salute. The story of this practice was recounted differently by those who were not interviewed by prosecutors or political commissions of inquiry. Juraj Karninčić, a retired captain and president of the Association of Captains of the Upper Adriatic, says:

The sail-by salute is a special experience, both for those who carry it out and for those who see an enormous ship pass in front of their town. I don't really know what I would compare this kind of emotion to. Leading people to understand that you have reached the peak in this profession also means thanking the place you come from ... I, however, am in favor of maintaining the old seafaring customs. When I was captain, I went close-in with nine or ten different ships ... I couldn't resist the temptation to do a sail-by salute. I am a bit nostalgic, yes, but I think it is essential in these cases to have total confidence both in the ship and in your abilities. Today, every cruise ship company wants to advertise by passing close to the coast. Dangerous or not, thousands of ships have performed the sail-by salute. And the companies want their ships to be seen, too. Whatever the case, it can't be denied that it is a dangerous practice ... It was a custom, one which few could resist. We just did it, that's all ... There were many Dalmatian captains who wanted to salute their hometown in this way and from the companies there was a kind of tacit consent … I always felt a very strong emotion in doing the sail-by salute with the ships I was captaining. You approach the coast and you hear the sirens, people greet you from the shore. An indescribable emotion. The important thing is to believe in yourself and in the ship and feel confident that nothing will happen. The captain is the most experienced person there and he must also be able to convey this sense of confidence to the entire crew… What happened to Schettino could happen to anyone who decides to go in so close to the coast.[21]

Captain Karninčić makes some important points: the sail-by salute is a common practice, carried out by thousands of captains. A very risky practice, however – so much so, that what happened to the captain of the *Costa Concordia* could have happened to anyone else. *To anyone else*, three words worth emphasizing. These are crucial declarations, on the one hand to understand the meaning of the practice within the world of navigation, on the other, to understand the great and ever-present risks that characterize it – and therefore how dangerous it was to tolerate sail-by salutes. Given the limited time for reaction, an always-possible human error in the execution of this maneuver was enough to transform a tradition into a disaster. The concept is a very clear and evident one, yet strangely enough this issue was not analyzed at all by the investigators, who, with no verification, restricted themselves to echoing the minimizing statements of the controllers themselves, or of those who were involved in the affair.

During the trial examination, Captain Schettino also stated: "Tourist navigation is something we often do" (Court of Grosseto 2015, 137), and: "However, it is something that has always been done, with due caution of course, and which anyway favors, let's say, the commercial aspect" (139). Such events at the time, moreover, were not prohibited by the legislation in force. According to some evidence, the *Concordia* had made at least fifty-two other sail-by salutes or very close-in transits off the island of Giglio,[22] and in 2005 Captain Palombo had made one himself, at a distance from the coast of 5–600 meters (139).

---

[21] "When captains did sail-by salutes", *La voce del popolo*, January 26, 2013.
[22] Francesco Viviano, "Sail-by salutes were an Italian custom. Why did no one stop them?", *La Repubblica*, January 17, 2012. It should be noted that there were no further confirmations of this data regarding close-in transits, nor further investigations by the judicial authorities.

In some cases, the courses really were highly dangerous: for example, when cruise ships passed through the very narrow space between the two stacks of the island of Capri. Yet such events were never sanctioned. Indeed, instead of being considered as extremely dangerous and not to be repeated, they were viewed in a positive light by the organization, eliciting praise and thanks.

The Normalization of Deviance

It is clear that, in this context, following the practice of the sail-by salute was not *wrongdoing* but *normal*: a paradoxical situation of "drift to danger" and "normalization of deviance". The first expression refers to "the effect of a systematic migration of organizational behavior toward accidents under the influence of pressure towards cost-effectiveness in an aggressive, competitive environment" (Rasmussen and Svedung 2000, 14).[23] The concept of "drift to danger" refers to the slow, constant, incremental movements of operational activities, such as tourist navigation, up to, and even beyond, the safety boundaries of the system. In these situations, an area of risk is broached where the objective limits to be respected (the safety route) can become subjective limits to be challenged. From a safety point of view, sail-by salutes were "danger signals" which, although known about, were instead encouraged (even if not in the form manifested on the night of January 13, 2012) by the company and local authorities, and tolerated by the systems of control (the Port Captaincies and the Coast Guard) and of regulation (the Ministry of Transport).

In the literature, it is well known how processes of socialization in organizations and in society can lead to the "normalization of deviance" (Skolnick and Fyfe 1993; Hochstetler and Copes 2001; Crelinsten 2003; Van Rooij and Fine 2018). This concept means a process that generates a constant erosion of normal procedures, in which violations, irregularities, and deviant practices are accepted as

---

[23] The drift to danger process tends to be slow, with multiple transitions occurring over an extended period. Each transition is usually small, so it can go unnoticed, with no significant problems visible until it's too late. The drift is not caused by people's wicked desire to cause accidents, or by a lack of attention or knowledge: it is, rather, a natural phenomenon that affects all types of systems. It is a model that emphasizes the importance of the history of a system in explaining why people work a certain way, what they feel is important in terms of safety, and what pressures can progressively erode it.

normal and conventional and, therefore, tolerated (Vaughan 2016). In the absence of accidents, these deviations "normalize", becoming usual practice.[24] People in the organization continue to honestly see their actions as normal, not deviant. The end result is a situation of slipping toward danger with no full awareness of this. As Weick stated "operators see nothing and seeing nothing" therefore "presume that nothing is happening" (1985, 118).

The processes of "drift to danger" and "normalization of deviance" damage the culture of safety by shifting the safety boundaries of the cruise route (toward the coast) without dwelling on why the original limits (the intended route) were set. In addition, they increase both the tolerance of errors that do not cause damage and the level of acceptance of risks in favor of interests related to efficiency and productivity. In this way, they lead the safety system toward a slippery slope in which accidents become increasingly possible.

Watzlawick, Beavin, and Jackson (1967) suggest the pragmatic paradox as an example of a dilemma. They show how an individual who occupies a certain role in a hierarchical organization can simultaneously receive orders to perform tasks or make decisions that transgress existing rules or are in conflict with previous orders. In the case of cruise navigation, an example of this is the request for safety on the one hand and the incentive to carry out sail-by salutes on the other. By deviating from the safe route in order to execute the sail-by salute,

---

[24] There are five important and seminal books, written from other disciplinary perspectives, which confirm the role of conformity in the etiology of organizational deviance and misconduct: *Obedience to Authority* (1974), by Stanley Milgram; *Crimes of Obedience* (1989), by Herbert Kelman and V. Lee Hamilton; *Ordinary Men* (1992), by Christopher R. Browning; *The Lucifer Effect: How Good People Turn Evil* (2007), by Philip Zimbardo; and *Moral Disengagement: How People Do Harm and Live with Themselves* (2016), by Albert Bandura. Each of these studies shows how individual actors explain and justify the horrible acts they commit by referring to the norms and hierarchy of the organizations to which they belong. They justify themselves by saying that they have not committed deviant acts but rather that they have followed orders without motivation, that they are only cogs in larger mechanisms, and other excuses. There is a sixth book that should be added to this list, *Eichmann in Jerusalem* (1964), by Hannah Arendt. I am, however, in agreement with Hilberg (1996, 150), who believes that, given the evidence and testimonies, there was no "banality" in this "devil", Eichmann. The thesis regarding the mechanism at work is right, but the particular case is wrong. On this, see Cesarani (2004); Haslam and Reicher (2007); Stangneth (2014).

an area of risk is entered, one not always adequately controlled, in which management methods mainly depend on the human factor and the technical equipment available. In such contexts, two scenarios can occur: in the first, the overconfidence of the command group shifts the line more and more toward the coast, increasing the danger (Moore and Healy 2008; Moore and Schatz 2017); in the second it becomes difficult, if not impossible, to swiftly correct any human errors.

Near-Miss or a Demonstration of Skill?

Weick and Sutcliffe (2015) argue that managing the unexpected is a continuous effort to define and monitor the weak signals of very serious and dangerous potential threats. The interesting thing is that sail-by salutes certainly could not be defined as weak signals, hidden amongst a multitude of other signals and threats. They were visible and intentionally realized events. Were they near misses or not?

The perception of subjective risk is influenced by several variables (Slovic, Fischhoff, and Lichtenstein 1985). These include (1) familiarity/habit, which leads to risk acceptance: thus, unlike new risks, which trigger a higher level of reaction, risks associated with work habits tend to be underestimated; (2) knowledge, whereby expertise leads to an underestimation of the risk. Consequently, the closer a negative event is approached and there is a positive outcome, the more the risk associated with the event will tend to be underestimated in the future. The problem, therefore, is that sail-by salutes were not viewed as warning signs of potential danger, but rather as signs of success.

Near misses, therefore, can be considered in two completely different ways: as proof that safety measures are working (positive asymmetry)[25] or as a danger signal (Dillon and Tinsley 2008). In the Costa Crociere system and the organizational field of reference, the first conviction prevailed. Sail-by salutes were seen as absolutely normal, certainly not as signs of potential danger if something unexpected happened. In addition to the normalization of deviance, "outcome bias" – the tendency to focus on the result in assessing the quality of a decision or behavior (Baron and Hershey 1988) – also contributes to making managers and frontline operators myopic in relation to near misses. If we focus on the outcome, the same dangerous behavior tends to be

---

[25] Positive asymmetry is the tendency to emphasize only examples of the best or most positive cases (Cerulo 2006).

evaluated differently depending on whether or not it is followed by an adverse event. If no adverse event occurs (when a sail-by salute goes well, for example), the focus on the successful outcome blinds us to the complex processes and factors that have determined this result. It might even have simply been a matter of chance.[26] In contrast, should the outcome involve damage or accident, all those prior events, which otherwise would not be considered or evaluated negatively, are automatically tinged with blame.

If the last two sail-by salutes carried out by the *Costa Concordia* are analyzed, the penultimate by Captain Garbarino and the last by Captain Schettino, an almost complete overlap between the routes can be observed (see Figure 3.2). Navigation speed was also about the same on both occasions. Comparing the two salutes, it emerges that in both cases there was an approach close-in to the coast, with just a very slight difference in trajectory (Court of Grosseto 2012a, 9–10).[27]

From the analysis carried out by *Lloyd's List Intelligence*, the information service that monitors and collects data relating to ship routes, it also emerges that on August 14, 2011, the *Costa Concordia* passed less than 230 meters from the coast of the island of Giglio. Of the two overlapping courses, the first was celebrated with letters of thanks; the second, marked by death and disaster, ended in a legal process. But in a context in which the first type of events is tolerated, sooner or later the second can also occur. Excessive confidence leads to hubris, exposing managers and professionals to failure in terms of assessing a given situation that is inherently risky, favoring wrong decision-making processes. Then, when things go wrong, the search begins for the individual culprit.

What was not clear to the various agents in the system is that navigation according to safety rules at a certain distance from the coast, and tourist navigation with the variant of the sail-by salute, constitute two completely different scenarios. These will now be examined in more detail.

---

[26] On the incidence of fate in the outcome of an undesired event, see Eusebi (2011).

[27] Taken from www.lloydslistintelligence.com. *Lloyd's List Intelligence* provides an interactive online service that offers detailed data on ship movements, real-time AIS positioning, and comprehensive information on ships, businesses, ports, and accidents, as well as credit reports, industry data, and analysis, including short-term market outlook reports. *Lloyd's List Intelligence* also provides a range of support services such as consulting, research, due diligence, market trend analysis and credit risk assessment for entire insurance portfolios.

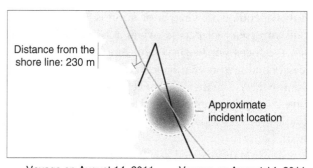

Distance from the shore line: 230 m

Approximate incident location

— Voyage on August 14, 2011 —— Voyage on August 14, 2011

Figure 3.2 The routes of the *Costa Concordia* on January 13, 2012 and August 14, 2011

According to Perrow (1999) a system is characterized by loosely coupling connections when its parts can vary independently and respond to each other, while maintaining their identity and their separateness, physical or logical, from others, as will be seen better in Chapter 4. A system is instead characterized by tight-coupled connections when each of its parts is closely connected to others, so that a change in one point generates an immediate change in other parts, with a rapid and uncontrolled propagation of the effects.

In navigation according to safety regulations, at a distance from the coast, the organization of the ship is, in fact, characterized by close connections. These require centralization of command, because decisions on the bridge have an immediate impact on the conditions of navigation. However, when the ship follows a route planned in advance, and the travel process is clearly visible and comprehensible (see Figure 3.3), navigation is also characterized by linear interactions – simple, based on familiar sequences, predictable, and understandable for the operator.

Passing from navigation according to safety rules to tourist navigation and the practice of the sail-by salute, the complexity of the system increases (see Figure 3.4).

The linear interactions become complex, characterized by unfamiliar, unplanned, unexpected sequences and, as the predictability of the course is reduced, at the same time, not visible and not comprehensible to the operator.

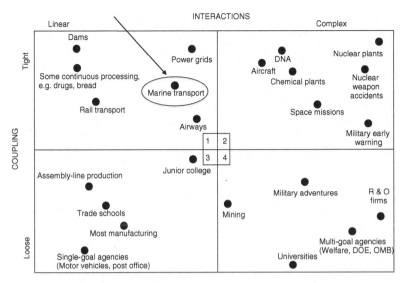

Figure 3.3 Interactions/coupling chart
Source: Perrow 1999, 327

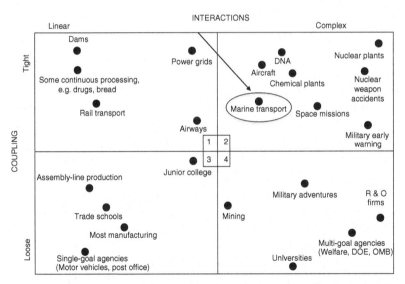

Figure 3.4 The practice of the sail-by salute increases the complexity of the interactions
Source: modified by Perrow 1999

In such situations, centralization and decentralization are required at the same time: the former to cope with close connections, the latter to deal with the complex, unplanned interactions that may emerge. The two requirements are mutually exclusive, therefore incompatible. In this case, the system characterized by tight connections and complex interactions becomes prone to accidents, as the chances of recovery in the event of an error are very limited. This is what happened to the *Costa Concordia*. If the errors had been made three miles from the coast, as scheduled by the official route, the accident would not have occurred.

The inquiry placed a great deal of emphasis on the error made in planning a route that went so straight toward the island. In reality, the choice was also linked to the desire to avoid sailing into the nature reserve that is located around the island of Giannutri. In a system that accepts the practice of tourist navigation, with no specified rules and methods, it is evident that decisions of this kind can be implemented. In such a system, they are considered as errors and/or violations only in the event of an accident: otherwise, they are completely tolerated under normal conditions.

The Silence of the Controllers and Regulators

Faced with the widespread nature of, and excessive confidence in, such a risky practice, the competent bodies had never issued any instructions to prevent, or at least regulate, the close-to-shore transit of ships of a certain tonnage. There was not even a penalty. In a situation of this type, the organization under control, believing that control must be carried out by the external controlling organization, continues, without knowing it, to operate in an increasingly risky way, if the latter does not carry out controls or set limits or enforce sanctions. The situation is similar to someone skiing off-piste without being fully aware of it. This is a clear problem of failure of control, within an obviously very problematic regulatory vacuum.

This is also the case here: with the silence of the Port Captaincies and Coast Guard, the company and the team on the bridge continued to perform increasingly dangerous sail-by salutes. In the past, the Captaincies had even authorized some close-in transits, as reported by Captain Mario Terenzio Palombo: "I understand that, from 2007 to 2011, there were four sail-by salutes at a reduced speed (about 5 knots) at Giglio agreed upon with the Port Captaincies and the shipowning company" (Public Prosecutor's Office 2013a, 343). Furthermore, from the data acquired thanks to the AIS system, the *Costa Concordia* performed dozens of close-in transits off the island.[28] It is difficult to deny, therefore, that the Captaincies were aware of close-by sailings and that they tolerated them.

In a situation where controllers do not carry out controls, the controlled can progressively move into areas of greater risk. It is a striking fact, mentioned above, that near Giglio there was a protected zone, the natural park of the island of Giannutri, where navigation was prohibited for environmental reasons (Public Prosecutor's Office, Court of Grosseto 2013b, 176). While navigation in certain waters was prohibited for environmental reasons, no doubts were raised, nor restrictive orders issued, regarding a risky practice, for safety reasons.

With reference to the American context, Perrow (2014) remarks that the status of the Coast Guard is very weak, and its objectives in conflict, such as the provision of maritime services on the one hand and police duties on the other. All this makes the organization vulnerable to pressure from companies and insurance companies (152). It was certainly a singular thing that the Port Captaincy involved in the investigative pool of prosecutors who were looking into the disaster was the same subject that did not seem to have done much to control, regulate, or avoid the repetition of similar unsafe seafaring practices.

The silence of the controllers is joined by that of the regulators: until 2012, there is no trace of any regulation of the so-called "sail-by salute" – a highly dangerous, yet well-known and widespread practice, so much so that it is considered a "seafaring tradition". The anti-"sail-by salute" decree-law,[29] was, in fact, signed by the Ministers of the Environment and Transport only in March 2012, after the disaster. The sudden approval of the anti-salute decree-law does raise a question: if the accident was caused by the behavior of a negligent and immoral captain, why change the law so quickly two months after the event? Was this not perhaps the belated recognition of the danger of such a long-tolerated practice?

---

[28] Francesco Viviano, "Sail-by salutes were an Italian custom. Why did no one stop them?", *La Repubblica*, January 17, 2012.

[29] D.M. of March 7, 2012 n. 56, which, for 2 nautical miles from the external coastal perimeters and within these perimeters, prohibits the navigation, anchoring and stopping of merchant ships over 500 gross tonnage used for the transport of goods and passengers.

Several years after the disaster, in June 2017, some organizations representing business and commercial interests on the island of Ischia (Federalberghi and Confcommercio) wrote to the Italian prime minister to request the restoration of the practice of the sail-by salute, as a typical "maritime greeting". Indeed, given its fundamental role in the island's tourist economy, its abolition had negative economic consequences for operators. At the same time, it was noted that the practice had not in fact completely disappeared and that it was still performed in some areas, such as the Amalfi coast.

In conclusion, the absence of controls, and the critical issues highlighted earlier, should have broadened the search for responsibility to a *systemic* level. Instead, it remained solely and exclusively at an individual level: a simpler and more convenient operation.

3.4.2 Phase Two: Approaching the Accident

The second phase of the event, at the center first of the judicial investigation and then the trial thereafter, began at 18:27 on January 13, 2012 and ended at 21:45, when the ship collided with the rocks. The various investigations and actors (the company, the regulators, the controllers, the media, and the judicial system) focused mainly on the individual actor – the captain, on his errors and violations, in a "short history" arc of time that lasted 3 hours and 18 minutes. Less attention was paid to latent factors (and none from the point of view of their consequences) or to the numerous organizational, regulatory, and control criticalities that certainly played a role in the genesis and dynamics of the accident. Focusing attention on the scapegoat tended to shift these elements and their interaction into the background.

The accident appears to have been triggered by a set of (involuntary) errors in evaluation and, consequently, in the decision-making processes. It is likely that these errors were favored by reduced situational awareness. Errors are always possible: "No system can completely avoid errors. Any discussion of reliability must start with that as axiomatic" (Weick 1987, 122). However, it is one thing if these errors are made in safe areas 3 miles offshore, as scheduled. It is a wholly different matter if they occur close to the shore, where the chances of recovering from the situation are almost completely eliminated by the limited mobility of the ship.

Organizational Criticalities

On the bridge on the day of the accident there were the captain (who was absent for some time, returning about eleven minutes before the collision), three officers, an officer cadet, the cartographer, and the helmsman. Subsequently, other people not involved in navigation operations arrived, including the ship's restaurant manager and hotel director. The sail-by salute had been requested by the restaurant manager the week before, but had been postponed by the captain due to the adverse weather conditions at that time.

Prosecutors and courts were very insistent with regard to the failure to communicate the change of route, which would constitute a violation. On the one hand, however, this variation was hardly an exceptional event and was instead frequent in this type of navigation and, on the other, it was not always communicated to the company and the Port Captaincies (as in the case of the penultimate sail-by salute near the island of Giglio). No particular sanctions or other types of warning exist for this kind of non-communication. Furthermore, even if it had been communicated, the Captaincies would not have prevented it. The reasons for the insistence on this aspect are not clear, therefore, apart from depicting the captain as a person who violated the rules – as if, in some fashion, a risky operation became less dangerous through being communicated.[30]

It was not the first time that the captain had made a sail-by salute near the island of Giglio. This is confirmed by the court-ordered evaluation, from which it appears not only that Antonello Tievoli, the restaurant manager, considered it entirely legitimate to ask the captain to approach Giglio for a simple "salute", but also that the captain was preparing to perform a completely "routine" maneuver (Court of Grosseto 2012d, 70–72). Habit facilitates a common tendency, the illusion of control (Langer 1975): in other words, an overconfidence in one's abilities and skills in relation to managing risky situations. This aspect may have led the entire team on the bridge – and certainly not just one person – to underestimate the real situation and to make a series of errors, both in terms of actions and evaluations, that then triggered the accident.

---

[30] See, in this regard, what emerged from the minutes of Schettino's testimony, Court of Grosseto, 2014h, part I, 29.

After all, in complex systems, performance is the result of the inter-related actions of the various team members. If this is true in favorable situations, the same holds for adverse ones. Failure is attributable to the work of the entire team, not to the conduct of one individual. In the case in question, the captain was not alone on the bridge, other officers were also present. While this was noted by the experts (Court of Grosseto 2012f, 69), it does not seem to have been given adequate consideration by the courts.

The team's overall attitude may have been favored by the "can-do attitude", a trend whereby past successes, in this case in carrying out the sail-by salutes, generate the conviction that these successes will be repeated in the future. On the one hand, this makes it more difficult to identify the limits of such actions: how near to the coast can you get? On the other, it makes people with negative perspectives reluc-tant to report the problem. This happens in particular in situations of commercial pressure and in the absence of significant controls, as will be seen below. Years of success in the practice of sail-by salutes had helped to create this dangerous belief, this dangerous faith.

It should be noted that the sail-by salute maneuver was carried out in calm seas, but in the evening and in front of a dimly lit island – in January, almost deserted. Furthermore, just over a minute before the impact, which occurred at 21:45:07, there was no sign of tension: the team joked that the ship was passing very close to the coast and nobody seemed to have any perception of imminent danger (Court of Grosseto 2015, 161). The captain's statement "Otherwise we go on the rocks" was followed by general laughter (Court of Grosseto 2012d, 82). The work group on the bridge did not, therefore, operate as a reliable and situation-aware team. No one prevented the maneuver or tried to warn the captain of the impending crisis. Nobody was aware of it, except, at the very last moment, the captain himself. Only one officer, two minutes before impact, tried to indicate the situation, but, obtaining no response, he did not consider it appropriate to make any further comment.

The figure of a ship's captain enjoys the highest status in an intensely hierarchical organizational context. It is worth pointing out that, from a historical point of view, marine navigation has always been charac-terized by semi-military organizational structures and highly central-ized decision-making processes, with a single person in command.

The Court showed that the captain had a style of command that tolerated no objection. However, no in-depth analysis was done to analyze whether this management and behavioral model was common in ship management or was rather an individual style of behavior. And if it had been an individual style, why had the company not put in place alternative measures? It should be borne in mind that the Navigation Code[31] depicts a hierarchical and pyramidal structure, at the top of which is the figure of the captain. During a voyage, the latter's decisions are difficult to question, not only by the crew, but even by the owner. Moreover, the ship was technologically very advanced – something that can generate a climate of false confidence, bringing about an increase in the acceptance of risks that is not always fully perceived (Schröder-Hinrichs, Hollnagel, and Baldauf 2012).

In the field of military and civil aviation, efforts have been made for decades to correct any behavior of this type with "crew resource management training", a set of specific training procedures for operating environments in which human error can have devastating results. Instead of verifying the presence and adequacy of this kind of training system, the court restricted itself to stigmatizing the individual behavior of the captain, forgetting that, in such an organizational climate, compliance with authority becomes the norm. In these conditions, if one person is wrong, everyone is wrong, and, as plane crash analysis has demonstrated for a long time, the consequences can be catastrophic (Weick 1990; Reason 1997; Catino 2006a). It should also be added that there was little training activity aimed at developing Bridge Team Management, a decision-making system that builds close collaboration between the captain and crew members in order to solve problems. It was, in the end, a clear failure of teamwork as a whole and certainly not of one person alone.

The court also found other critical issues relating to communications and the use of language. While the official language in use was Italian, many sailors, including some on the bridge, did not know it well, nor did they have a good knowledge of English. This made communications problematic, increasing organizational vulnerability.

Technological and Regulatory Criticalities
As well as organizational criticalities, technological and regulatory criticalities were also present. Internationally and within the EU, the safety of maritime navigation has been a topic of great importance

---

[31] In particular articles 295 and 321.

for years. Various international organizations have promoted multiple initiatives that place safety at sea as a fundamental objective of maritime navigation policy, in order to protect passengers, crew members, and the marine environment. These initiatives include the introduction of maritime traffic monitoring systems in straits and in access areas to ports.

The relevant documents on the subject include the International Maritime Organization (IMO) guidelines on the Vessel Traffic Service (VTS),[32] a service aimed at improving the safety and efficiency of maritime traffic and protecting the environment. The VTS system, in essence, thanks to an exchange of information between the competent authority and the ship, makes it possible to govern traffic in the areas most at risk in order to prevent accidents or damage to human life and the environment, even guaranteeing navigation aid in some cases. These guidelines are expressly referred to by the so-called SOLAS[33] and certain European directives,[34] which require states to introduce the system (Russo 2011).[35]

However, while there is no lack of solicitations, from the point of view of the implementation of these regulations, there is still a certain sluggishness: to date, since 2001, the year the detailed regulation of the VTS came into force in Italy,[36] there are only twelve VTS centers

---

[32] Adopted with Resolution A.857(20) of November 27, 1997.

[33] London Convention on the Safety of Life at Sea of November 1, 1974.

[34] The most important of these is the Directive of the European Parliament and of the Council 2002/59/CE, adopted on June 27, 2002.

[35] Where it is operational, the Vessel Traffic Service provides various services: an information service on a series of variables useful for navigation, such as weather conditions, hydrogeological conditions, and any other factor that might be a source of danger; the navigation assistance service, which allows the Authority, where it deems it necessary or at the request of the ship, to provide directives on the route and speed in order to avoid grounding and accidents; finally, the traffic organization service, through which the Authority assigns the spaces to be occupied to the ships and indicates the speed limits (Russo 2011). Highly specialized and trained personnel are, of course, required for the correct functioning of the system: in this regard, the IMO dedicates an entire annex to this aspect, which indicates the specific training requirements. Annex II, Resolution A.857 (20) of November 27, 1997.

[36] With the law of March 7, 2001 n. 51, the task of establishing the VTS implementing provisions by decrees was assigned to the Ministry of Infrastructure and Transport, in agreement with the Ministry of the Environment. The Port Captaincies were made responsible for the operational management of the service.

installed in the country, and coverage of the port areas in central Italy is low. In particular, at the time of the *Costa Concordia* accident, the island of Giglio had been waiting for at least three years for the system to become operational. Admiral Ferdinando Lolli stated[37] that the agreement to install the radar and make the VTS operational was stipulated with the Selex and Finmeccanica companies in 2005 and should have been concluded in 2009. Today, several years later, there is still no sign of the VTS on Giglio.

The Port Authority is equipped with a control system called the Automatic Identification System (AIS), mandatory for all ships of gross tonnage above a certain weight, which makes it possible to detect the route, speed, and position of the vessel and control its movement via satellite. However, this system does not provide any navigational support and at most constitutes an additional source of data and information to be processed, in order to avoid possible collisions with other ships. In the investigation relating to the *Costa Concordia* accident (Public Prosecutor's Office, Court of Grosseto 2013b, 188 and following), it is explained that in reality the AIS system is not designed to control safety in a way that would have prevented the ship's collision with the reef. The AIS system

is used to identify other ships, representing the dynamic scenario of the vessel (routes, speed, condition, etc.), simplifying the exchange of information; it is therefore used above all in an anti-collision function with other naval units. The AIS system installed on land makes it possible to have an image of the maritime traffic in a given area and, if necessary, to exchange messages with ships. On the other hand, not all ships and not all shore stations are equipped with an AIS system (and even ships equipped with AIS may not have it in operation). In conclusion, the AIS is an additional source of information: it does not replace, but only supports, navigation systems such as radar or VTS. (192)

In short, then, it seems that if the *Costa Concordia* had found itself in proximity to another ship, the system would have in some way performed its safety function. As it was, however, the only system that might have proved effective was the VTS, which was not yet

---

[37] Alessandra Arachi, "They have been waiting for the system to control traffic at sea for three years. The VTS could have corrected the Concordia's course", *Corriere della Sera*, January 16, 2012.

operational on Giglio. Logically, the reason for this difference is not entirely clear. There seems to be a certain technological inadequacy in providing a system, the AIS, which, if not interfaced with the VTS system, the only one able to offer concrete navigational assistance, is of little use. All the more so if we consider that the Livorno Port Captaincy was unable to observe what was happening in the stretch of sea where the *Concordia* was wrecked because, with a rather large area to monitor, as required by law, it constantly monitored only the zones considered most at risk (Court of Grosseto 2012d, 156–157). As a result, the scale of the AIS monitor had been reduced, so the Captaincy would not have noticed either the ship's change of course or its collision with the rock. The Port Captaincies might only have become aware of the ship's variation from its predetermined route through the coordinated action of two systems, the AIS on the one hand, and the VTS on the other – even better, if supported by a VTMS service (Court of Grosseto 2012d, 156), a satellite system that, through the integrated use of various devices and radar, allows the monitoring of traffic "in real time".

The question therefore arises: did these "shortcomings" in technological equipment not make it necessary to issue orders prohibiting navigation at a distance too close to the coast, given that reaction times following possible errors on the bridge would have irreversibly undermined safety conditions? Doubts arise, furthermore, as to why these critical issues were not adequately evaluated during judicial proceedings.

All this, despite the evident absence of an effective traffic control and regulation system and of coordination and integration between the various subjects involved. There was no effective interdependence between the ship and the Port Authority, but only a "generic" type of interdependence – in other words, each contributed to the overall aims of the transport system, but without continuous safety-directed interactions or communications.[38]

---

[38] Thompson (1967) has distinguished three types of interdependence in organizations: (1) *generic* ("pooled"), when work is interrelated only in the sense that it contributes to the overall goals of the organization; (2) *sequential*, when A's output constitutes B's input, as in an assembly line; and (3) *reciprocal*, when mutual adaptation between the parties is required in order to carry out an activity.

Following the incident, the limitations of two other digital instruments emerged: (a) the electronic nautical charts interfaced with the ECDIS system, which require constant updating and must be consulted taking into account the level of zoom and the type of software used; and (b) the GPS antenna, which is installed above the bridge but which, given the length of the ship, does not provide a completely correct indication of its position (Gaeta 2012, 43).

Criticalities of Control
Analyzing more than 200 marine accidents, Charles Perrow (1999, 189) argued that:

The marine world does not take kindly to international regulation ... It is not a system that breeds cooperation. Captains are masters of their fate and do not want their freedom impinged by another captain; nations are similar. Nations have little experience with national regulatory systems in the marine world ... In contrast, the air transport system was regulated from beginning by each nation because the planes fly primarily within the nation.

Unlike the aviation system, in the context of maritime navigation there is no subject appointed to carry out traffic regulation and control activities such as the Air Traffic Controller, who assigns each aircraft its own lane and provides information on altitude. The flight of a commercial aircraft is continuously regulated and controlled by the controller by radar system, from the taxiing phase at the departure airport to the final taxiing stage at the destination airport. In addition, in order to avoid possible collisions, an ad hoc system was introduced: the Traffic Alert and Collision Avoidance System (TCAS). This system, thanks to a communication and coordination service between aircraft (Resolution Advisory Complement), sends a signal to the pilot when there are "intruders" in the vicinity and there is a risk of collision, indicating the maneuvers to be carried out in order to avoid the collision. In case of non-compliance by the pilot, a system for correcting the indications on maneuvers is also provided. So, the case may be that two aircraft risk a collision and the pilot of the first, through the TCAS, indicates to the pilot of the second the chosen maneuver (for example, a pull-up) in order for the latter to make the opposite choice (a dive). If the first pilot does not comply with the indication given, the indications given to the second aircraft, thanks to a communication system between the two TCAS, are corrected in real time (Reversal Resolution Advisory).[39]

Maritime traffic, on the other hand, has no such sophisticated forms of control. Ships must communicate, and be authorized to travel, the courses they will take and any changes to them. But there is no continuous communication, with orders given and authorizations issued. In addition, maritime navigation is less technologically advanced – something partly due to a certain mistrust on the part of captains and operators. Navigation aid systems are mostly information systems that manage the sometimes very large flow of data to be processed. They do not provide any support service for decisions. This means that the captain, in a potentially dangerous situation, must receive, process, and analyze a huge flow of information coming from the different systems and decide how to act in order to ensure navigational safety with no form of support.[40]

3.4.3 Phase Three: The Management of the Emergency

The third phase, crisis management, began immediately after the impact against the rocks and ended at 05:45 the following day, with the great majority of passengers rescued. This last phase, together with the second, was the main subject of the investigations conducted by the various agents. Di Lieto (2015) highlights some significant organizational criticalities, including:

- inadequate training for the specific integrated navigation system;
- lack of training in non-technical skills that can enhance teamwork;
- absence of a company policy and operating procedures for sail pasts;
- inadequate teamwork procedures;
- ambiguity stemming from the coexistence of traditional and integrated methods for controlling and monitoring the route;
- usability issues with the Integrated Navigation System's user interface;
- ambiguity deriving from the use of both Italian and English languages on the bridge, even though Italian is the only official one. (2015, 59)

---

[39] With regard to the air traffic control system and the TCAS, see H. Abdushkour et al. (2018, 2).

[40] Ibid., for a more accurate comparison between the air traffic control and maritime systems.

The software dedicated to the calculation of the trim and stability of the ship (NAPA) was installed in the computer located in the safety center adjacent to the bridge, and this computer was not working. This was an essential instrument for assessing the stability of the ship in the event of flooding, as it could provide data on the ship's thrust reserve, draft, and trim. That night, following the blackout, it broke down and could not be restarted due to the critical issues relating to the operation of the emergency power supply (Court of Grosseto 2013b, 361). The impossibility of assessing the stability of the ship prevented the captain from deciding what to do with greater awareness in terms of the real effect of the damage suffered by the vessel – something that certainly influenced the night's events. The judicial agents did not, however, take this criticality into due consideration either, objecting, in a note in the request for indictment (Court of Grosseto 2013b, 361) that the software had not been approved by the Italian Naval Registry or by another body recognized by the Italian administration. There is something incredible about this: an operational instrument that could have been of vital importance for decisions in the emergency phase did not work and the prosecutors, instead of analyzing this organizational criticality and the role it was unable to play, restricted themselves to pointing out that this software was not authorized. Should there or should there not, then, be a working instrument to support decisions in emergency situations? And if so, is this then also the captain's responsibility?

Another significant organizational criticality highlighted concerns the tightness of the watertight doors. In this regard, certification irregularities emerge from the conversations between a company manager and another captain, intercepted by the Grosseto Carabinieri Investigative Unit: "These watertight doors we have are from that fucking company that, bloody hell, they should be put in prison"; "the people who certify the ships should be thrown into jail"; "Because these watertight doors here, they hold like they're made of Teflon. Two years, and they already need to be changed!"[41] Inexplicably, these interceptions would not be taken into consideration during the trial.

---

[41] "False tests and casual checks, how the Costa bypassed safety", *La Repubblica*, December 22, 2012.

Another important critical issue, though not considered decisive either by court experts or prosecutors, concerns the emergency generator, located at the highest point of the ship, deck 11. This should have come into operation immediately after the failure of the engines but instead it did not function. It would have allowed the use of some very important instruments such as navigation lights, communication systems, equipment and instruments for navigation, emergency bilge pumps, rudders, and emergency devices capable of securing the elevators (several people were found dead in elevator shafts). Basically, both the experts and the prosecutors believed that the operation of the diesel generator would not have prevented the sinking of the ship (Public Prosecutor's Office, Court of Grosseto 2013b, 146). While this is certainly true, it would also certainly have made a different and more effective management of the emergency possible. For example, the absence of communication systems made evacuation operations more complex and, at such a critical moment, the locking of the rudders meant that the ship could not be steered.

Personnel Training and Communications

An important critical issue that emerged from the inquiry concerns the training of personnel in the management of emergencies. The prosecutor spoke about "a Dantesque level of chaos" (Public Prosecutor's Office, Court of Grosseto 2013b, 303) in the operations carried out in order to abandon the ship and responsibility was essentially attributed to the captain for not having been able to manage the emergency event. This assessment is based on the concept that an emergency must be managed through procedures. An emergency, however, cannot be reduced to the orderly execution of procedures by organizational atoms: the reliable management of an emergency requires the training of a reliable team. It is a question of organization, not of bureaucracy ("there were procedures") or individual heroism.

Thinking that it is possible to manage an emergency through rules and procedures means not having a clear idea of what an emergency is. In emergencies such as the *Costa Concordia* incident, information is constantly changing and the level of awareness of the situation is limited and does not correspond to the evolution of the facts. The agents act in a situation of "bounded rationality" (Simon 1957; March and Simon 1958; Cyert and March 1963) not of absolute rationality, typical of the ideal type referred to by those who sit in judgment. The logic of the prosecutor noted only that there were procedures and that the captain violated them. He did not try to reconstruct the real context in which these decisions were made: rather, after re-analyzing them in the cold light of day and with a certain level of "hindsight bias", he concluded they were wrong.

From what emerged in the trial (although hardly in a particularly detailed manner), fire-fighting drills were held on the Costa Concordia, but anti-breach drills were not, probably in the belief that this second type of emergency situation was wholly unlikely. But it is well known that "thinking that a disaster is impossible makes unthinkable disasters possible". The more it is considered impossible for an event to occur, the fewer remedial measures are put in place that could prevent or contain it, and, unintentionally, the conditions for its occurrence are pre-established.

At an organizational level, the cruise company's own crisis unit appears not to have been adequately prepared to deal with similar situations. In particular, from reading the documents of the proceedings, it is difficult to actually identify the real role of this body in emergency situations. In this regard, the statements of the FCC (Fleet Crisis Coordinator) are striking, stressing that the crisis unit should not give suggestions to the captain, as "this is not only something not to be done, but which could be counterproductive" (Public Prosecutor's Office, Court of Grosseto 2013b, 422). However, a number of doubts tend to arise about the operational usefulness of such a body in a critical situation. Not surprisingly, the prosecutors themselves, referring to the management of the emergency on the ground by the crisis unit, spoke of "unprecedented ineffectiveness" (Court of Grosseto 2013b, 617). The *Concordia* accident does not seem to have been the only one to shine a light on critical issues in this regard. In the request for indictment, reference is made to other incidents at sea that occurred both before and after January 13, 2012 when the intervention of the crisis unit did not prove effective (Court of Grosseto 2013b, 619).

Another interesting element in this regard was highlighted by the experts. In the event of a breach, the company's procedures required the captain to contact the Fleet Crisis Coordinator and a technician. From a phone call between two engineers who formed part of the crisis unit, it emerged that they themselves were not even aware of the technician's telephone number: a clear sign of lack of coordination between key subjects indicated in the procedure (Court of Grosseto 2012f, 65).

In addition, it emerges from the captain's testimony that the delays in communicating with the authorities, and consequently in activating the emergency procedures, were due to the fact that, while deciding, the crisis unit and the captain had also to take into account the possible costs for the company – specifically, regarding the stipulation of contracts with tugs (Court of Grosseto 2014g, part I, 16).

The report from the administrative inquiry promoted by the local maritime authority[42] highlighted, in the first place, as the cause of the accident, the crew's lack of knowledge of the ship and of the tasks to be performed in the event of an emergency: "The lack of knowledge indicated, however, emerges more clearly precisely in those components of the crew with specialized assignments and responsibilities who should have provided suitable instruction to the remaining crew members" (Port Captaincy of Livorno 2012, 132). These criticalities also emerge in the legal proceedings. In particular, experts found the emergency procedures put in place for the *Costa Concordia* to be inadequate. Several crew members barely knew the specific task assigned to them in the safety rota, others were not even aware of having a role in an emergency (Court of Grosseto 2012d, 51). In this regard, it should be noted that the captain himself, in a master audit that closed on December 31, 2011, had made suggestions about actuating the familiarity of crew members with their assigned roles in the safety rota, which he saw as insufficient, but received no response from the company (Court of Grosseto 2014h, part I, 21–22). The absence of adequate staff training raises a number of doubts with regard to the effectiveness of procedures.

The trial also revealed that no psychological stress-tests were carried out aimed at preparing the ship's command team to manage emergency situations (Court of Grosseto 2014h, part I, 39). As Patrick Lagadec (1993) states, to manage a crisis you need to be able to learn quickly; and to learn quickly during the crisis, you need to have learned a great deal already. This was a critical latent factor in education and training. It was not the captain's panic that created the chaos, but rather the disorganization and unpreparedness on the part of untrained and inadequately trained personnel to deal with emergency situations that

---

[42] This investigation, conducted in accordance with the navigation code, was aimed at ascertaining the causes, and any responsibility on the part of the crew on the bridge, in the creation of the accident.

predisposed the conditions for chaos. Ex post moral judgment regarding the behavior of personnel, and of the captain in particular, should have taken this important organizational factor into account.

Instead, despite having detected a certain lack of preparation, the attorney's office did not ask itself if the training of operators was adequate, or if they did periodic exercises, as happens for example with aircraft pilots in simulators. There was no in-depth analysis, merely the comparison between *being* (behavior as it was) and *having to be* (behavior as it should have been according to the figure of the model agent) in an ideal context rather than a real one. In the trial, too, when the topic came up, the tendency was for prosecutors to bypass the issue, without going into any particular detail (Court of Grosseto 2014h, part I, 39). However, without adequate and up-to-date preparation, people manage emergency events, especially ones as unique as this disaster, with the resources they have, chaos and panic included.

In addition, certain issues of non-compliance were found (Court of Grosseto 2012d, 50–51), in particular regarding the use of the language on board for work communications not in line with the International Safety Management code (53). Some of the staff had taken basic courses more than five years before, with no evidence that they still remembered what they had learned. Most of the personnel assigned to emergency duties were thus completely unprepared. Neither had the part of the crew assigned to the lifeboats been properly trained: out of forty-eight people, only thirteen were in possession of an updated certificate for lifeboat use, and as many as thirty-five were without one (47). The last drills for launching the lifeboats had been carried out in an incomplete manner and on only one side of the ship.

In short, many non-conformities existed in terms of the role these figures were supposed to play during the emergency phase. Moreover, a number of officers and staff members were unable to adequately understand the Italian language, and some did not even understand English. The language problem was also a decisive point for the experts, who stated that it was "evident that the working language established by the management company (Italian) was used by Italian and foreign personnel (those able to understand it) and that the remaining foreign staff operated using the English language. This sometimes led to the need on board to give orders in both languages, causing confusion and delay in the execution of emergency operations" (Court of Grosseto 2012d, 53). This gap undermined conditions of reliability and safety.

What happens, in fact, when orders are very rapid, given the specific situation, and do not allow room for errors or requests for clarification? "Confusion and lack of clarity in information remain constant throughout the crisis" (93–94). With respect to this criticality, however, no consequences in relation to the causal dynamics were taken into consideration. Indeed, although the evaluation indicates a lack of procedures for verifying language knowledge during the recruitment phase as an organizational criticality, the suggestion is that it was the captain's responsibility to employ personnel capable of understanding the instructions given during the approach maneuver to Giglio, an extreme situation involving rapid orders (Court of Grosseto 2012d, 53, 73). According to regulatory requirements, however, *all* crew members should have been able to understand his instructions. Karl Weick (1990) showed that communications give structure to organizations, particularly in critical situations. If communications in organizations cannot be carried out reliably, as happened in the *Costa Concordia* disaster, entropy increases and events become chaotically difficult, if not impossible, to manage reliably and safely.

3.4.4 Beyond Human Error: Agent Model or Organizational Model?

About 80 percent of marine accidents are attributed to human error, and they are the result of excessive speed in poor weather and errors in navigation (Perrow 1999, 224).

However, the analysis of the accident, and in particular of the second and third phases, has highlighted numerous organizational criticalities and error-inducing conditions that were completely underestimated in the investigation and trial. In other words, there was no model organization and consequently there could not be a model agent. The judicial agents, however, restricted themselves to drawing up a precise list of these critical issues, without looking more closely at their interactions or their possible impact on the course of events.

The prosecution theory – amplified by the media, confirmed by the courts and, naturally, happily accepted by the other organizational agents involved (the company, the Captaincies, the Ministry of Transport, etc.) – was based on the belief that, at some point, a single man was responsible for a series of incorrect behaviors, including gross errors, violations, and morally deplorable actions. An ordinary person, in other words, departed completely from the previous behavioral patterns of his everyday life and thereby became responsible for a disaster. It was a "bolt from the blue" and therefore wholly unpredictable. This analysis, however, recounts a different version of what happened. With regard to the emergency phase, from the moment of impact against the rock until all the people on board were taken to safety, except for the thirty-two who lost their lives, the captain did everything he *could* do. He did not, probably, do everything he *should have* done, but this difference between *could* and *should* has to be evaluated in terms of the actual operational context of that particular night. If Schettino's behavior did not measure up to the situation and errors were made, this must be considered and judged within a fallacious organizational context. It is not, therefore, a matter of criminal behavior, but rather of human insufficiency in the face of an exceptional event in less than optimal organizational conditions. As stated previously, there cannot be a "model agent" in the absence of a "model organization".

The starting point is that no system can completely avoid error. As already reiterated, any discussion of reliability must begin with this axiomatic statement (Weick 1987, 122). Explanations of complex events that in the analysis take only the individual level into account are limiting and simplistic on the one hand; and, on the other, they tend to produce scapegoats. They are simplistic and limiting in that they abstract individual behavior from the operational context which generates it and which gives meaning to the behavior. As Rasmussen explained:

In most work situations, the individual actor is faced with many degrees of freedom with respect to the composition of normally successful work procedures. The flexibility and speed of professional expertise evolve through a process of adaptation to the peculiarities of the work environment ... During this adaptation, performance will be optimized according to the individual actor's subjective process criteria within the boundaries of his individual resources. (Rasmussen 1993, 10)

In work, shortcuts and tricks of the trade frequently evolve and are very efficient under normal conditions. They are, however, judged as serious human errors when, in certain specific circumstances, they give rise to accidents.

In the case of the *Costa Concordia*, the responsibility for the accident was traced back to a single deviant case, the deranged behavior of a morally reprehensible figure. Without questioning the factors that may have fostered the event (the practice of the sail-by salute), if not determined it (the critical management of the emergency), responsibility was shifted from an organizational and institutional level to an individual level. This type of reconstruction is distorted because it reproduces, in an artificial environment, a complex experience of professional life that was part of a wider context.

Events such as the *Costa Concordia* accident are complex organizational phenomena that cannot be attributed to a single cause or to a single person. We cannot, therefore, treat an event of this type as an isolated fact and understand it adequately – its longitudinal dimension has to be considered. The disaster must be studied as an organic whole that is product and process at the same time, embedded in a specific context and in a specific social system, within which it takes shape.

As shown in the previous sections, the accident was a failure at different levels: individual, organizational, inter-organizational, and regulatory (see Figure 3.5).

The *Costa Concordia* event shows all the characteristics of an organizational accident, with a long incubation period, during which warning signs were not only ignored, but considered as behavior and action to be rewarded. The practice of the sail-by salute responded to a logic of appropriateness to a set of expectations that had become institutional, an "indispensable tradition". Was a good captain the one who did sail-by salutes or the one who refused to do them? In this way, the various subjects, over time, developed a definition of the situation (the custom of the sail-by salute) that allowed them to go on as if there was nothing dangerous or wrong about it.

The accident was not a random, anomalous, unpredictable event. It seems to have, rather, originated in the creation of the practice of the sail-by salute and then in the history of the organization and its broken safety culture. In addition, it seems to have lain within a fallacious system of controls and regulations.[43] In a safety culture dominated by an unwarranted optimism based on the "can-do" attitude, anomalies

---

[43] Organizational culture refers to the core values, norms, beliefs, and practices that characterize the functioning of a particular organization. At the most basic level, the organizational culture defines the assumptions that employees adopt while carrying out their work – defines "the way we do things here". The culture of an organization is a powerful force that persists even following reorganizations and the departure of key people.

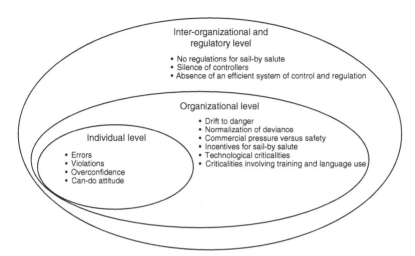

Figure 3.5 The various levels of failure

such as sail-by salutes were not seen as warning signs, but as consistent with the organization's commercial aims. Therefore, there was an obvious conflict between commercial and marketing objectives, on the one hand, and safety, on the other.

On this point, what emerged during the trial is of particular interest. The captain was accused of having allowed a number of guests to go onto the bridge, in violation of company regulations and safety measures. However, it was learned from the trial that guests, including groups with dozens of people, were also welcomed onto the bridge during navigation at the request of the company itself, and for a fee (Court of Grosseto 2014f, part I, 40). So the practice was prohibited by company regulations and at the same time encouraged by the management and even subject to a fee (60 euros for the "bridge tour"). No consequences followed on from this revelation, which was certainly a matter of organizational responsibility; only the accusations against the captain for what happened that night.[44]

As for the management of the emergency, according to the regulations in force, before giving the order to abandon the ship, the captain should have had the purser carry out a muster call (with megaphones

---

[44] Court of Grosseto, Court of Assizes, Hearing Report made by sound recording, Criminal Proceedings, N.R.G. 1023/13 – R.G.N.R. 285/12, 03/12/2014, 38–41.

and lists of names) of all the passengers and crew: 4,229 people spread throughout 220 meters at the various meeting points. Doing some basic arithmetic, it would be possible to call, simply by saying the name and surname of each passenger, about 25–30 people per minute. The whole process, then, maintaining the same rhythm and without stopping, would take between two hours and ten minutes and two hours and twenty minutes. If, in addition to calling out the names, it was also necessary to check the passengers' response, in order to ascertain their presence, the time required would be doubled at least. Time would, in any case, have certainly been taken away from managing the emergency. Among other things, investigations revealed that, between the passengers on the list available to the captain and those who were actually on board, there was a difference of over five hundred people. The muster call would therefore have taken even more time, given that hundreds of people would not have responded and it would have taken a long time to realize the difference between the list and reality. Compliance with this rule would clearly have endangered the lives of passengers. Failure to comply with an absurd rule, instead of being considered an important decision in terms of speeding up emergency operations, was considered a sign of negligence on the part of the captain.

In conclusion, if the focus is too closely on risky frontline actions, or if only the emergency management phase is analyzed, it is harder to realize that this was an organizational accident, in which criticalities and deficiencies in the navigation operations control system emerged. Examples include the organization's inability to keep ships within safety limits, an incorrect incentive system, an inadequate safety culture, and a critical control system. The size of the problems relating to the allocation of responsibility is evident.

Finally, it is also worth mentioning that, in maritime incidents involving ships and ferries, the average mortality rate is very high.[45]

---

[45] With no claim to statistical validity, an estimate made from 25 cases of shipping accidents gives an average number of 633 deaths per accident. This is a sample that certainly requires better specification, but to date the *Costa Concordia* accident ranks in penultimate place in terms of number of victims: *Titanic* 1912, Atlantic Ocean, 1,496 dead; *Empress of Ireland* 1914, Quebec, 1,012; *Andrea Doria* 1956, Massachusetts, 46; *Tamponas* 1981, Java, 580; passenger ship 1986, Bangladesh, 600; *Admiral Nakhimov* 1986, Black Sea, 448; *Dona Paz* 1987, Philippines, 4,340; *Scandinavian Star* 1990, from Oslo

In the light of the conditions and scarce resources available, and given the number of victims (relatively low, compared to the total number of passengers on the ship), perhaps the management of the emergency was not as disastrous as the courts believed. The captain's maneuver to approach the mainland had also certainly created excellent conditions in terms of being able to go ahead with the rescue of the people on board. For the prosecutors and the courts, this was all just luck. Given the convictions they began with, it could hardly have been otherwise.

3.5 The Social Construction of the Scapegoat

Criminal investigations and media coverage play a crucial role in the social construction of the scapegoat by pointing out misconducts and framing events (Palmer et al. 2016; Roulet and Clemente 2018). In the case of *Costa Concordia*, the conventional explanation of the accident provided by the mass media and magistrates is based on an erroneous theory of rational choice in decision making: a captain as an "amoral calculator". The long history that incubated the accident was not taken into consideration. Instead, it was a disaster in compliance with the rules, not reducible to the action of an immoral person who went insane in one night. It was also certainly a disaster generated by a series of errors, but based on compliance with typical risky practices within a critical safety culture. It is clear that the first explanation, based on the error-making operator, produces greater advantages for multiple agents.

In Chapter 1, I argue that in order to be credible, a scapegoat in organizations must have played a role in the affair for which he is held responsible, even if, for the sake of convenience, he is also made to bear the guilt of others. A person does not suddenly become a scapegoat: as discussed in Chapter 2, the attribution of responsibility is a

to Fredrikshavn (Denmark), 159; *Moby Prince* 1991, Livorno, 140; ferry 1993, Haiti, 500–700; *Estonia* 1994, Baltic Sea, 852; passenger ship 1996, Lake Victoria, over 800; *Kursk* 2000, Barents Sea, 118; ferry 2002, Gambia, 970; ferry 2003, Bangladesh, 600; ferry 2006, Java Sea, over 500; ferry 2006, Red Sea, over 1,000; *The Princess of the Stars* 2008, Philippine coasts, over 800; *Bulgaria* 2011, Volga, 122; *Costa Concordia* 2012, Isola del Giglio, 32; ferry 2014, Bangladesh, 200; *Sewol* 2014, South Korea, 295; *Norman Atlantic* 2014, Greece, 9; ship 2015, Bangladesh, 78; *ARA San Juan* 2017, San Jorge Gulf, 44.

social process (Palmer 2014) that the accused organization can influence through communication (Coombs and Holladay 2002; Coombs 2007; Bundy and Pfarrer 2015; Bundy et al. 2017). The scapegoat emerges through a process of "manufacturing", or even "counterfeiting" (Goffman 1974).[46] This is a process that involves the intentional effort of one or more individuals to manipulate the action so that one or more people are induced to have a false perception of what happened – for example, by stating discrediting and defamatory facts (Gangloff et al. 2016). In order for the manufacturing process to take place, certain conditions are required: agents promote or exploit discrediting facts; an event (or more than one) that occurred during the accident is "framed";[47] and sometimes even the dismissal of the "guilty individual" is framed (Cornelissen and Werner 2014). The public in general believes these facts, reinforcing the work of the agents who promote them. In the scapegoating process that took place after the *Costa Concordia* accident, there were various agents involved, some internal to the navigation system, others, as will be seen in the following sections, external, such as the mass media and the judiciary.

3.5.1 Character Stigma, Discrediting Events, and Degradation Ceremonies

Garfinkel (1956) develops the concept of "degradation ceremonies" to denote a mainly communicative process aimed at lowering the social status of a person within a group or society in general, in order to shame that person for violating norms, rules, or laws, inflict punishment upon them and deprive them of rights and privileges.[48] In this way, the public recognizes in a given social actor qualities that are decidedly worse than the model of normality. As we have seen in this

---

[46] "Manufacturing" and "counterfeiting" are two concepts developed by Goffman (1974) which help to explain the process of construction (or manufacturing) of the scapegoat, the "scapegoating process", even though Goffman does not speak specifically of this phenomenon, but rather of the very important concept of stigma.

[47] Regarding the emphasis given by the media to certain specific facts of an incident or crime in order to influence public opinion, known as "framing", see Sara Sun Beale (2006).

[48] Chris Greer and Eugene McLaughlin (2011) refer back to the concept developed by Debord (1970) of "public execution in the society of the spectacle".

regard, one of the three types of stigma identified by Goffman involves the individual characteristics, the personality, of a subject, perceived as weak-willed, dominated by passions, dishonest, etc. (1963, 4).

The case of the *Costa Concordia* accident is emblematic in this regard. The investigation and the public statements of the investigators, on the one hand, and the mass media, on the other, focused on problems relating to the event's chief protagonist that were moral, rather than strictly legal, in nature. It was a moral, rather than a criminal, trial. Furthermore, the judicial investigation, first, and the trial thereafter, were both characterized by the numerous presence of third parties with respect to judicial procedures, and by mass media information that was extensive and, as will be seen, one-sided, at the same time. In this regard, the analysis of the media coverage of the *Costa Concordia* case, carried out with reference to the arc of time extending from the day of the accident (January 13, 2012) to the ruling of the Supreme Court of Cassation (May 12, 2017), brought some elements of particular interest to light. Out of a total of 292 articles analyzed, published by the two most widely circulated Italian national newspapers, *La Repubblica* and *Corriere della Sera*, about 90 percent (264 articles) focus exclusively on the individual factor and on the figure of the captain as the cause of the disaster. Only the remaining 10 percent (28 articles) investigate in some way the organizational factors and criticalities that played a role in the dynamics of the accident, as previous sections here have shown. Even before the evidence deriving from the inquiries was available, almost all of the articles featured an exclusive focus on the individual human factor, which were mainly based on the assumptions of the Prosecutor's Office, thus functioning as a kind of megaphone.

It is reasonable to believe that the extensive media coverage had an influence on the investigation and the trial, which saw the involvement not only of legitimately participating agents (judges, lawyers, defendants) but also of the general public. It was as if there existed not just the official panel of judges to answer to, but also a parallel panel of judges made up of this audience. This placed real public pressure on the magistrates, leading to the swift identification and sanctioning of the guilty, and raised many doubts with regard to the emotional poise of both investigators and magistrates.

As Giglioli pointed out, a process of degradation is more effective when (a) the facts in question "... are labeled in an exemplary manner,

(b) the more the accuser manages to identify himself as the representative of the interests of the community, and (c) the more the audience present will be of the right size" (1997, 23). Even before the actual dynamics of the facts had been understood and, above all, even before a trial was held, the narration provided by the media "framed" the captain as the story's sole protagonist, in a moral tale where Schettino appeared as the immoral reprobate to be punished.

It is a known phenomenon that the perception of a situation by the media and the public reinforce one another, eliminating definitions of the situation that are alternative to the definition that is establishing itself as dominant. In this way, a "spiral of silence" is generated for alternative hypotheses (Noelle-Neumann 1974). As Garapon (1996) states, the media, as an instrument of public indignation and anger, risk spreading a sense of fear and victimization and thus risks favoring the scapegoat mechanism.

As previously mentioned, the scapegoating process requires that one or more discrediting facts of a given event be "framed", and that the general public believe them, reinforcing the work of the agents who promote them. In the case of the *Costa Concordia*, there were two interconnected, emblematic discrediting events that fostered, if not determined, scapegoating: the abandonment of the ship by the captain before all the passengers had left the ship and his failure to go back on board. These two events played a decisive role in the whole story, not so much from the point of view of the sentence imposed (one year and eight months out of sixteen years overall), but for the image they created and the stigma they generated in relation to the figure of the captain. They immediately helped to create a real belief in the captain's guilt – a granite belief. Although less serious as alleged violations compared with others, his abandonment of the ship and failure to go back on board had a volatile impact on the interpretation of the other offenses the captain was charged with.

The First Discrediting Event

First, the abandonment of the ship. This became necessary because the ship had keeled over on to its starboard side, where the captain was: had he remained on board, he would have drowned and could not have helped anyone. This act, incorrectly communicated by the media as committed out of cowardice rather than necessity, immediately generated moral condemnation of the captain – condemnation that in some ways exceeded the criticism relating to his incorrect (according to the prosecution) handling of the ship. The fact acquired great visibility at a national and international level following the publication, on January 17, 2012, of the recording of a telephone call that took place on the evening of the shipwreck, in which Gregorio De Falco, an officer of the Captaincy of Livorno, ordered the captain, in no uncertain terms, to go back on board. From that moment on, sufficient demonization was triggered to identify Schettino as guilty of everything. His behavior was swiftly defined as "cowardly" by the media, with national newspapers running headlines like "Captain coward", "He abandoned 300 people", "He even abandoned the disabled", and "Schettino fled for the lifeboat".[49]

The recording of the phone call, with simultaneous translation and transcriptions, was also reported by numerous newspapers and broadcasters around the world, accompanied by indignant comments.[50] There was also no shortage of cultural stereotypes and generalizations deployed by the international press: "Was anyone surprised that the captain involved in the *Costa Concordia* tragedy was Italian?" and, "he is a man with a theatrical style, gesticulating as he speaks".[51] On the basis of the phone conversation, Officer De Falco was portrayed by the media as the good, high-principled hero figure, the noble example who partly restored honor to the seafaring world by trying to encourage the captain to return to his ship. The latter, meanwhile, is portrayed as inadequate to his role, reluctant to carry out his duty and to rescue the passengers, essentially "an unlikely Lord Jim, dishonored by his escape".[52]

---

[49] "Captain Coward", *Libero*, January 18, 2012; "He abandoned 300 people", *Il Messaggero*, January 18, 2012; "He even abandoned the disabled", *Corriere della Sera*, January 18, 2012; "Schettino fled for the lifeboat", *Corriere della Sera*, March 4, 2012.

[50] "Recording reveals coastguard told captain to 'get back on board'", *BBC News*, January 17, 2012; "Port Authority to cruise ship captain: 'Get on board, damn it'", *CNN News blogs*, January 17, 2012; "Costa Concordia: coast guard to captain: 'Get back on board the ship!'", *The Telegraph*, January 17, 2012.

[51] "If *Der Spiegel* calls us all Schettinos", *Il Fatto Quotidiano*, January 26, 2012.

[52] So runs the headline of an article in *La Repubblica* of January 27, 2012, referring to the famous character in Joseph Conrad's novel.

In addition, the image of a "cowardly" captain was solidified in the collective imagination through a specific "memory hook" (Fine 1996, 1163): the catch phrase "Get back on board, damn it!" pronounced by De Falco during the conversation with the captain and also enthusiastically reported by the major media around the world.[53]

It is significant to note that, since the phone conversation was part of the official documentation of the Captaincy, it should not in fact have been made public – certainly not as soon as it was. The timing of the publication is interesting: the conversation appeared as an independent contribution in the *Corriere Fiorentino* newspaper on the morning of January 17, 2012, just four days after the accident – with amazing promptitude, in other words. The story of how the call spread is truly unique. The journalist who disseminated it states that on January 16, 2012, while he had temporarily moved away from his car, "someone" deposited a pen drive – through the open window, since the journalist is a smoker – on the car seat. And the drive contained an excerpt of the conversation between Schettino and De Falco. The journalist delivered the pen drive to the editorial staff and the next day the recording made its way into the world through the *Corriere Fiorentino*. It is worth pointing out that the pen drive only contained an extract of the conversation – the part containing the phrase "Get back on board, damn it!" that was soon to become world-famous.

Who had an interest in circulating that decontextualized sentence using a journalist who made himself available for the purpose? Some images from Italian TV news *TG1* of January 17, 2012, filmed at the Grosseto public prosecutor's office, show Commander De Falco rejecting all journalists, except the author of the scoop (Schettino and Abate 2015, 418). Information so artfully disclosed tends to create prior consent to accusatory theories, even before the real dynamics of the facts have been clarified. A second conversation between Schettino and De Falco, on the other hand, one calmer and more constructive in tone, was only made public much later. The different timing of publication of the calls was not random and suggests, rather, the existence of a very specific strategy.

---

[53] The phrase quickly became so famous that a web agency started producing T-shirts, receiving orders from all over the world. ("Italy's 'Get back on board, damn it!' T-shirts a hit", *Reuters*, January 20, 2012).

It is important to notice that the negative media construction of the captain's behavior caused a high-impact, negative "horn effect", with related consequences in terms of reading and interpreting the facts.[54] Negative traits are known to be easier to acquire but harder to lose than positive traits (Rothbart and Park 1986). Added to this came the fake news, later clarified and denied, that the captain left the ship after taking off his uniform in order to blend in with the passengers. In the meantime, however, this fake news continued to circulate, reinforcing the captain's negative image.

The case of the abandonment may appear controversial, but it should at least be remembered that it happened at 00:17, just a few moments before the ship overturned, as the patrol boat of the Guardia di Finanza (the Financial Guard) was warning the boats that were taking people to safety to move away due to the imminent capsizing of the ship. When the captain got on the lifeboat, after having helped to free it, the "ship listed wildly" (Court of Grosseto 2015, 396). The second in command ended up in the water under "the rain of objects falling from the increasingly sloping decks of the Concordia" (397) – the vessel was at an inclination of over 25 percent (415) and rapidly worsening.

As emerged from the evidence, in the last few moments, as the ship rotated on itself and collapsed onto one side, the surface of the bridge was gradually transformed into a slide and then into a vertical wall. For this reason, the second in command had thrown himself into the sea. It is in this specific context that the captain had no alternative but to move away as quickly as possible from the ship, together with the last passengers left on that side, and only after having helped to disengage the last lifeboat, which otherwise risked being left unused after the ship had keeled over. The investigative unit of the Carabinieri of Grosseto also confirmed that the captain abandoned the ship at precisely that moment of extremity. Not only was staying aboard on that side of the ship practically impossible, given the inclination of almost ninety degrees, it was also certain that the captain would have died had he not left the ship just then, given the position the vessel was in. This is a point worth repeating: the only other behavior possible in this situation was to die. Yet this evidence was never communicated correctly by the media.

---

[54] A "horn effect" is a cognitive bias whereby the perception of a person is unduly influenced by a single negative trait.

It should be remembered that, after an unsuccessful attempt, the captain never returned on board. He remained on the reef about 30 meters from the ship, in telephone connection with some people involved in the rescue, such as the Provincial Command of the Carabinieri of Grosseto, who had asked him to stay where he was in order to coordinate operations as a visual reference. According to the prosecution, on the other hand, his contribution to handling the rescue was virtually zero.

The Second Discrediting Event
The second emblematic discrediting event in the construction of the negative image required for scapegoating was Schettino's failure to get back on board the ship. De Falco, the officer of the Port Captaincy of Livorno, not having understood the way in which the ship had keeled over, ordered the captain to go back on board from the starboard side, which was by then underwater. Obviously, this was impossible. Instead of containing the chaos, the officer was, in this way, contributing to its exacerbation. The captain's uncertain tone during the phone call stemmed from a communication from De Falco that was in fact completely meaningless, even though expressed in imperative, not to say aggressive, terms. This was not an aspect, however, that would be taken into consideration by the media: for them, as well as for their readers and viewers, it was all too clear who the hero was and who the villain.

In order to actually get back on board the ship – by the port rather than, as De Falco insisted, the starboard side – the captain would have had to be taken by a boat to the far side of the vessel in relation to the point where he found himself at that moment: on the reef between the ship and the island. He would have had to climb a boarding ladder without equipment or suitable footwear and then, somehow, do his best to both save those who were still on board and coordinate the emergency. What this actually would have involved is far from clear, given the condition of the ship: tilted over on one side and partly submerged, completely in the dark, bereft of any audio communication system that might have been made it possible to contact the missing people. Any attempt to return to the ship seems to be more of a moral imperative than a concrete operational possibility with some chance of success. The captain would have had to sacrifice himself in order to save his image, even though doing so would save nobody's life. The result, probably, would have been to add his own name to the list of those who had to be saved, rather than effectively trying to play a role in the rescue process.

According to SOLAS regulations, the captain is responsible for, and first guarantor of, safety. But this is an optative requirement of a generic regulatory code and what it really means in a situation of extreme emergency such as that of the *Costa Concordia* is not at all clear. If anything, it becomes an ex post judgment from afar, made by those unaware of the real operational context. Furthermore, while it is true that rescuers did subsequently arrive on board the vessel, these were personnel specialized in emergencies such as firefighters, in groups and not alone, with the correct equipment and with the ship now in a stationary condition.

In short, the issue of Schettino's failure to return to his ship was analyzed and judged without the real factors being taken into consideration: that, on the one hand, the action was incredibly difficult, if not impossible, in the conditions as they were, and on the other, utterly useless. As a gesture, while it might have seemed heroic, it would have had no concrete result in terms of saving lives. Thus, the abandonment of the ship and the failure to get back on board, thanks to the circulated recording of the call between De Falco and Schettino, became a crucial element of the "ritual of degradation" that targeted the captain's moral status. The mass media, rather than providing correct information regarding the dynamics of the event and the various organizational and inter-organizational factors that fostered it, instead played the role of "moral entrepreneurs" (Becker 1963), encouraging the launch of a crusade against the captain.

Moral Evaluation vs Legal Evaluation

In the *Costa Concordia* case, in the eyes of public opinion, the captain quickly became "the scoundrel of scoundrels"[55] and "the bogeyman in a story that could not be any darker".[56] In the days immediately following the accident, the mass media on the one hand and, on the

---

[55] Goffredo Buccini, "Concordia, the survivors as they pass. Schettino fled for the lifeboat", *Corriere della Sera*, March 4, 2012.
[56] Giusi Fasano, "Captain in cell – Abandoned ship and alarm given late", *Corriere della Sera*, January 15, 2012.

other, the Public Prosecutor of Grosseto, in charge of the investigation, intervened on several occasions in order to declaim the captain's guilt and discredit his character. On January 15, it was stated that the approach to Giglio was a maneuver that the captain had wanted to make and which he had ordered, while he was also accused of having abandoned the ship when there were still many people on board that needed to be saved.[57] The media deployed a variety of highly-colored expressions for the sole purpose of constructing an immoral image of the captain and highlighting his negative character traits: "human error and stupidity that render all technology and all knowledge useless", "there is the disconcerting sequence of carelessness, of manifestations of incompetence, of fatuity, of irresponsibility, of cowardice ... which call for severity without leniency", "the night of lies and madness of a confused man. Or, worse, deceitful", "Schettino, the exhibitionist at the helm who drove the ship like a Ferrari", "a panicking child", "a shoddy, exhibitionist captain", "the befuddled bravado of an inadequate captain",[58] "pathological insensitivity",[59] etc.

While still lacking a precise picture of the dynamics of the accident, the prosecutor had already identified the one person responsible. On January 16, during a press conference, the prosecutor commented: "we were struck by the conscienceless nature of the hazardous maneuver that the captain of the *Costa Concordia* made near Giglio".[60] A "conscienceless" maneuver that was actually periodically repeated – not an exceptional and rare violation but "an indispensable tradition", as Giglio's then mayor described it. Yet, throughout the investigation, no serious in-depth analysis was ever made into the dangerous practice of sail-by salutes: instead, it was considered a single, deviant act.

---

[57] "Harsh words from the prosecutor: 'The captain abandoned ship with still many people on board that needed to be saved'", *La Nazione*, January 15, 2012.

[58] "A chain of errors and carelessness", *Corriere della Sera*, January 15, 2012; "Severity now", *Corriere della Sera*, January 16, 2012; "Are there any injuries or deaths? No, it's all fine. The captain lies in phone calls with the Captaincy Office. Impatience from the mainland: do you want to go home?", *Corriere della Sera*, January 17, 2012; "Schettino, the exhibitionist at the helm who drove the ship like a Ferrari", *La Repubblica*, January 17, 2012; "De Falco, the voice of duty", *La Repubblica*, January 17, 2012; "Individual responsibility", *La Repubblica*, February 5, 2012.

[59] "The Captain Schettino show. Lies instead of truth", *Corriere della Sera*, February 28, 2014.

[60] "Giglio shipwreck, Prosecutor Verusio: 'Inexcusable unscrupulousness'", *La Nazione*, January 16, 2012.

On January 18, 2013, in a radio interview, the prosecutor defined the captain's behavior as "heinous", "unspeakable and unforgivable".[61] A firm belief that seems to say little about the facts and a great deal about the character of the suspect, which, if anything, should have been the outcome of an investigation and certainly not its preliminary premise. Throughout the course of the investigation and even after the trial, the prosecutors continued with similar statements: in the case under examination "it must be noted that the 'human' factor was an exclusive element in the dynamics of events and it must again be reiterated that the defendant Schettino bears the almost sole burden of the horrific chain of mistakes made".[62] In the end, the expressions being used are of the type: "careless idiot",[63] "he had an exuberance that led him into insincerity", "it was a flagrant error bordering on the unbelievable", "testicular evaluations",[64] "unforgivable and unspeakable conduct",[65] "he lied shamelessly and without repentance"[66] in the indictment, which ends with the "apocalyptic" comment: "God have mercy on commander Schettino because we can have none".[67]

In the request for indictment[68] there are numerous moral judgments that add nothing to the disputed facts, but seem to betray the intention to construct a negative and immoral image of the defendant: "Unequivocal deficits in management and communication skills … non-crystalline vocation for transparency in inter-company relations" (157); "painful stammering" (319); "embarrassing inadequacy" (323); "the captain's inertia" (367); "obtuse immobility"

---

[61] The programme *24Mattino*, on Radio24, www.youtube.com/watch?v=42uszE8S5O0.

[62] *La Nazione*, May 15, 2013.

[63] Words of the prosecutors of Grosseto reported by Alfredo Faetti, "Schettino, 26 years requested, the prosecutor: 'He was a careless idiot'. And he: 'I don't run away.'" *Il Corriere Fiorentino*, January 26, 2015.

[64] "*Concordia*. Prosecutor: In four years, Schettino went from being captain of oil tankers to large cruise ships", *La Repubblica*, January 22, 2015.

[65] "The prosecutors accuse: Schettino saw badly at night, he played it by ear", *La Repubblica*, January 23, 2015.

[66] "Schettino is a careless idiot, he deserves 26 years", *La Repubblica*, January 27, 2015.

[67] Words of the prosecutor Stefano Pizza, reported by *Il Sole 24 ore*, January 26, 2015.

[68] Public Prosecutor's Office of the Court of Grosseto, February 25, 2013a.

(368); "shameless immodesty" (405); "shocking imprudence... colossal incompetence... petty disposition... ignoble motivations... boastful bon viveur", in just eleven lines (493); "disarming cynicism" (589), "shocking imprudence ... colossal incompetence ... petty disposition ... ignoble motivations" (in four lines, 591); "the captain's apathy" (655); "ignoble abandonment of the bridge" (678); "ignoble choice" (679). In the appeal, too, the prosecutors were not sparing with judgments of a moral nature, underlining the captain's tendency to self-exaltation and "inappropriate star-like posing" (Florence Court of Appeal 2016, 140 and 145).

In addition to all this, there is an odd reconstruction of the captain's dinner on the night in question, in which it is stated – as reported by a witness – that the captain drank only sparkling water (Florence Court of Appeal 2016, 194). It is then suggested, however, given that the decanter available to diners was no longer full, that he drank wine instead (195). This statement proves nothing, its only possible use being to instill the doubt that the captain had drunk some wine before again taking command of the ship.[69] Two pages are spent discussing dinner and wine, while only two lines are dedicated to the fact that, between 21:43:00 and 21:43:15, the alarms set on the radar were deactivated – no one knows by whom, nor on whose order (213). Their operation could have alerted the team on the bridge to the imminent danger, providing time for a counter-maneuver. But there is no in-depth analysis, only two lines. The dinner also inevitably attracted headlines from the media as sensational as they were mistaken: "The captain and the dancer, wine and frivolity on the bridge", "The merry drinkers", "Schettino was not lucid", etc.[70]

Furthermore, it is of particular interest that, both in the request for indictment (155 and following) and in the first instance verdict (146 and following), there was included a summary of the professional evaluation made in 2002 and 2003 by the former Captain Palombo, a historic figure in the Costa Crociere group, together with the professional evaluation made by the company dating back to 2007–2008. The text states that Palombo evaluated the captain as "professionally

---

[69] It is worth remembering here that, in the first judicial interrogation, the captain had already declared that he neither smoked nor drank (Court of Grosseto 2012, 101).
[70] *La Repubblica*, January 20, 2012; *Corriere della Sera*, January 31, 2012.

valid" but with "some gaps relating to the management of personnel and discipline on board" and with a tendency to lie and place the blame on others. Similar deficits in people management, teamwork, and communication are highlighted in the company's evaluation (without, however, specifying the average values of these evaluations for the personnel).

However, investigators and magistrates do not say whether those professional assessments, dating back in some cases to a decade before the accident, were still valid and, if so, how it was possible that the company gave command of a ship with more than four thousand people on board to a captain so lacking in terms of non-technical skills. Either these skills were not necessary, and therefore it is not clear why these evaluations were reproposed in the text, or the evaluations themselves were considered unreliable, or the company was grossly negligent in not taking them into account. None of this is investigated, just as nothing is said about the fact that the evaluator himself, Captain Palombo, had become famous for being the "reinventor" of the sail-by salute, as we have already seen, and as he himself recounts in his memoirs (Palombo 2008, 149). Again, no attention is given to, or mention made of, this relevant fact. And, one has to ask, if the professional profile of the captain really was the one described above, why, on the company's website on the day of the accident, was there a post in which he was praised for, among other things, the sail-by salute he had performed near the island of Procida? Was he, as the world was later led to believe, a deviant, or was he a fine professional to be commended with an encomium on the company website?

It is interesting to note that in the request for indictment the psychological professional profile serves to argue that "These unequivocal deficits in management and communication skills, together with the non-crystalline vocation for transparency in inter-company relations, have found dramatic confirmation – with easy hindsight – in the tragic events of January 13 2012" (Public Prosecutor's Office, Court of Grosseto 2013b, 156). Meanwhile, in the first instance judgment, "this apparent diversion into Schettino's past" (148) is traced back to the reason for that night's sail-by salute, as a tribute to Captain Palombo.

In order to establish the defendant's guilt, the public prosecutors resort to a rhetoric of degradation that serves to build an image of incompetence and immorality. A hasty and elementary psychologism is employed in order to construct an (im)moral image of the captain that is functional for the accusatory hypothesis. This is evident in the captain's testimony. The prosecutors, at a certain point, accuse the captain of not having consulted, in line with the Damage Control Plan, the Stability Manual, and the Instruction Manual dealing with the stability of the ship in the event of a breach, as required by procedure. Now, it is not clear what the usefulness would be of underlining the failure to consult a manual in a critical and emergency situation, if not that of constructing the (immoral) image of a man inclined to violate regulations. Consulting the manual would certainly not have changed the course of events, but, on the contrary, would probably have generated further delay (Court of Grosseto 2014f, part III, 11–12).

In general, what clearly emerges is a prosecution strategy aimed at focusing attention on the presumed tendency of the captain to violate procedure, to place himself above it, regardless of any assessment of the adequacy of the individual contested regulations to effectively deal with an emergency situation. Many doubts are raised, however with regard to their actual usefulness.[71]

The character and moral traits of the captain certainly did not suddenly make their appearance on that night and in those circumstances. This provokes a legitimate question: if the captain really was such a worthless figure, how is it possible that Costa Crociere had entrusted the lives of over four thousand people to such an individual a number of times over several years and with no doubts ever being raised? And why, it is worth repeating, was there a post praising Captain Schettino on the company website on the very day of the accident? These are questions that perhaps the investigators should have asked themselves, at least in order to find answers to their own questions. But this did not happen.

Precomprehension and Bias in the Investigation

The investigation and court decisions thus suffered from multiple cognitive biases, held together by the fact that one individual was regarded as the cause of the accident. In particular, three biases can be found in this case.

The first is "tunnel vision": that set of systematic tendencies that prevent us from being accurate in the perception, and consequently in

[71] See Court of Grosseto (2014f) and Court of Grosseto (2014g).

the interpretation, of events (Findley and Scott 2006). Once a suspicion is developed, the tendency is to give more weight to the evidence that favors it, giving less or no importance to any opposing evidence. In the case in question, the focus was immediately on a single suspect, the captain, and the evidence that then built the case was selected and filtered – minimizing, if not actually ignoring, evidence that pointed in the direction of other investigative hypotheses.

Connected to "tunnel vision", there is a second cognitive error: "confirmation bias" or "forensic confirmation bias" (Kassin, Dror, and Kukucka 2013). From the very first moment, a working hypothesis was formulated that treated the captain as the "real" suspect. The process continued by considering the suspect as the "true culprit" instead of testing this hypothesis and analyzing other factors that could contribute to explaining the accident in a more complete way. Evidence was unilaterally selected and interpreted that would later justify his conviction. At the same time, evidence that would have shown a significantly different distribution of responsibility was undervalued and ignored. Conclusions were reached through the search for, and flawed interpretation of, information that supported the preconceived thesis. In short, what was supposed to be the *output* of a path of analysis, of an investigation, was actually, right from the start, the *input*.[72]

Confirming this trend is the fact that the fifty questions posed in the evaluation were mainly aimed at investigating the "short history" – those few hours between the departure of the ship on the last leg of its voyage and the end of the emergency phase. In this way, the investigation framework was simplified and consequently the involvement of other organizational agents became more difficult, with all the attention focused on the captain, and, to a negligible extent, the command team.

---

[72] The problem of the so-called implicit bias is a very important issue that particularly concerns public prosecutors and law enforcement agencies in the investigation phase. The United States Department of Justice in 2020 announced the establishment of a training program to teach these subjects to recognize and manage implicit bias. The program will be an integral part of the ordinary training course and will be based on the results of the most recent research in the field of social sciences. Regarding this initiative, see: www.justice.gov/opa/pr/department-justice-announces-new-department-wide-implicit-bias-training-personnel; more generally, on the bias problems that characterize the decision-making processes of judges, see Guthrie, Rachlinsky, and Wistricliff (2001).

In the three degrees of judgment, the prevailing search for factors capable of confirming the investigation's guiding hypothesis, such as information about the captain's lack of professionalism and morality, is clearly evident, while information that could work against this thesis, such as critical organizational factors, remains in the background with no in-depth analysis. Confirmation bias is maintained in two interrelated ways: (1) the way information is sought, as expectations influence the amount and type of information the person looks for (Trope and Liberman 1996); (2) the way in which information is processed, as expectations influence the interpretation, memory and judgment of new information (Fiske and Neuberg 1990).

Finally, a third cognitive error present in this story is the "fundamental attribution error": the cause of a person's behavior is traced back to presumed moral, internal, qualities, underestimating instead the influence that the environment or context may have had in determining such behavior (Ross 1977; Nisbett and Ross 1980).[73] In this way, it was assumed that what the person *did* actually mirrors what he *is*. If the captain was immoral, given that he abandoned the ship (even though it is clear that things were not quite so straightforward), then the *previous* decisions and actions that led to the disaster will also be immoral and therefore wrong.

It follows that the evidence that gradually emerged regarding latent factors, the numerous organizational criticalities present, did not in the least affect the original belief. There was a situation of cognitive hysteresis, or psychological fixation, in which people fail to revise their initial assessments in the face of new evidence, in particular evidence that diverges from expectations (Woods et al. 2010). Here, this included the significant errors by the helmsman, the failure of the emergency generator which prevented a more effective management of the event, the problems to do with operator training, deficiencies in language knowledge etc. – all factors detailed in previous sections. The repeated errors of the helmsman in the crucial phases of the event were deemed irrelevant by the Prosecutor's Office, and in any case were seen to be caused by the captain himself, responsible as he was for giving multiple orders in a short period of time (Public Prosecutor's

---

[73] On the fact that we tend to overestimate personal, *dispositional* factors (genes, personality traits, personal pathologies, etc.), and underestimate the influence of *situational* factors, see Ross and Nisbett (2011).

Office, Court of Grosseto 2013b, 220). Even the fact that the helmsman moved the rudder in the opposite direction to the direction given in the order just a few seconds before impact was the captain's fault, not the helmsman's. Nothing was said about the fact that the helmsman not only did not understand Italian (the ship's official language), but that he also had a fairly poor grasp of English – something that could have played an important role in his erroneous behavior. This was an organizational criticality certainly not attributable to the captain, but acknowledging this would perhaps have deprived the prosecution of an extra weapon.

It is a controversial point, this error of the helmsman, who for 13 seconds moved the rudder in a direction opposite to the captain's instructions, pushing the ship towards the rock, instead of moving it away. The attorney's office claimed that this made no difference to the event and that, given the previous events and the hysteresis of the rudder, the collision would have occurred anyway.[74] In reality, there was no rudder hysteresis: as is clearly visible from the black box data, the rudders moved smoothly, following the captain's orders. The verdict on this aspect states:

"The court experts and the expert witnesses of the State Attorney's Office and the prosecution have, however, stated that it is not possible to establish with certainty what would have happened had there not been the error of the helmsman, the effect of which undoubtedly was to attenuate, for a fraction of time, the effectiveness of the maneuver that the captain was attempting to reduce the angular momentum of the bow of the ship and try to stop the listing of the stern to port. Perhaps the collision would have affected other compartments of the ship located further aft, but it should be noted that this desperate maneuver attempted by the captain was ordered when the ship was already so close to the rocks, and with the stern practically committed to the shallow water, as to make it practically useless". (Court of Grosseto 2015, 202).

In reality, other (civil party) experts argued that the impact would either not have occurred or would have occurred in a very different part of the ship, further aft and with completely different dynamics of

---

[74] "Rudder hysteresis" refers to a delay in the movement of the rudder, and consequently of the ship, from the moment in which the helmsman moves the rudder following the order from the captain.

the accident and of the emergency. Given its importance, this other possible evolution of the situation merited more detailed study. Furthermore, it must be remembered that the type of ship referred to by the courts experts was the wrong type. The mathematical model was in fact based on a ship from several decades before, with only one rudder at the center between the two propellers. Therefore, the assessments of the effect of the helmsman's error ordered by the judge for the preliminary investigations and carried out by the coordinating admiral of the expert panel, referred to the behavior of a two-prop ship with only one rudder. However, the *Costa Concordia* had two rudders, not one, and thus had greater agility and fluidity of maneuver. A ship with two rudders has a much more immediate reaction capability. The head of the experts, who only admitted the mistake during the hearing, was in fact forced to confirm that a ship with two rudders would have impacted at most at the stern, if the helmsman had carried out his orders correctly. The collision, therefore, would have occurred in the last section of the ship, giving rise to a completely different emergency situation. Faced with such an error in data analysis, the calculations concerning the impact should have been redone, but this was not the case. The courts did not feel that this had to be taken into account. Indeed, the argument continued to be that the helmsman's errors were induced by the captain, who had expressed himself in a breathless fashion. Since in the last moments before the impact the captain was carrying out an evasive maneuver, a kind of enormous counter-steering, it was obvious that, given the situation, a breathless fashion was perfectly apt. The problem, according to the courts, lay in this and not in the fact that the helmsman did not understand English very well and Italian not at all. Thus, the problem was a training one, a matter of selection of resources, and organizational. But the fixed belief from the outset that the captain was the only truly responsible figure made it possible to interpret this fundamental circumstance in a simplistic and distorted way.

Another element of interest, albeit not considered at all closely during the trial, concerns the much-discussed theme of the lookout. With the helmsman moving to the helm, on the night of the accident, the role of lookout remained uncovered. With regard to this, the captain pointed out to the prosecutors that he had repeatedly reported to the company the need to provide for the presence of more than one sailor on the bridge, just in case, but had never received a reply (Court of

Grosseto 2014f, part I, 55–56). This further organizational lapse does not seem to have aroused the curiosity of the prosecutors.

If the captain was guilty, why bother widening the extent of the investigation? The case was already closed only a few days after the event. A trial should be a path from doubt to certainty. In this case, there were few doubts from the very beginning, only certainties to be confirmed and justified. It is well known in the literature, as Asch (1946) has shown in his configurational model, that in the formation of impressions, the first stages influence the interpretation of the following information, modifying as they do the interpretation of the whole configuration (Fazio, Eiser, and Shook 2004; Brambilla et al. 2019). The investigators formed an initial belief, even in the presence of very little definite data on what certainly was a complex event, and this conviction governed, in a short-sighted way, the following investigative activity.[75] Following the questioning of the captain, held on December 2, 2014, the attorney's office reported to a journalist on the sidelines of a hearing what sentence would be requested – before the trial phase was over, before the witnesses were heard. And the next day's newspapers took up these declarations,[76] hunting for evidence that supported the conclusion reached and without taking into account any doubts and hypotheses that might somehow undermine the initial belief.[77]

In the attorney's office's request for indictment, part of the text reads:

"[…]even more than for the crime of shipwreck, a shocking imprudence and a colossal incompetence – together with the ignoble desire to hide his responsibility for the cause of the accident until the end and to avoid following procedure, also for ignoble reasons of economic convenience – there exists a remarkable series of behaviors, both active and omissive, which are the first and fundamental cause of the death of twenty-seven passengers and five crew members and the injuring of hundreds of people" (Request for indictment – pursuant to Article 416 of the Italian Criminal Code – by the Public Prosecutor's Office at the Court of Grosseto, February 25, 2013, 591–592).

---

[75] On the so-called cognitive biases that public prosecutors and courts may be influenced by, and in particular on confirmation bias, see the study by D. Kim Rossmo and Joycelyn M. Pollock (2019).

[76] "Costa Concordia, the Public Prosecutor: more than 20 years for Schettino", *Il Messaggero*, December 3, 2014.

[77] With regard to this phenomenon, see Lord, Ross, and Lepper, 1979; Anderson, Lepper and Ross, 1980.

A Simple Solution to a Complex Case

The interpretation given to the abandonment of the ship created an image of the captain as a figure of moral reproach even before judicial sentencing. Through a sort of horn effect, this single event determined a completely negative image of the person even before light had been cast on how things had actually occurred. It helped, indeed, to give direction to a certain interpretation of the facts: if he had been so immoral as to escape, surely he must be guilty of everything. All of this created an opportunity for some agents to construct a scapegoat by making use of the person found with "the smoking gun". After all, it is well known that language of the "bad apple" kind creates a sense of the origin of the problem and also suggests the way it should be solved. Punishing one or more people is always easier than encouraging a complex systemic response.

The emphasis on the event of the abandonment of the ship, read in a simplistic and unilateral way, transformed the accident into a "scandal", not because of the dangerous repeated practice of sail-by salutes, encouraged by the company and tolerated by the controllers, but because of the behavior of the captain. A scandal ends with condemnation of the guilty and whosoever is deemed unworthy of having held a particular office is removed. Someone else is appointed in their place; no changes are made to the organization or to the control and regulation system.

It is also important to underline that the media played a fundamental role in building up the negative image of the captain. As is well known, more than rigorous analysis and law, it is the media that judge reality, not limiting themselves to representing facts, but modeling and amplifying them through distortion, emphasizing what seems to be most successfully communicable. On this point, Chris Greer and Eugene McLaughlin claim that: "Due process and journalistic objectivity can give way to sensationalist, moralizing speculation about the actions and motives of those who stand accused in the new media spotlight" (2011, 27). It follows that reader and viewer are not so much interested in verifying the truthfulness of the news, but are struck by the narrative and its emotional effectiveness (Berger and Luckmann 1966, 147–162). This leads to a delocalization of the judicial context in the media (Garapon 2001), with the press taking over a trial, especially its investigation phase. Indeed, it has been highlighted (Garapon and Salas 1996) that, thanks to the media, a "trial outside the walls" develops alongside the trial in the courtroom, in which a battle takes place under the eyes of public opinion. Here, the media reconstruct judicial activity by frequently exaggerating the facts relating to the investigation, in an attempt to capture public attention by highlighting emotion and scandal. With reference to the 1986 *Challenger* incident, Diane Vaughan wrote:

> Perhaps the most obvious lesson is about the manufacture of news and the social construction of history in an age when most people are distanced from events and depend on published accounts for information. Even when incredible resources are brought to bear on understanding a public failure involving an organization, the explanation is likely to be more tangled and complex than it appears. Both the consumers and producers of information about public events should beware of the retrospective fallacy. (2016, 393)

In conclusion, the media's search for sensationalism and ratings (Battisti 1982, 55–56) and their use of "strong" language and expressions (such as "Captain coward") created a negative media image of Schettino in just a few days, both as a captain and as a man. This image was superimposed onto the Grosseto prosecutor's interpretation, creating a dynamic of mutual reinforcement and confirmation between media narration and judicial action. At the same time, the stigmatization and blamestorming of the captain opened a window of opportunity for the other agents involved in various capacities in the accident, creating favorable conditions for the construction of a scapegoat.

Finally, the role of the media should be emphasized, often providing highly spectacular commentaries in the period immediately following an accident, while the role of the public prosecutor is central and prevails over that of the defense of the accused. Media attention tends to decrease greatly during the trial phase, when power relations between prosecution and defense tend at the very least to find a certain balance. All this certainly also represents a problem beyond the circumstances of this particular case.[78]

On the margins of this analysis, it should be pointed out that the case of the *Costa Concordia* highlights some distortions resulting from the transition within the Italian legal system from an "ordinary" type

---

[78] On this point, Ray Surette (2003, 42) stated: "In their content, the media focus on the extreme front end of the process, from the planning and committing of a crime, through its discovery and investigation, to the crime's resolution".

of trial (which takes place through legal process, with a designated place for its development, its own specific rules, and closed to external influence) to "trial by media".[79] This latter focuses mainly on the preliminary investigation phase, which is without rules, is asymmetrical, and takes place in the media, where emotionality prevails, rather than official legal premises.[80] The relations between media and justice, on the one hand, and the influence of the mass media on investigative and judicial decision-making processes, on the other, are extremely important and require a more in-depth analysis: this, however goes beyond the objectives and confines of the present work.[81] In a famous American ruling, *Nebraska Press Association* v. *Stuart* (1976), Judge Brennan warned that uncontrolled and prejudicial reporting before the trial could have negative effects on the trial's fairness.[82]

In conclusion, the analysis of this complex case has highlighted, or at least illuminated, the very reasonable doubt that a moral evaluation of the defendant took the place of actual evidence: that, first, the belief underlying the verdict was formed and then justification was found for this. This belief was based on the construction of a psychological–ethical double of the defendant, who was deemed to be guilty even before his guilt was proven.

3.5.2 *The Agents of Scapegoating and Their Converging Interests*

To understand the processes that lead to organizational scapegoating, we should first identify the main agents involved and the role that they play. In the literature there are studies on scapegoating within

---

[79] Lauren Chancellor (2019, 435) refers back to the definition by Katherine Rozad (2013) of "trial by media": "a market-driven form of multidimensional, interactive, populist justice in which individuals are exposed, tried, judged and sentenced in the court of public opinion".

[80] Leonardo Sciascia wrote that "When public opinion appears divided on some sensational legal case – divided into those who believe that the defendant is innocent and those who believe they are guilty – this division does not in fact occur based on the knowledge of procedural elements against the defendant or in their favor, but on impressions of liking or disliking – like betting on a football match or a horse race"("La vieja doblez de la vida italiana", *El País*, May 3, 1987).

[81] See Forti and Bertolino (2005).

[82] *Nebraska Press Assn. et al.* v. *Stuart, Judge, et al.* No. 75–817. Argued April 19, 1976. Decided June 30, 1976; download from: https://supreme.justia.com/cases/federal/us/427/539/.

individual organizations. This case is different, however, in that, as emerged from the organizational analysis, the *Costa Concordia* accident gave rise to an *arena* in which the interests and strategies of the various agents involved came together. In the accident there are at least six different agents who, for various reasons, had an interest in recounting the story of the accident as caused, mainly, if not exclusively, by the behavior of a single person. We can distinguish three kinds of agents involved. First, the *promoters* who triggered the scapegoating: the judicial system, prosecutors, and the panel of judges; the mass media, national and local newspapers, and television. Second, the *beneficiaries*, those who benefited from identifying a scapegoat by avoiding their involvement: the company, Costa Crociere; the Port Captaincies. Third the *helpers*, those who, without being directly involved in the event and in the trial, favored the construction of the scapegoat: the Port Captaincies; the regulator; the Ministry of Transport – RINA; and the local authorities and bodies, and municipalities.

Some agents brought civil actions in the trial – for different reasons and purposes, of course, all perfectly rational in terms of their own interests: the company, the Port Captaincies, the Minister of Transport, and the local authorities. Obviously, it is not suggested here that there was concertation between the various agents within the arena, but only a common convergence of interests. It was not, therefore, a *planned* strategy, but an *emerging* strategy, produced by the convergence of the individual strategies of the various agents. Pursuing (legitimate) individual or organizational objectives, the emerging outcome was the inter-organizational construction of the scapegoat (see Table 3.1). Objectives such as, for example, diverting blame onto the individual, on the "rogue employee", to avoid legal consequences and minimize costs and reputational damage (the company); focusing attention on human error to mask the fact that nothing that had been done to prevent the risky practice of sail-by salutes and to maintain the status quo (the Captaincies, the Ministry and local authorities);[83] ascertaining

---

[83] Although crew negligence, or damage resulting from crew negligence, is covered by insurance, it is very much in a company's interests to make the liability for negligence converge on an individual rather than on a team of officers. In the latter case, the event would reflect a negative standard throughout the entire fleet.

Table 3.1 *Agents in the scapegoating arena*

Agents	Role played	Interests	Strategy
Judicial system	*Promoter* – judicial investigation: contributors to scapegoating	Solve a complex accident quickly and easily	Focus investigation mainly on the human factor, on the captain's actions
Mass media	*Promoter* – triggers, initiators and main agents in scapegoating	Keep attention on the presumed symbolic culprit of the event	Create idea of scandal by emphasizing spectacle, customizing news
Company	*Beneficiary* – civil party in the trial and civil liability	Divert blame and lighten sanctions	To place organizational criticalities and the role played in encouraging the practice of sail-by salutes in the background; give the appearance of victims ("passing the buck")
Port Captaincy	*Beneficiary* and *helper* – judicial police investigation: collection of evidence and evaluation of this in the inquiry; civil party in the trial	Mask awareness of the risks of sail-by salutes and of the fact that nothing was done to ban or regulate them	Produce knowledge avoiding involvement and responsibility
Minister and RINA	*Helper* – administrative investigation; civil party in the trial	Mask awareness of the risks of sail-by salutes and of the fact that nothing was done to prohibit them or to control them with regulations	Limit the investigation to human factor only

Table 3.1 (*cont.*)

Agents	Role played	Interests	Strategy
Local bodies	*Helper* – civil party in the trial	Mask having encouraged sail-by salutes, despite the risks and having done nothing to prevent them	Avoid blame by diverting attention; appear as injured victims of the accident

individual responsibility in order to solve a complex problem quickly and easily (the judicial system);[84] and building the media process and creating a spectacle in order to keep the attention and indignation of public opinion at a high level in relation to the event's symbolic culprit (the mass media). In this context, certain limits of criminal law emerge whereby the accident, like a disaster or case of misconduct, is reduced through judicial procedure to a case of individual deviance from a pre-established norm.

Thus, in the case in question, the cognitive errors and "short view" that characterized first the investigative work, and then the decisions of the courts, also constructed the judicial culprit, and scapegoat, for the benefit of the interests of the other organizational agents, protecting them from legal and organizational consequences. Once investigations are concluded, the statements of the attorney's office are significant for only a little more than a year after the accident: "The story presents no unsolved mystery", "the determining cause of the shipwreck, deaths and injuries is unfortunately dramatically attributable to the human factor".[85] In fact, as Bucher (1957) states, if conventional explanations regarding the nature of an accident do not provide a convincing version of what happened, an attempt will be made to trace and assess the responsibility of those who should have controlled the situation. For the organizations involved in the event, therefore, the need emerges

---

[84] The prosecutor, concluding the investigation in December 2012, said he was "very satisfied with the short timeframe in which the investigation was brought to an end", in "*Concordia* investigation closed with nine names. Also in the prosecutor's sights, the hero officer", *La Repubblica*, December 21, 2012.

[85] "*Concordia*, Schettino and 5 others tried and Costa try to plea bargain for a million", *La Repubblica*, February 26, 2013.

to identify a scapegoat to blame for what happened. Finding flaws in design involves high redesign costs; finding flaws in management has legal consequences; blaming frontline operators preserves the system. With reference to the navigation system in the United States, Perrow pointed out that, "Shippers and insurers have a common interest in defining all casualties as the result of operator error, limiting the ability of customers to recover damages under law, but thereby enabling unsafe ships with overworked crews to sail and retarding the development of safety devices and practices" (2014, 152). But this is a simplistic way to bypass the complex problem of causation, a convenient shortcut. As Tom Douglas states, "To blame someone or something for what is happening equally tends to produce a sense of having solved the problem of cause" (1995, 192–193). In this particular case, for example, focusing attention on the captain's errors and shortcomings helped blur a number of organizational gaps. Immediately after the accident, the company, despite being well aware of the practice of sail-by salutes and encouraging it, and although the dynamics of the accident were not yet clear, identified the captain as the only culprit and the human factor as the only cause – the "passing the buck" strategy.[86] The statements from the company's top management were significant: "We work together following strict principles and laws. Then there is the human factor", "The navigation code attributes absolute power to the captain, the ship-owner cannot intervene to modify his decisions".[87] They even went so far as to state, with regard to the practice of sail-by salutes: "This does not exist in Costa Crociere".[88] In the request for indictment, however, quite a few doubts emerged in relation to the "complete transparency" of the company's policies, also with reference to accidents prior to that of January 13, 2012 (Court of Grosseto 2013b, 624).

[86] On this point, "*Concordia*, official statement: errors of judgment by the captain", *La Repubblica*, January 15, 2012; "And Costa throws Schettino under the bus", *La Repubblica*, January 16, 2012; "Human error, procedures not respected", *La Repubblica*, January 16, 2012; "War between Schettino and Costa", *La Repubblica*, January 20, 2012. See also "Costa accuses Schettino, alarms disabled", *Corriere della Sera*, January 17, 2012.

[87] "Captains have too much power. Alarm seriously delayed", *Corriere della Sera*, January 20, 2012.

[88] "Gabrielli: 'Costa warned about waste' (i.e., the disposal of the ship's waste following the shipwreck). The company: 'Sail-by salute not authorized,'" *La Repubblica*, January 25, 2015; see also "Watertight door open and unread e-mails. The new mysteries of the *Costa Concordia*", *Corriere della Sera*, January 12, 2013.

The effectiveness of this strategy of individual blame and "passing the buck" onto the captain, even before the results of the inquiry were known, is demonstrated by the fact that, in the months following the accident, the company recorded a 28 percent increase in bookings compared to the previous year.[89] The same strategy was also adopted by the Ministry of Infrastructure and Transport, which, to conceal the failure to intervene in the practice of the sail-by salute, a highly risky and widespread practice, limited the field of administrative investigation – promoted in order to identify the causes of the accident – solely to the human factor. This also emerged clearly from the statements by the then minister, who, in commenting on the accident, spoke of "incredible human error" and "non-compliance with policies and regulations" on the part of the captain.[90]

From the minutes of the special evidence pretrial hearing, there emerged the role played by the controllers, the Port Captaincies (Court of Grosseto 2012e, 19). The latter, in charge of investigating the causes of the accident, immediately intervened with "self-absolving" declarations designed to divert blame onto the captain: "We knew absolutely nothing, but the Captaincy was not warned on other occasions either, given that (the sail-by salute) is a maneuver that falls within the responsibility of the captain"; "The responsibility for the sinking of the *Costa Concordia* near Giglio certainly lies with the captain".[91] The Captaincies, therefore, far from being neutral, played an important role in the scapegoating. It is only necessary to consider the fact that the information collected during the investigations and then used by the experts came from the activity carried out in part by the public prosecutor and in part by the judiciary police, which was constituted by the Captaincy itself. It should also be noted that the panel of judge's experts for preliminary

---

[89] "Foschi and the recovery of Costa Crociere", *La Repubblica*, May 1, 2012; "Costa pride to the forefront. Foschi: Now we're stronger than before", *La Repubblica*, June 10, 2012; "Just over five months after the *Concordia* tragedy, the only company flying the tricolor flag shows clear signs of recovery, producing 2.2 billion euros of economic impact in the nation and 230 million in Liguria", *La Repubblica*, June 25, 2012; "Costa, after the disaster, business restarts. In May, boom in requests for cruises", *La Repubblica*, July 1, 2012.

[90] "Number of shipwreck victims rises to 11. Captain under house arrest", *La Repubblica*, January 17, 2012.

[91] "Costa, searches resume. Brusco: Schettino wasted an hour of precious time", *La Repubblica*, January 26, 2012.

investigations was made up of officers belonging to the navy, the Port Captaincy Corps, and engineering professors. This, on the one hand, posed a problem regarding expertise in the investigation – as there were no expert figures such as merchant ship or passenger ship captains or organizational accident experts. And, on the other, it reveals an evident conflict of interest, considering that the members of the panel were figures belonging to the very organizations whose role should have been the subject of further study in the experts' report. This conflict of interest inevitably had a limiting effect on the panel's faculty of judgment. This is not, it should be reiterated, to claim that there was intentionality in excluding certain lines of investigation a priori or in highlighting certain facts rather than others, but rather that there existed a "self-serving bias" in terms of how facts were analyzed. How could members of the organizations that were in some way responsible for a control system identify the deficiencies in that very system?

There is striking proof of this in the statements of the commander of the Genoa Port Captaincy: "I can testify that Costa Crociere, despite the tragic accident of the *Concordia*, is the true synthesis of safety, hospitality and development. Our controls are very strict, but no irregularities have ever been found on board. I can say with absolute certainty that yesterday, today and I am sure also tomorrow, Costa, for us as overseers of safety at sea, is a model to follow".[92] A further important element in this regard emerged from interceptions by the investigative unit of the Grosseto Carabinieri, which registered the existence of "opaque connections" and "dangerous relationships" between shipowner, Port Captaincies, and the Italian Naval Registry (RINA) regarding "manipulated controls".[93] In particular, it can be perceived that RINA's checks and observations meshed with a "grueling negotiation between the parties to find common ground".[94] The statements of the head of the Crisis Unit regarding the inspection initiated by RINA are significant: "Our K1 (Foschi) certainly spoke with

---

[92] "*Costa* pride to the forefront. Foschi: Now we're stronger than before", *La Repubblica*, June 10, 2012.

[93] "Fake tests and easy-going controls. How Costa got round safety checks", *La Repubblica*, December 22, 2012; "Controls and inspections, the dangerous relationships", *La Repubblica*, December 23, 2012.

[94] "*Concordia*, from suspicious interceptions to casual checks", *Corriere della Sera*, December 22, 2012.

RINA's K1. They came to an understanding".[95] No value, however, was given to these interceptions during the trial.

From the analysis of accidents such as that of the *Costa Concordia*, therefore, fundamental problems and organizational and institutional learning needs emerge, as, consequently, do the limits of criminal law as the only instrument to account for complex events of this type. Such limits relate both to provision of justice for what happened, which is the responsibility of the judicial system, and to improvement of the system. The latter is not the responsibility of the judicial system, but its conclusions inevitably condition subsequent actions: if the captain is the culprit, why change the system? With the bad apple removed, the system is healthy.

Following an incident of this seriousness, it should have been necessary to start a process of analysis of the marine transport system and its criticalities in order to implement remedial and improvement measures. Instead, all attention was immediately focused on the wrongdoing of one individual, the captain – the only figure, moreover, to be sacrificed. The attorney's office responded to the plea bargaining request put forward by Schettino's lawyers with: "Don't even think about it".[96] The prosecutors were quite happy, however, to offer plea bargains – ones that were far too advantageous to be refused – to the lawyers of the other defendants: something that hardly looks accidental.

[95] "Fake tests and easy-going controls. How Costa got round safety checks", *La Repubblica*, December 22, 2012.
[96] "*Concordia*, five plea bargain; Codacons fury: scandalous", *La Repubblica*, May 15, 2013.

4 | How to Spot Organizational Scapegoats

4.1 The Organizational Dimension

At this point, it is important to discuss how organizational scapegoats can be identified. First of all, it is essential to recognize the role played by the organizational context in the genesis and dynamics of the negative event involving the scapegoat.

For an organization, the benefit derived from explanations that identify the immediate cause of a negative event (accident, misconduct, wrongdoing) in an individual decision is that people can be fired, punished, or transferred to other positions: the organization can then move forward without making any particular changes (Vaughan 2016). The idea of operator error as the cause of an accident has undoubted advantages for organizations but it does not remove the system's conditions of risk and does not prevent the event from repeating itself, even if in different forms and ways. The human factor is a symptom rather than the cause. It is very likely that other people in the same situation may make the same mistake: changing people, or sanctioning them, does not eliminate the underlying conditions of risk.

We can therefore say that, if an event repeats itself independently of the agents that cause it, it is the context that is prone to failure, not the individual – who thus becomes a scapegoat. Replacing the person who has failed with another means the same failure may occur with another actor. The "human error" label should serve as a starting point for analyzing how and why an organizational system fails, not as a conclusion. In order to distinguish whether an event is mainly determined by a person or a series of factors pertaining to the context, the following question must be asked: could another person in that situation have made the same mistake? If the answer is positive, it is the context that determines the event, regardless of the person on duty.

The common image of deviance rarely includes organizational agents (Simmons 1965; Liska 1987). After all, organizations don't think and act, individuals do. However, individuals interact with organizations as well as with other individuals, and organizations interact with other organizations (Coleman 1974). Organizations are not a mere collection of people. Rather, large organizations are a collection of positions that significantly influence the thoughts, decisions, and work-related actions of the people occupying these positions. As James S. Coleman wrote:

The ... structure exists independently of the persons occupying positions within it, like a city whose buildings exist independently of the particular persons who occupy them ... In an organization that consists of positions in a structure of relations, the persons who occupy the positions are incidental to the structure. They take on the obligations and expectations, the goals and the resources, associated with their positions in the way they put on work clothes for their jobs. But the obligations and expectations, the goals and resources, exist apart from the individual occupants of the positions. (1990, 427)

Individuals in families, Coleman argues, are not easily replaceable because the building blocks of families are the individuals themselves, not the positions they hold. In large organizations, however, the building blocks are the positions, not the people. Positions deeply influence people's course of action and decisions. Organizations can provide fertile ground for the origin of deviant actions (Ermann and Lundman 2002, 9), for example, by limiting information and accountability, or by dividing activities into multiple parts, so that no one has an overall view of the whole work process and its results. Organizational elites can also indirectly cause deviant actions by establishing norms and reward and punishment systems that, albeit unintentionally, encourage deviance. Finally, the elites themselves can consciously use the hierarchical chain to command deviant activities.

Henry Finney and Henry Lesieur (1982), Ronald Kramer (1982), Diane Vaughan (1983), and James W. Coleman (1987) were among the first to propose an integrated model that highlights the interconnections between competitive environments, external norms, organizational structures, aims and processes, regulatory failures, and individual decisions to commit violations. All these elements make the organization the central unit of analysis. In this context, organizations

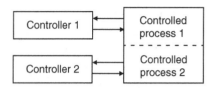

Figure 4.1 Control in a boundary area
Source: Leveson 2011, 98

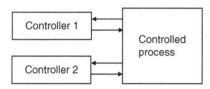

Figure 4.2 Overlapping control
Source: Leveson 2011, 98

are the link that mediates between the external institutional environment and individual action.

To better understand the role of individual and organizational contributions, we can try to analyze two different situations that involve a control activity. The first concerns control in boundary areas (see Figure 4.1). In this case, there are two controllers and each controls a specific process or scope of activity: controller 1 controls process 1; controller 2 process 2. However, there is a boundary area (the dotted line) between the two processes where it is not clear whether control responsibility pertains to controller 1 or controller 2. It could therefore happen that, given this uncertainty, each controller believes that control in that specific area pertains to the other – the final outcome being that no one is in control.

In the overlapping control situation, two or more operators control the same process, in a control redundancy situation, but the relationship and communication modes are not defined (see Figure 4.2).

It may happen that each of the two operators, not having carried out the control, believes that their colleague has done this: thus, in this case, too, the control mechanism is fallacious.

The two cases show very clearly that, with a change of personnel, the control system does not change and does not improve. In other words, the fallacy lies not in the person on duty, who will then be sanctioned in case of failure or accident – the organizational scapegoat – but in

Figure 4.3 System with three components in series

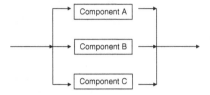

Figure 4.4 System with three components in parallel

the way in which the work system has been designed and organized. Leplat (1987) showed that in a steel factory, up to 67 percent of accidents occurred in areas of co-activity, where control responsibilities were not correctly specified and where overlapping control led to operator confusion. This can also happen at an organizational level, when two or more organizations are involved in the same process or in neighboring processes. Social psychologists call this "diffusion of responsibility" (Latané and Darley 1970; Brown 1986): if everyone is responsible, then in fact no one is. A process of "social redundancy fallacy" (Snook 2000) takes shape, where increasing controllers does not improve the control activity but, rather, exposes it to potential control failures.

Continuing with the subject of errors in organizations, two different situations can be distinguished. An organization makes *type 1* mistakes when it carries out an action that *should not have been* carried out: for example, when a patient is given a drug that they should not have been given because it was the wrong drug or because the patient suffered from a particular allergy. An organization makes *type 2* mistakes when it fails to perform an action that *should have been* carried out: for example, when a patient is not given a certain diagnosis or is not given a certain therapy.

Empirical evidence shows how these two types of errors do not occur casually, but are related to work processes, to the ways in which work is divided and coordinated, and to the ways in which redundancy is designed. In this regard, two different situations can be distinguished: the system with three components in series (see Figure 4.3) and the system with three components in parallel (see Figure 4.4).

In the first case, the three components in series operate separately and the output of one component becomes the input for the next. This ensures greater verification of the activities performed, even if it can be detrimental to the speed of execution. In the system with the three components in parallel, on the other hand, in relation to a specific input, the three components operate simultaneously. This increases the speed of execution, but at the expense of the possibility of control. For example, we can trace the two situations to two distinct areas in a hospital: the area of scheduled operations (system with three components in series), and the area of emergency medicine (system with three components in parallel).

The consequence of this is that the type of error depends somewhat on the type of system: the system with three components in series reduces type 1 errors (performing an action that should not have been performed) but tends to increase type 2 errors (not performing an action that should have been performed); the system with three components in parallel, on the other hand, reduces type 2 errors but tends to increase type 1 errors. For example, in an emergency room, promptness of action avoids type 2 errors, not doing something that must be done, but at the same time makes type 1 errors possible, performing an incorrect action that should not be done. For instance, the wrong drug might be administered or a medicine might be given to an allergic person because, given the emergency nature of the situation, it was not possible to make checks in time.

Under these conditions, people can make mistakes regardless of the state of their "morale". Mistakes depend on contexts and changing people does not change the potential for accidents. Sanctioning people without modifying contexts and rendering them more reliable means creating organizational scapegoats.

4.2 The Role of Procedures and Regulations

Organizations establish rules and procedures to determine different aspects of organizational life: processes and working methods, relationships with external subjects (customers, suppliers, etc.), working hours and shifts, production objectives, safety, and many other aspects. Procedures can be considered as "stabilizers of expectations": they are designed to transform the uncertain into the certain, based on a scheduled sequence of facts, actions, and relationships. Sometimes, they can be misaligned with reality or obsolete with respect to changes that have occurred. Or, they can be in conflict with one another, produced by different organizational units, with a low level of information coordination. In this case, a window of opportunity is opened for their violation.

A large area that gives rise to situations prone to failure, regardless of the people occupying specific roles, is composed of "situational violations". These are cases in which an operator finds himself operating in a condition of conflict between different and conflicting systems of rules. Following one specific rule, in other words, involves violating another. A frequent case in companies is the conflict between production procedures and safety procedures (Reason 1997; Catino 2006a). The former are designed to ensure that an organization's output is efficiently achieved. Safety procedures, on the other hand, tend to define behavior and action by limiting their range of action, sometimes accruing strength and legitimacy from accidents that have taken place. The problem that frequently emerges is that whoever designs the rules for production is different from whoever designs the rules for safety. The consequence is that the human operator finds himself within a space made up of conflicting rules: following the production rule violates the safety rule and vice versa. This is a situation similar to the aforementioned "pragmatic paradoxes" of Watzlawick et al. (1967), in which an individual, in order to carry out one order, must necessarily violate another.

There is an illustrative case of such situations in the activity of coupling and uncoupling wagons on certain types of trains (Free 1994; Reason 1997, 49–51). According to the *British Railway Rule Book*, the railway operator cannot stay between two wagons when the train is in motion. An obvious and common-sense rule, one might say; indeed, the question arises as to why such a thing should even be standardized. Only when the train is completely stopped can the wagons be coupled or uncoupled. However, the buffers – which serve to absorb impact and maintain the correct distance between the wagons – are short, and when fully extended the operator cannot engage or disengage them, particularly if the train is in a slightly uphill or downhill position. The only solution is for the driver, with considerable skill, to put the locomotive slightly into reverse. This reduces the tension between the buffers and the operator can hook or unhook the wagons. However, a paradox emerges: if the operator follows the operation rule, he violates the safety rule; if he follows the safety rule, he cannot carry out the task. The result is that the operator, however he acts, makes a mistake, violating a rule. There have been several accidents, some fatal. However, what determines the accident is not only the violation, but the execution in a situation of low attention or low coordination with the driver.

Situations of this type bring out two important lessons. The first is that the person who violates a rule is forced to do so by the situation, otherwise he could not achieve the result. Therefore, the propensity to violate does not change if the person is changed. The violation is situational – that is, the operator is *forced* to carry it out. The second lesson is that if you want to reduce accidents, it is not enough to call for compliance with the rules, which conflict with each other. It is necessary to understand why the operator carries out that type of behavior and try to help safeguard the risky action. For example, if the accident is fostered by a distraction or lack of communication with the driver, it may be useful to have a third person coordinating the activity, or to equip the operator and driver with a radio. This reduces communication problems and improves coordination. However, this requires overcoming a certain organizational hypocrisy and recognizing the risky action as worthy of greater safeguarding. If no changes are made, the risk is that the violations necessary to carry out the activities become routine – a part of the worker's typical repertoire of action.

4.3 Organizational Decoupling

An important organizational perspective for understanding the situations that favor the creation of organizational scapegoats is represented by neo-institutionalism. In a seminal essay, Meyer and Rowan (1977) analyze the conformation of organizations to the surrounding institutional environment, highlighting how this process of *isomorphism* in organizations leads to the creation of formal structures. Organizations tend to conform to the external institutional environment according to this isomorphic process, equipping themselves with formal structures which, rather than being effective and efficient, are nothing more than myth and ceremony.

To reach this conclusion, Meyer and Rowan draw on previous research on American educational organizations (Meyer 1977). The separation between a school's didactic and administrative areas makes it difficult to carry out checks on the real effectiveness of teaching, and, because of this difficulty in evaluation, the school would adopt substitutes, such as external procedures and criteria, assuming that these really guarantee the effectiveness of the didactic activity. The school, teachers, students, educational content, and so on are evaluated by external committees on the basis of rigorous, formalized criteria. Not being able (or not knowing how) to measure effectiveness, objective evaluation parameters are employed, even though these do not ensure the actual effectiveness of measurement, but rather what is conventionally considered to be educational effectiveness. In other words, in the absence of concrete empirical evidence, parameters and procedures resemble myths or ceremonies, with which compliance is required. The greater the conformity, the more the legitimacy of the organization increases and the greater the chances of obtaining funds or reducing cuts.

On the basis of this empirical evidence, Meyer and Rowan identify two types of organizations: (1) those that do not possess intrinsic criteria of efficiency and that therefore, in order to survive, must adapt to the needs of legitimacy deriving from the external environment (e.g. schools, political parties, etc.); and (2) those that possess intrinsic criteria of efficiency, which in some way must be respected in order for the organization to survive (for example, companies, banks, etc.). The first type of organization presents a particular managerial problem, as on the one hand they must follow the logic of efficiency, and, on the other, they must conform to the pressures coming from the external institutional environment, which may not include an efficient solution for the organization.

In certain situations, therefore, these pressures are conflicting and conforming to one might threaten conforming to the other. What to do? Meyer and Rowan identify a solution in "decoupling": two parallel structures are developed, one formal, aimed at respecting institutional rules, the external myths; one informal, aimed at making things really work, following the rules of efficiency and results. The two authors therefore suggest that decoupling makes organizations capable of maintaining standardized and legitimate formal structures, while their internal activities vary according to practical considerations.[1] This separation

---

[1] By "formal structure", we mean both the structural aspects (positions, organizational architecture, etc.), and programs, policies, and decisions (Boxenbaum and Jonsson 2008, 90). For an in-depth study of neo-institutional theory, see Greenwood et al. (2008) and, for a discussion of decoupling, Boxenbaum and Jonsson (2008).

can only last if the controls are reduced to a minimum and ceremonialized with a more than substantial ritual conformity. Decoupling, therefore, is a strategy to balance the demands of organizational efficiency with the needs of the organization for external legitimation: to bridge the gap between policies and practices, on the one hand, and between means and ends, on the other (Bromley and Powell 2012).

With the main points of the neo-institutional theory on decoupling clarified, let's move on to analyze the implications for organizational deviance and the creation of scapegoats. The role of organizations and their leaders and managers is decisive for the implementation of organizational strategies and decisions that can facilitate the deviance of participants. Organizations are not mere neutral contexts within which deviant behavior occurs. Through decoupling, organizations are able to satisfy the external environment's demands for legitimacy, while leaving the members free to act to achieve goals effectively and efficiently. However, in this way space is created for deviant behavior on the part of the members of the organization, in the attempt to reconcile the misalignment between the demands for efficiency in pursuing results and the demands of the external environment.

In short, decoupling, while it allows an organization to manage the tension between external demands for legitimacy and internal demands for performance, also creates the space for deviant behavior on the part of participants. The latter then become convenient scapegoats if things go wrong, or when their deviant behavior, which grew out of an organizational tension that was certainly not created by the participants, is discovered. Deviance, claim Monahan and Quinn "is the dark secret of decoupled organizations ... Individual 'bad apples' and 'poor leadership' became convenient scapegoats for deeply entrenched organizational strategies and processes" (2006, 377–378). All this leads to a series of organizational issues that go beyond the question of who is to blame.

In conclusion, in situations where the external environment is characterized by conflicting norms, leaders and managers of organizations can implement solutions with structural adaptations that on the one hand absorb the conflict and on the other become the context for deviance and for the creation of scapegoats. In such situations, deviance tends to be normalized (Vaughan 2016) and informally accepted as the way things are done. The idea of decoupling is connected to the conception of organizations as "loosely coupled systems", which will be discussed in the following section.

4.4 Loosely Coupled Systems and Scapegoats

In Chapter 3, the distinction was introduced between "loosely coupled systems" and "tightly coupled systems" in organizations (Weick 1976; Orton and Weick 1990; Perrow 2014). This distinction is relevant not only from the point of view of organizational functioning, but also in terms of the production of organizational deviance, the problems related to responsibility, and the creation of scapegoats. Loosely coupled systems "are well designed to scapegoat employees successfully without detection" (Laufer 2008, 146).

First, let's briefly review the main characteristics of the two types of organizational connection, in order to identify the implications in the genesis of organizational deviance and in the creation of scapegoats.

We refer to tightly coupled systems when each part of an organization is closely connected to the others, so that a change at one point generates an immediate change in other parts of the system. One example is a nuclear power plant, where the malfunction of one part can immediately generate repercussions on the other parts of the system in a rapid and uncontrolled way. In contrast, in loosely coupled systems, events respond to each other while, at the same time, maintaining their own identity, as well as their physical or logical separateness from the others (Weick 1976).[2] This occurs, for example, in school organizations, which Weick represents with the use of an evocative metaphor:

Imagine that you're either the referee, coach, player or spectator at an unconventional soccer match: the field for the game is round; there are several goals scattered haphazardly around the circular field; people can enter and leave the game whenever they want to; they can throw balls in whenever they want; they can say "that's my goal" whenever they want to, as many times as they want to, and for as many goals as they want to; the entire game takes place on a sloped field; and the game is played as if it makes sense (March, personal communication).

If you now substitute in that example principals for referees, teachers for coaches, students for players, parents for spectators and schooling for soccer, you have an equally unconventional depiction of school organizations. The beauty of this depiction is that it captures a different set of realities within educational organizations than are caught when these same organizations are viewed through the tenets of bureaucratic theory. (Weick 1976, 1)

---

[2] The expression "loose coupling" has already been used in the literature by other authors, such as Glassman (1973) and March and Olsen (1975).

It might be wondered how an organization of this type is able to move forward and do what it is expected to do. Such organizations, if analyzed and evaluated with rationalistic assumptions, typical of bureaucratic theory, seem chaotic and irrational contexts. Instead, to observe its functioning, it is necessary to employ different approaches and conceptual tools, such as the concept of loose coupling. In the case of a school organization, Weick (1976) argues, the position of school assistant is loosely connected with that of principal. The two agents are in some way linked to each other, but each maintains their own identity and independence and the bond that holds them together can be occasional, limited to specific, not very important, situations. According to Weick, these connections allow the various subsystems of an organization to be held together, avoiding the centrifugal forces that might dissolve them. But such couplings are loose in the sense that the parties retain their own autonomy of action, and the decisions and actions of one party have vague, occasional, and nondeterministic repercussions on the others. Unlike organizations with tight couplings, in those characterized by loose couplings the coupling between the elements is not deterministically established (given A, then B), but is, in fact, loose (given A, sometimes B, but also C, F, H, etc.).

In organizational realities, loose couplings bestow various benefits on organizations in terms of flexibility and adaptation to environmental changes (Weick 1976).[3] Organizations characterized by loose couplings may therefore be best suited to compete in highly uncertain environments characterized by rapid change. However, in addition to the benefits of such an organizational solution, some dysfunctions persist. For example, environmental uncertainty favors loosely coupled systems, which could in turn favor illegal behavior (Keane 1995).

---

[3] Loose couplings allow the units of an organization to persist over time – that is, to maintain the traditional working methods of that subsystem or, on the contrary, to experiment with innovations in the subsystem, without the effects being immediately transmitted to the entire organization; they are a sensitive mechanism of perception of the environment, as perception is expressed by different, loosely coupled elements and therefore relatively independent in terms of the perception itself. They facilitate local adaptations to specific circumstances, quickly, inexpensively, and effectively; guarantee greater adaptability to changes in the environment; make it possible to isolate a possible subsystem problem, preventing it from spreading to other parts of the organization; facilitate the self-determination and autonomy of the actors, thus promoting their accountability; and they can potentially reduce coordination costs, because there are fewer coordination needs and lower levels of conflict.

Some members of the organization may attempt to illegally influence elements external to the organization, bribing public officials, violating pollution laws, using misleading advertising, or performing other illegal actions. Collusion, for example, could be seen as an attempt to reduce financial and organizational uncertainty. The greater the uncertainty, therefore, the greater the incentive to try to reduce it illegally.

A loosely coupled organizational structure, says Keane (1995, 173), may be more prone to corporate corruption than a tightly coupled structure. This is because, in such structures, the head office may be less attentive to what happens in the different organizational units, and consequently respond less promptly to reports of incorrect acts by the subsidiary organizational units. In addition to this, there is lesser internal control, typical of these structures, which could make the organization more vulnerable to illegal behavior. As Vaughan pointed out in this regard (1983), if the ability of senior management to control and monitor a business unit is weakened, it becomes very likely that this organizational unit will give rise to illegal transactions. Keane, in addition to reporting many cases of companies operating in different production sectors (1995, 173–175), states that loosely coupled organizational structures are more prone to scapegoating due to the obfuscation of responsibility in the organizational process.

An example of these dynamics is the spill of more than 40 million liters of oil from the *Exxon Valdez*, which occurred in 1989 when the tanker hit a reef on the shores of the Prince William Sound, an inlet in the Gulf of Alaska. As requested, the ship had deviated from normal trade routes, due to some small icebergs encountered at the mouth of the strait. Despite navigating in potentially dangerous waters, on the evening of the accident the captain temporarily left the bridge, leaving the ship in the hands of the third officer and a crew member. Due to a series of errors in the chain of command, and insufficient monitoring of navigation, around midnight the ship made a turn too slowly, running aground on the reef and dispersing much of its cargo at sea. The captain was deemed to be solely responsible for the event: he had left the bridge to tired and insufficiently experienced officers and, in addition to negligence, he was accused of having drunk alcohol and therefore of not being in full control of his faculties. This accusation would later turn out not to be wholly substantiated, but it immediately served to turn the figure of the captain into a perfect scapegoat, with follow-on aspects of negative connotations and even stigmatization and ridicule.

By reducing the accident to individual actions, little attention was consequently paid to various structural and organizational problems. For example, the fact that it was a single-hulled, rather than double-hulled, ship which would have offered greater resistance to impact in the event of an accident – an accident that would not therefore have happened or would not have caused such extensive damage. The agreements between the governments relating to traffic in those areas requested transport by double-hulled ships, but no checks had been carried out. No attention was even paid to the malfunctioning of the Coast Guard radar, which did not allow the operator to view the ship's dangerous course. It was therefore impossible to intervene to alert the team on the bridge of the danger. The lack of control by the Coast Guard certainly contributed a weakness to the reliability and safety of navigation in those waters. In addition, although it had long been promised, no technologically up-to-date iceberg monitoring equipment had been installed. As a result, the *Exxon Valdez* was sailing out of the normal sea lane to avoid small icebergs believed to be in the area. This, however, took the tanker into other risky waters. The company that operated the pipeline, Alyeska Pipeline Co., a consortium of seven oil companies, was very late in providing relief immediately after the accident (fourteen hours, instead of the scheduled two). Coordination problems and a lack of available equipment and personnel then hampered the prompt removal of the spilled oil, which was carried out with considerable delays. Emergency plans did exist, but more in the form of a desired evolution of the accident situation than an effective and timely reaction to the accident. All these factors, however, took second place to the fact that the captain was responsible for the disaster.

In conclusion, loosely coupled systems seem more predisposed to potential abuse in terms of liability, as they can be an excellent tool for evading legal liability, including through the identification of one or more scapegoats. This theme of the relationship between types of organizational structures and propensity for scapegoating is of particular interest, not only theoretical, even though it certainly requires more in-depth analysis and more detailed empirical evidence.

4.5 Guilt, the Chain of Command, and Formative Contexts

When complex organizational events occur, such as accidents, scandals, or crises, we must ask ourselves whether these events are the result only of "bad-apple" individual action, or the result of bad organization. In particular, two relevant factors emerge: (a) the chain of command, composed of those who in some way establish (b) the "formative contexts" (Lanzara 2016) within which the so-called bad apples act. Formative contexts are relevant in that they shape people's perceptions and meanings, the ways they organize and act in a given situation. Formative contexts are composed of structural elements, such as the system of formal authority, roles, tasks, and the communication system; and of cognitive elements, such as the assumptions that govern the strategies and actions of the agents. The context is formative in that it leads people to see and do old things in innovative ways or, on the contrary, conditions them, imprisoning them in habitual ways of doing things (Lanzara 2016). Replacing people without changing formative contexts and the chain of command means continuing to do the same things, with different people.

There follows a description of two very different cases, and the relevant role played by the two factors in both.

4.5.1 The Abu Ghraib Case

The Facts

The scandal of the abuse and torture of Iraqi prisoners by American soldiers in the Abu Ghraib prison in Iraq came to light on April 28, 2004, when some images were made public during the CBS *60 Minutes II* program.[4] The photos showed naked men huddled together as if in a human pyramid, with two grinning American soldiers posing; dogs set on prisoners; a hooded prisoner, his hands tied with electric wires; prisoners on a leash dragged like dogs; simulated executions; acts of sexual violence; and other extreme scenes. The next day an article by Seymour Hersh (2004a) was published on the *New Yorker* magazine website, with some disturbing photos. These sadistic and grotesque

---

[4] The scandal began when specialist soldier Joseph Darby handed the Army Criminal Investigators a copy of a CD containing photos of the abuse. Darby had copied images from the computer of specialist soldier Charles Graner, one of the personnel most involved in the abuse. The military leaders and the Secretary of Defense were immediately informed of the facts and General Sanchez requested an investigation to be conducted with subjects outside the Abu Ghraib prison. The investigation was given to General Antonio Taguba (see Taguba 2004).

images immediately created a political storm for the Bush administration and aroused widespread revulsion in American and world public opinion. It seemed incredible that American soldiers sent to Iraq on a mission to bring freedom and democracy could have been responsible for such horrible acts, and even – recklessly – taken photographs of them, as if for souvenirs or trophies. All this, in clear violation of the laws and agreements of the Geneva Conventions.

President Bush said he was deeply sorry for what had happened and that offenders would be identified and brought to justice. The official explanation lightened the charge as being caused by a few "bad apples", "rogue soldiers", stating that there was no evidence that the abuses were systematic. In an interview, General Richard B. Meyers, Chief of Staff, expressed bewilderment and amazement at the images of criminal abuse, saying he was certain that there was no evidence that they were systematic facts. He believed that these were isolated accidents and the work of a handful of miscreants. However, the event had just entered the public domain following the release of the video, and there was certainly no time to conduct a thorough investigation that could confirm that claim. In reality, what General Meyers argued, rather than shedding light on the individual or systematic nature of the abuse, provided clear indications of the intention to lighten the charge and place the blame on a few bad apples.

Eleven low-ranking soldiers were tried by military court and were sent to prison. General Janis Karpinski was cautioned, removed from command, demoted to the role of colonel and given early retirement. She was the only senior officer to be convicted of prisoner abuse, more for what she did not do than for what she did. Abu Ghraib prison was permanently closed on August 15, 2006.

Formative Context and Contributing Organizational Factors

Were the tortures and abuses in Abu Ghraib committed by only a few bad apples who took advantage of the power they had over prisoners? Were those found guilty solely responsible for such acts, or were they scapegoats, created to shift attention and blame from management and wider systemic and organizational problems?

Various inquiries have highlighted a series of contributing factors that established the formative and situational context within which those inhumane acts took place. Individual behavior must be analyzed and understood in relation to the wider environment of the regulations and the organizational context in which they took shape. Contributing factors existed, therefore, at several levels: (a) at the *environmental* level, a political–strategic system formed by the highest-ranking military and political people; and (b) at the *organizational* level, relating to the specific situation of the Abu Ghraib prison.

Environmental level: At the level of the political–strategic environment, at the origin of everything was the spread of a new military paradigm in the aftermath of the 9/11 terrorist attack in 2001, which President Bush called the "war on terror". Within this new paradigm, the relationship between means and ends, between what was lawful and what was not, was reformulated. In other words, the drive to obtain results was very strong, even at the expense of constraints on the means to be used. Some members of the Bush administration, notably Vice President Cheney and Secretary of Defense Rumsfeld, believed that an imminent terrorist attack was highly likely, creating a strong sense of urgency. They wanted results immediately, with no particular restrictions on the means. The phrase "the gloves are off" was repeated several times in the chain of command (Mayer 2008). Colonel Jordan[5] stated in a meeting: "We're taking the gloves off. We're going to show these people, you know, that we're in charge" (Zimbardo 2007, 420). In August 2003, General Geoffrey Miller was sent from Guantanamo (Cuba) to Iraq, with the aim of applying the methods used in Guantanamo in Abu Ghraib in order to make interrogations more productive. Miller was convinced that prisoners in Iraq were treated too well and that this affected the results. He believed that "if you allow them to believe at any point that they are more than a dog then you've lost control of them".[6] Prisoners, in his opinion, had therefore to be treated like dogs in order to make them understand who was really in charge.

General Miller had stated: "We're going to change the nature of the interrogation at Abu Ghraib", and this meant "taking off the kid gloves" (in Zimbardo 2007, 336). Taking off the gloves that cushion the blows in a boxing fight means hitting the opponent hard – no constraints, no rules. Simply put, it means having a free hand. According to General Karpinski, General Miller and Lieutenant

---

[5] Colonel Steven L. Jordan was appointed director of the Joint Interrogation Debriefing Center at Abu Ghraib prison.

[6] "Iraq abuse 'ordered from the top'", *BBC News*, June 15, 2004, http://news .bbc.co.uk/2/hi/americas/3806713.stm.

General Sanchez, to whom Miller reported, had defined a new line for dehumanization and torture in Abu Ghraib (Taguba 2004). Added to this, there was the pressure for results. As Colonel Warren stated, there had been several phone calls from Washington with a single message: "produce, produce, produce" (Gourevitch and Morris 2008). The insistent message was that the war against Al-Qaeda was primarily an intelligence war, and victory or defeat depended on information. Interrogations with the prisoners thus constituted a fundamental source of information.

Beginning in January 2002, President Bush limited the validity of the Geneva Conventions and on February 7 issued a memorandum that they did not apply to the conflict with Al-Qaeda. Although these Conventions were also valid for the conflict in Afghanistan, the Taliban were considered illegal fighters and therefore did not merit the status of prisoners of war (Strasser 2004). Various communications gradually transmitted by various departments (US Department of State, Department of Justice) and by members of the White House team made it clear that a special regime was put in place for the prisoners at Abu Ghraib and Guantanamo: a free zone, a kind of legal limbo where laws and international agreements regarding prisoners and war victims did not apply.

If the intense pressure to obtain results was clear, there was less clarity in relation to implementation procedures – in other words, how to obtain these results through interrogations. In a month, up to five drafts on procedures circulated, each one a little different from the others, and this created a great deal of uncertainty about what to do. The standard operating procedures for dealing with prisoners and handling interrogations were rather ambiguous, and when clear they were quite extreme in terms of methods. These ambiguous procedures, coupled with orders with uncertain boundaries (such as: "the detainee must be worn down"), produced a system prone to failure. What does it mean to "wear down" a prisoner? What are the limits to achieving this goal? This wasn't clear. A memo from Rumsfeld referred to the "authorized harsh interrogation methods for prisoners at Guantanamo" (Monahan and Quinn 2006, 371). Orders of this type provide very wide margins of interpretation and methods of implementation, and everything was left to the discretion of the military. Thus, the use of unmuzzled dogs to scare and intimidate prisoners became a common practice, considered lawful by prison guards as it was authorized by their superiors.

Kenneth Roth, director general of the League for Human Rights, says that giving the green light to interrogations under duress paved the way for abuse. The line between permitted and prohibited actions was blurred by differing legal opinions and the paucity of clear written procedures. At the same time, there was a need to adapt to the new war paradigm imposed by Al-Qaeda terrorism, in which the enemy did not adhere to the rules of the more famous land warfare (Mayer 2008). All this had created a "moral inversion": since the terrorists were so violent and dangerous, the military felt justified in approaching this war differently from others, redefining the rules accordingly (Balfour, Adams, and Nickels 2020, 79). Despite the fact that Guantanamo interrogation practices, euphemistically defined as "augmented techniques", had to be personally authorized by the Secretary of Defense, in migrating from Afghanistan to Iraq these practices were neither limited nor protected. The result was that the policies approved for use only with Al-Qaeda prisoners and the Taliban, who were not protected by the Geneva Conventions, were also effectively applied to prisoners who instead did fall under the protection of such international laws.

Organizational level: As for the contributing factors at the organizational level, various investigations conducted by the military (Taguba 2004; Fay and Jones 2004) and *The Abu Ghraib Investigations* (see Strasser 2004) highlighted a series of "systemic problems" at the operational–management level. A first, fundamental element was the fact that the military police (MP) assigned the management of prisoners to military intelligence (MI). The change marked a shift from the prevalence of a logic aimed only at prisoner management to a logic centered on interrogations. The relations between the two subjects were compartmentalized, while a continuous and closer coordination should have been necessary. Moreover, the prison guards were completely unprepared to manage a situation as complex as that of Abu Ghraib because their training was completely insufficient (Taguba 2004, 48). The military police in charge of detaining prisoners received no specific training on how to handle them. Manuals and publications on the subject were available online, but the computers available to the military did not have access to the Internet (Strasser 2004).

Another critical element was that, even at this level, the standard operating procedures for handling prisoners and managing interrogations were inadequate, incomplete, unclear, and fluid. All this created a situation of ambiguity for the guards in terms of what was lawful with regard to achieving objectives and what was not: "By not communicating standards, policies, and plans to soldiers, these leaders conveyed a sense of tacit approval of abusive behaviors toward prisoners"(Strasser 2004, 81).

Another very important problem concerned the absence of effective leadership and control. As emerged from *The Abu Ghraib Investigations* (Strasser 2004), the commanding officers and their staff at various levels were held accountable for what happened, particularly for what they had *not* done to prevent this kind of behavior from happening and repeating itself. In the inquiry cited it was argued that "Military and civilian leaders at the Department of Defense share this burden of responsibility" (Strasser 2004, 40). It was this weakness of leadership, both of the Commanding General of the 800th MP Brigade and the Commanding Officer of the 205th MI Brigade, that allowed the abuses of Abu Ghraib to take place. These commanders knew, or should have known, what was happening and should have prevented it. The investigation called for disciplinary action against these leaders,[7] but nothing happened as a result.

Heading Abu Ghraib and other prisons in Iraq was Brigadier General Janis Karpinski, who had no experience in running any kind of prison. Despite this unpreparedness, Karpinski found herself having to manage three large penitentiaries, seventeen prisons throughout Iraq, dozens of very dangerous prisoners, eight battalions of soldiers, hundreds of Iraqi guards, hundreds of inexperienced reservists, as well as the special Tier 1A interrogation center: a workload totally excessive in quantity and complexity for such an inexperienced officer. Furthermore, General Karpinski, due to the dangers and poor living conditions, did not reside in Abu Ghraib, but at Camp Victory, near Baghdad. For a great deal of the time, she was away from the prison and often traveling to Kuwait. There was, therefore, a lack of daily hierarchical monitoring of what was going on in the Abu Ghraib prison (Zimbardo 2007, 335). The absence of guidance and control favored the spread of inappropriate behavior and intensified ambiguity with regard to how to conduct interrogations. The investigation (Strasser 2004) found that the failure of General Karpinski's leadership favored the construction of the series of conditions that led to the

---

[7] In particular, sanctions against generals Fay, Jones, Sanchez, Abizaid, and Kern.

abuses, such as the failure to define appropriate standard operating procedures for the management of prisoners and interrogations.

The various investigation reports highlighted the problems deriving from the involvement of several agencies and organizations in the interrogations, with consequent coordination and integration problems between the military, on the one hand, and between the various specialist contractors (analysts, linguists, interrogation agents) on the other. Furthermore, 35 percent of the contractors had not received any training in military interrogation techniques (Strasser 2004, 73). In addition, given the lack of clarity on the chain of command, uncertainty existed with regard to the different responsibilities of the various roles involved in the interrogations. In his report, General Taguba (2004) had underlined the critical role played by two civilian contractors involved in the abuses in Abu Ghraib and raised many doubts in relation to the use of this type of collaborator. Working with military intelligence in the prison, they were in fact giving orders to the military police. The military outsourcing process had blurred the boundaries between military and civilian personnel, introducing independent individuals into the military environment who were sometimes not subject to compliance with any rules.

Finally, the creation of the *Joint Interrogation and Debriefing Center* introduced a further level of complexity in the management of interrogations, which was already under stress. The center was an ad hoc organization, made up of six different units and lacking a normal command and control structure (Strasser 2004, 71). The absence of guidance, of leadership, was dramatically evident. The director of the center, in fact, a weak leader with no previous experience in terms of interrogations, handed over the responsibility for the main activities to subordinates without worrying about the training of the operators.

All these contributing organizational factors, relating to leadership, control and coordination, and the training of operators, created the contextual conditions that led to the abuses.

Bad Apple or Bad Barrel: The Scapegoat

The official military investigation into the Abu Ghraib events resulted in a report made by General Antonio Taguba that attributed responsibility to high-ranking officers for having requested and adopted violent techniques in interrogations. Nevertheless, none of them were charged for this. Rather, eleven low-ranking soldiers were tried and went to prison, and one general was demoted. In short, the case was filed away with the simplistic conclusion that a few bad apples had misinterpreted the orders of their superiors, orders that had nothing to do with the extreme behavior at issue. There was no consequence for the chain of command, for high-ranking officers and for Rumsfeld, for giving the orders, setting up the formative context, and putting in place the practices that led to abuse (Hersh 2004a, 2004b; Strasser 2004; Preston 2011).

There are many doubts that the events of Abu Ghraib were attributed only to the few individuals who carried them out, the conclusion reached in the trial. According to Monahan and Quinn (2006) the practices of abuse were not the result of the actions of individual bad apples or the failure of leadership at an individual level: in fact, they "were empowered, so to speak, by structural arrangements at the prison" (370). Human Rights Watch stated in *The Road to Abu Ghraib* report (2004) that the systematic abuses were not the act of a few, but the result of administrative policies that sought to circumvent the Geneva Conventions, as well as the United Nations *Convention against Torture*. Both the *Schlesinger Report* (Schlesinger 2004) and the *Fay Report* (Fay and Jones 2004), however, while recognizing multiple causes of abuse on prisoners, including inadequate policies attributable to different levels, found no evidence that the torture derived from official policies (Balfour et al. 2020, 73–74). Philip Zimbardo, on the other hand, argued that responsibility must be sought at the highest levels, including President Bush and his advisers, for the role they played in redefining torture as a necessary tactic in the war on terror. Defense Secretary Rumsfeld, according to Zimbardo, "is charged with creating the interrogation centers where detainees were subjected to a host of extremely coercive abuses for the dubious purpose of eliciting confessions and information" (Zimbardo 2007, 378). In the view of Balfour et al. (2020), the case is a matter of "administrative evil". In Hersh's opinion, too, (2004b), the roots of the Abu Ghraib scandal can be traced back, not simply to the criminal tendencies of some military personnel, but to the faith that President Bush and Donald Rumsfeld had in secret operations and in the use of coercion in the fight against terrorism. It emerged, in fact, that the White House had authorized extreme forms of torture in interrogations, including water-boarding.

The soldiers could, of course, have opposed orders of this type: they had not only the right, but the duty to do so. Had this not worked, they could have turned to someone higher up the chain of command. However, this went against the imperative that orders must always be followed or trouble will ensue. A situational violation, in other words: to follow orders would have violated some rules; and not to follow them would have violated others. However, they acted, they would have been in the wrong.

In conclusion, the actions carried out by the guards did not derive so much from dispositional elements – that is, from the criminal tendencies of a group of soldiers – but drew legitimacy from a sort of political mandate by the then Secretary of Defense Donald Rumsfeld who, in order to obtain sensitive information quickly, made it lawful to resort to means bordering on torture (Hersh 2004a, 2004b; Strasser 2004; Bower 2007). These actions were later justified as unavoidable compromises, which formed part of the "rules of the game" (Gourevitch and Morris 2008). Actions and decisions by the soldiers took shape within an area where boundaries and limits were not clear; objectives therefore became the justification for actions of any kind.

When the scandal broke, Rumsfeld's immediate response to the release of the photos was to minimize their importance, even though he later had to acknowledge his sole responsibility for what had happened. In fact, during the congressional hearing he acknowledged that: "If there's a failure, it's me ... These events occurred on my watch. As Secretary of Defense, I am accountable for them, and I take full responsibility".[8] Rumsfeld then offered his resignation to President Bush, who rejected it. On the same day (May 20), Bush appeared in public with Rumsfeld and other members of the government, reiterating that the Secretary of Defense was doing a great job (Woodward 2006, 306). It was a gesture of great loyalty by the president to one of his closest collaborators. It was also to recognize that "from a blame-avoidance perspective, a senior member of Bush's own inner circle could hardly be fired without appearing to justify those who sought to attach blame at the highest levels of the administration" (Preston 2011, 166).

An effective blame avoidance strategy consists of finding an individual or organization unable to defend themselves – suitable, therefore, to act as a lightning rod or scapegoat. But this wouldn't have worked in Rumsfeld's case, since the hunt for a scapegoat would only have continued to go higher and higher. Only after the midterm

---

[8] Evan Thomas, "No Good Defense", *Newsweek*, May 16, 2004.

elections, which resulted in the Republicans losing the majority in the Senate, was Rumsfeld replaced by Robert Gates. The growing unpopularity of the Secretary of Defense and his inability to function as an effective lightning rod to divert blame away from the White House convinced Bush to implement a change. The reason given was that a change of strategy in the war in Iraq had to be followed by a change of leadership: "When I decided on a new strategy, I knew that in order to make the strategy work, for people to understand that it was new, there had to be new implementers of the strategy" (in Woodward 2008, 196–197).

It wasn't just a matter of bad apples, says Zimbardo, but bad barrels (2007, 331). According to Fiske, Harris, and Cuddy these were, among other things, predictable events: "Abu Ghraib resulted in part from ordinary social processes, not just extraordinary individual evil" (2004, 1484). This was a theory reflected in the results of Zimbardo's *Stanford Prison Experiment*, where it was demonstrated that some people can easily adopt destructive behavior toward others. In the experiment, conducted in Stanford, Zimbardo (2007) and his colleagues selected twenty-two people to take part in the simulation of a prison. Eleven of them, chosen at random, had to play the role of prisoners, the other eleven had to act as guards. Without receiving any specific orders, the guards began to become aggressive and commit gratuitous abuse. The rights of prisoners became privileges to be acquired through obedient behavior. The experiment became more and more extreme and was stopped after six of the fourteen days scheduled. It emerged clearly how the dynamics of a social situation can strongly influence the individual behavior of "normal" people. There were no differences between the guards and the prisoners, but after less than a week two social groups had formed that expressed deviant pathologies and behavior:

Neither the guards nor the prisoners could be considered "bad apples" prior to the time when they were so powerfully impacted by being embedded in a "bad barrel". The complex of features within that barrel constitute the situational forces in operation in this behavioral context – the roles, rules, norms, anonymity of person and place, dehumanizing processes, conformity pressures, group identity, and more. (Zimbardo 2007, 197)[9]

---

[9] For a critical reading of the experiment and its implications, see Haslam and Reicher (2007).

Something similar had happened in Abu Ghraib. The soldiers accused and convicted of the crimes committed were certainly not innocent scapegoats, far from it. As Mary Fulbrook wrote, referring to the crimes committed by the Nazis and their allies, "Human beings make individual moral choices and have personal responsibility for their actions – even when they are forced to act in conditions not of their own choosing, and even when the range of choices available to them is unbelievably constrained and limited or is perceived as such" (2018, 539).

The contributing factors highlighted here, therefore, neither excuse nor absolve the individuals who committed those inhumane and illegal acts. They were fully aware of what they did, and even went beyond what would have been useful for intelligence purposes. But they had not created the political, organizational, and procedural environment within which this behavior took shape. As Balfour et al. write, "When organizational dynamics combine with a tendency to dehumanize and/or demonize a vulnerable group, the stage is set for the mask of administrative evil" (2020, 83). The individuals who committed those acts were the heirs to that system, that formative context created by others. In this, they were convenient scapegoats to divert guilt from other levels and responsibilities. And if only they were held accountable and therefore condemned, no serious discussion about what needed to change was initiated. The formal structures that facilitated the deviance remained intact.[10]

[10] Events of this kind have not only affected the US military. After a four-year investigation, on November 19, 2020, the Inspectorate General of the Australian Armed Forces confirmed with the so-called "Brereton Report" (Brereton 2020) that between 2005 and 2014, and in particular in 2012, some soldiers of the special units operating in Afghanistan (SAS) killed and tortured civilians. A kind of initiation rite even emerged for those who had to carry out the first killing, which involved shooting prisoners. SAS commanders gave the orders and the soldiers carried them out, in a competition between patrols. Even in the presence of warning signs, no remedial measures were put in place to avoid similar events. (The Brereton Report is available here: www.defence .gov.au/about/reviews-inquiries/afghanistan-inquiry. Facts of this type show a common matrix that deserves a systematic and comparative analysis, one not limited to the individual military teams of the countries involved. In light of this report, in fact, the Afghan Human Rights Commission asked that other countries involved militarily in Afghanistan also conduct similar investigations. In particular, it asked the United Kingdom to conduct a thorough investigation into some suspicious killings committed by its special units (Rory Callinan, "Calls for UK to investigate possible war crimes in Afghanistan", *The Guardian*, November 20, 2020).

4.5.2 The Dieselgate–Volkswagen Case

The Facts

In 2007, Volkswagen ("The people's car") launched "Strategy 2018", a very competitive strategy designed to make the German car maker the number one car manufacturer in the world, with the creation of new models and the conquest of new markets in the United States, Russia, and China. The leaders of this strategy were Ferdinand Karl Piëch, chairman of Volkswagen, and Martin Winterkorn, the CEO. The ambitious goal was to reach ten million cars sold every year, a significant increase compared to six million at the time. And the clean diesel market was going to be an important asset in achieving that goal.

Eight years later, in 2015, Winterkorn was forced to resign and Volkswagen was hit by one of the worst environmental scandals ever, for intentionally deceiving customers and controllers by manufacturing and selling cars equipped with software that could cheat exhaust gas emission tests. Millions of cars sold emitted gases that were forty times higher than the legal limits set in the United States. The plan had the strong backing of Volkswagen chairman Piëch and involved popularizing diesel in the United States through a campaign to promote clean diesel. There were, however, complications.

The engineers realized they were faced with enormous difficulties. Laboratory tests had shown that the exhaust gas recirculation system in the engine of the new models caused problems, prematurely wearing down the particle filter. This would have involved frequent (and expensive) filter replacement for customers to keep emissions within the standards required to pass the relevant test. In particular, the Environmental Protection Agency (EPA) in the United States would not have certified the cars, thus preventing their sale. It became very difficult to combine the conflicting objectives of having a "clean" car while staying within the time frames and budgets defined (Ewing 2017, 119). Whatever the solution, it would have increased production costs and made the car less competitive on the market in terms of price. How, then, to pursue the goal of becoming the number one car manufacturer in the world?

A possible solution was found. The engineers noticed that one of the many Audi software functions used for Volkswagen cars, a function called the "noise function", allowed the system to recognize when the car was being tested in the laboratory on a roller. The computer, therefore, could temporarily adjust emissions according to the test (Ewing 2017, 120).

The testing process was largely predictable, so the software could identify when the vehicle was being tested and when it was on the road. A group of engineers, therefore, decided to modify the software, produced by Bosch, in such a way that during the test the emissions were acceptable, reduced thanks to the automatic activation of a device. This involved changing just a few lines of software code within the engine control unit – "only" a few lines of the code to be revised among millions of others. The software was able to reduce emissions for exactly the time it took for the test. Immediately afterward, the engine returned to normal operation, and the car polluted up to more than forty times the limits set and detected during the test. It seemed like the perfect solution, even if it wasn't legal.

This information was discussed in a brief meeting in the Research and Development Building in the Volkswagen Factory complex in Wolfsburg. During the meeting it was explained how the software could recognize the external situation and then activate the instrumentation to reduce emissions during the test. In short, the car would only behave "legally" when emissions were being checked. Some objected with regard to the illegitimacy of such a ploy. Others objected that, after all, other companies did the same, and that therefore Volkswagen would have to imitate them in order not to lose competitiveness. The second opinion prevailed and the cars with the modified software were put into production.

The new cars passed emissions tests for seven years. Everything seemed to be going well, until three PhD students from West Virginia University realized that something was wrong. The three students had devised a detection system to carry out emissions tests not only in the laboratory but directly on the road and in various driving situations, in order to obtain more realistic results. Obviously, they were astonished by the data obtained, immediately noticing a clear difference between the results detected on the road and those detected in the laboratory. In 2014, they published their study, maintaining the anonymity of the manufacturer of the cars tested, since the research was for academic purposes and there was no intention of creating problems for Volkswagen.

But the secret did not stay a secret for very long. The California Air Resource Board (CARB), one of the regulators on emissions and pollution, was informed of the study and immediately asked Volkswagen to provide an explanation. At first, CARB, which had always had good relations with Volkswagen, only hypothesized a few technical problems that would soon be solved. But the company's immediate behavior was one of denial, their responses evasive. At the same time, Volkswagen tried to discredit the results of the published study. A few months later, the company said it had done some retesting and that the emission inconsistencies depended on technical issues that would quickly be resolved. They would therefore recall the cars sold in order to fix the problem. CARB requested the new test data for the inspected vehicles, but, when this was not forthcoming from Volkswagen, they did the tests themselves. Panic in the company skyrocketed.[11] It soon became impossible for Volkswagen to continue to deny the evidence, and in September 2015 some managers confessed to the deception, admitting that the software had been modified so that the car, during testing, would function differently and produce fewer emissions. On September 18, the scandal became public knowledge, as did the consequences.

It was a case of "corporate hypocrisy": on the one hand, the promise of clean diesel and on the other, deceit, with the large-scale adoption of defeat devices. Suffice it to say that in 2014, just a year before the scandal, Volkswagen was ranked by the world-famous Reputation Institute[12] in the Global CSR Reputation Winner top ten.

About 450,000 diesel cars sold in the United States were recalled immediately, but that was only the initial number, which was soon destined to grow. The company's share prices went down by 37 percent within days, resulting in a $20 billion loss in market capitalization. In addition, there were civil lawsuits for compensation and then criminal investigations. The media was naturally quick to publicize what had happened, with serious consequences for the image and reputation of the company. CEO Winterkorn resigned, stating: "I personally am deeply sorry that

[11] Patrick McGee, "Unsealed papers in VW scandal reveal panic among engineers", *Financial Times*, September 9, 2016.
[12] Reputation Institute, 2014, Global CSR RepTrak 100: Annual Corporate Social Responsibility Reputation Ranking.

we have broken the trust of our customers and the public".[13] Matthias Müller, the CEO of Porsche, was appointed in his place. Müller, however, had been head of Volkswagen's Product Division from 2007 to 2010, just around the time the company launched its clean diesel campaign – not exactly very promising as a sign of change.

The car company was forced to pay around $30 billion for their scheme, including reimbursements for customers, civil lawsuits, fines, and other costs. Eight managers, none at a high level, faced court proceedings in the United States, while other investigations were conducted in Germany. However, Germany did not grant extradition and Volkswagen warned the managers not to travel to the United States or they would risk being arrested, as happened to Oliver Schmidt, who was picked up while passing through the United States on his way to Cuba.[14] Another German Volkswagen employee, resident in the USA, was sentenced to forty months in prison in August 2017. It was believed that he was aware of the fraudulent project and was somehow involved in its planning.[15]

Although Volkswagen had indicated that it was willing to cooperate with the authorities and promised transparency, it refused to give the US Attorney General access to its email correspondence. Referring to German law, it would not share the results of the company's internal investigation and would not communicate the names of the people suspended or fired for the fraud, which, in any case, did not include any top managers.[16] The company's lack of cooperation was underlined by the Attorney General of New York, Eric T. Schneiderman, who in January 2016 stated: "Volkswagen's cooperation with the states' investigation has been spotty – and frankly, more of the kind

---

[13] Jack Ewing and Coral Davenport, "Volkswagen to stop sales of diesel cars involved in recall", *New York Times*, September 20, 2015.

[14] Jörn Poltz and Andreas Cremer, "Senior VW managers warned not to travel to U.S.: sources", *Reuters*, January 13, 2017.

[15] Eric D. Lawrence, "VW engineer gets 40 months in prison for role in diesel scandal", *USA Today*, August 25, 2017.

[16] Richard Milne, "Volkswagen has suspended 10 senior executives in emissions probe", *Financial Times*, October 22, 2015; Danny Hakim and Jack Ewing, "VW refuses to give states documents in emissions inquiries", *New York Times*, January 8, 2016; Jay Ramey, "VW still won't publish diesel investigation findings, citing more fines", *Autoweek*, May 15, 2017.

one expects from a company in denial than one seeking to leave behind a culture of admitted deception".[17]

Although the company admitted its faults, the top managers tried to shift responsibility onto a handful of "rogue engineers" who had operated without their knowledge. Winterkorn himself claimed that the irregularities in the diesel engine involved "terrible mistakes made by only a few ... I am not aware of any wrongdoing on my part".[18] In a video, he says: "It would be wrong to cast suspicion on the honest hard work of so many because of the terrible mistakes of only a few. Our team doesn't deserve that".[19] Similar claims came from Michael Horn, a Volkswagen division head, who denied any corporate responsibility, stating, in relation to the modified code, that: "This was a couple of software engineers who put this in for whatever reason ... To my understanding, this was not a corporate decision. This was something individuals did".[20]

Bad Apples, Bad Barrels, or Bad Orchards?

In this case, too, we can wonder: was it just the self-interested and fraudulent behavior of a few individuals, as Volkswagen claimed (bad apples)? Or was it something that originated at a higher level, with the involvement of the chain of command, the top management (bad barrels)? What was the role of Volkswagen's corporate culture in creating a formative context that fostered this behavior? What was the role of the wider environmental context and of the industrial system itself (bad orchards)? For example, the fact that no road tests were carried out offered the opportunity and incentive to deceive – there had already been previous cases of emission fraud by other car manufacturers.

Volkswagen's attempt to shift the blame to mid-level employees was not entirely successful, and several courts accused the company's leadership: "This is a case of deliberate, massive fraud perpetrated by

---

[17] Danny Hakim and Jack Ewing, "VW refuses to give American states documents in emissions inquiries", *New York Times*, January 8, 2016.

[18] Peter J. Henning, "The potential criminal consequences for Volkswagen", *New York Times*, September 24, 2015.

[19] Winterkorn, Martin (September 22, 2015): Video statement of the former CEO of Volkswagen AG.

[20] Jim Puzzanghera and Jerry Hirsch, "VW exec blames 'a couple of' rogue engineers for emissions scandal", *Los Angeles Times*, October 8, 2015.

Volkswagen management", stated Sean Cox, a Detroit Federal Court District Judge, imposing a $2.8 billion fine.[21]

Carl "Chris" Collins, at that time a Republican Senator, said: "I cannot accept VW's portrayal of this as something by a couple of rogue software engineers". The ex-administrator of the National Highway Traffic Safety Administration, Joan Claybrook, stated: "Suspending three folks – it goes way, way higher than that ... There are not rogue engineers who unilaterally decide to initiate the greatest vehicle emission fraud in history. They don't act unilaterally ... They have teams that put these vehicles together. They have a review process for the design, testing and development of the vehicles".[22]

As time passed, American justice became more and more convinced that a fraud of this size could not only not take place without the knowledge of top management, but not even without its direct involvement. This suspicion was confirmed by Volkswagen's organizational model of corporate culture: top-down, centralized, and hierarchical. New York Attorney General Eric T. Schneiderman said very clearly in this regard that: "The allegations against Volkswagen, Audi and Porsche reveal a culture of deeply rooted corporate arrogance, combined with a conscious disregard for the rule of law or the protection of public health and the environment".[23]

The *New York Times* conducted an in-depth investigation into the fraud and was able to show that the two top managers, Winterkorn and Müller, attended a meeting on November 8, 2007, where the issue of emissions was the main topic on the agenda. The *Times* managed to obtain attachments to two emails containing presentations given to the managers at that meeting. From these presentations, it was clear that the new engines would not meet US emission standards and this would mean an extra cost for filter replacement of about 270 euros per car. The email was sent to the managers present at the meeting, but Volkswagen argued that there was no evidence that the top managers had actually read the presentation (Ewing 2017, 177). Following this line of denial, Volkswagen said that the software change was not considered a big problem by top managers because in the past other

---

[21] Jack Ewing, "VW engineers wanted o.k. from the top for emissions fraud, documents show", *New York Times*, May 17, 2017; Jan Schwartz and Victoria Bryan, "VW's Dieselgate bill hits $30 bln after another charge", *Reuters*, September 29, 2017.

[22] Ibid.

[23] Press release from New York Attorney General, July 29, 2016.

problems with emissions had incurred sanctions in the United States that were regarded as insignificant. Therefore, they paid no attention to it.[24] It was as if to say that, given the limited risks, the top management was not interested in the problem.

This line of defense, however, was growing weaker and less and less convincing. In December 2015, Volkswagen was forced to admit for the first time that the fraud was caused by a chain of errors within the company and not just by the actions of a few isolated engineers.[25] At the same time, Volkswagen continued to try to make sure that their top management was not touched by any responsibility for what had happened.

Organizational Factors

To understand the genesis and dynamics of the "Dieselgate" case, it is necessary to analyze three organizational factors that played a role in this story: (1) the governance structure, (2) the organizational model, organizational culture, and leadership, and (3) the definition of objectives and the system of regulations.

(1) *The governance structure.* Volkswagen was governed by a strange mix of family control, government ownership, and the influence of employee representative associations. As with other German companies, half of the twenty places on the supervisory board went to the unions and the other half to shareholders. Two of the latter places went to representatives of the Lower Saxony state government. The board's role, in reality, was more a matter of appearance than of substance; as a former Volkswagen manager stated: "They lacked the ability to ask any deep technical question – and you see that in the current scandal". Attention to job protection was considered essential. As long as jobs were not threatened, the group's top management had a relatively free hand to manage the company, and no particular controls affected its work.[26]

---

[24] Nathan Bomey, "Volkswagen: we thought scandal wouldn't cost much", *USA Today*, March 2, 2016.

[25] Nils Pratley, "Volkswagen takes its cue from the bankers' book of excuses", *The Guardian*, December 10, 2015; Graham Ruddick, "VW Admits Emissions Scandal Was Caused by 'Whole Chain' of Failures", *The Guardian*, December 19, 2015.

[26] Andreas Cremer and Tom Bergin, "Fear and respect: VW's culture under Winterkorn", *Reuters*, October 10, 2015.

(2) *The organizational model, organizational culture, and leadership.*
Organizational leadership played an important role, in particular the figure who was certainly the most important at Volkswagen, the engineer Ferdinand Karl Piëch. Grandson of Ferdinand
Porsche, the inventor of the "Beetle", with Volkswagen since
1971, Piëch was CEO and chairman of the Volkswagen group
from 1993, leaving the position of CEO in 2002. He was then
chairman of the company's Supervisory Board from 2002 to
2015. He was an extraordinary manager, very competent with
regard to the technical aspects of the cars they produced, with
company objectives that were clear and not very negotiable. He
had an authoritarian style of command and was not inclined to
listen to others. Traits of nepotism were visible in matters of selection and recruitment – his wife, for example, an elementary school
teacher, was appointed to the supervisory board.[27]

Piëch quickly made it clear that he wanted more than just market leadership: he wanted "total dominance, and he was prepared to deploy
new tactics to achieve it, whatever the consequences" (Ewing 2017,
60). According to David J. Herman, chief executive of Opel and of the
European unit of General Motors, Piëch had introduced a new and
ruthless approach to the competition: "If you want to trace the origin
of the company ethic", said Herman, "I think you need to go back to
that period" – the period, in other words, when Piëch developed a new
corporate culture in which market domination was the only goal to
pursue, and it had to be achieved by all means necessary.

Ferdinand Piëch had a reputation for pushing engineers to the limit
in order to achieve goals. And when a reporter asked what would happen if they couldn't reach these goals, Piech replied: "Then I will tell
them they are all fired and I will bring in a new team. And if they tell
me they can't do it, I will fire them, too" (Ewing 2017, 89).

Piëch had no qualms about firing people he deemed incompetent or
not entirely in line with his way of thinking. Before the end of 1994,
less than two years after his arrival, he had replaced the entire board
of management – a total of nine top executives. His reputation as
a tough guy created a climate of fear and mistrust within the Audi

---

[27] David Crossland, "VW chief keeps control in family more out of wisdom than
nepotism", *The National Business*, March 23, 2012.

management team, and it would have been hard to find a manager that would have dared to criticize his decisions (Ewing 2017, 59). When an engineer protested that it would be impossible to do a certain job, Piëch replied: "If you don't want to do it, you don't have to" (Ewing 2017, 90). The implications were clear: for Piëch, denial and failure to pursue a technical goal were not possible options.

After his resignation in 2002, Piëch remained chairman of the supervisory board, and Bernd Pischetsrieder took over the position of CEO. The latter sought to introduce reforms independently from Piëch, with higher ethical standards of behavior, more effective internal controls, and an organizational climate of greater participation and openness. This did not last long. In 2006, Piëch replaced Pischetsrieder with Martin Winterkorn, who had previously headed up Audi and had a reputation for being far more obedient to Piëch's wishes – he was seen in fact as the latter's executive hand. With Winterkorn in charge, the goal of production volume market leadership resumed, meaning Volkswagen had to surpass two giants, General Motors and Toyota. Presenting "Strategy 2018", the 2007 masterplan, Winterkorn said that Volkswagen (VW) would become the biggest car manufacturer in the world. Diesel was part of this plan.

Volkswagen managerial culture was a despotic one, with the company ruled by an iron fist in rigid, top-down style.[28] It was a culture that was not very tolerant of errors or opinions that in some way contradicted or cast doubt on decisions taken at the top, even if there was some foundation for the contradiction or doubt. Just the fact of bringing bad news had a direct impact on the person who reported it, even if they were not directly involved in the genesis of the negative event. Arndt Ellinghorst, a former Volkswagen manager, gave an effective description of working for the company: "It was like North Korea without labour camps".[29] The VW culture was famous for being based on "anticipatory obedience" – in other words: "In that system, one isn't obedient – and worthy of being promoted – if one simply follows orders. You obey by not having to have explained what the guys on top desire".[30]

---

[28] Jack Ewing and Graham Bowley, "The engineering of Volkswagen's aggressive ambition", *New York Times*, December 13, 2015.
[29] Ibid.
[30] Andreas Cremer and Tom Bergin, "Fear and respect: VW's culture under Winterkorn", *Reuters*, October 10, 2015.

Due to this strongly authoritarian leadership, staff were under constant pressure to meet management expectations. Engineers were too anxious about pointing out the difficulties they encountered in following up on market leadership goals, and this blocked two-way communication between management and workers. The latter had only to obey the orders of management. Engineers played an important role: they were trained to solve technical problems and at this they were excellent. However, the people responsible for controlling and making sure that the engineers followed regulations lacked the necessary expertise on the subject of emission technology.

As Ewing wrote (2017,191), Piëch had created a culture within Volkswagen that revolved around him and a handful of protégés. A centralized authority created bottlenecks in the decision-making process and during his leadership Winterkorn perpetuated this system. The rest of the organization was paralyzed under a top-down, hierarchical command. Engineers dominated, and this meant excellent products could be created, but at the expense of other areas. It should be remembered that, under Piëch's leadership, Volkswagen had been involved in illegal, if not criminal, behavior, such as the Lòpez scandal, and this had already highlighted a certain flexibility with respect to rules and regulations to the advantage of achieving market objectives. In conclusion, Volkswagen was an example of "toxic culture" (Van Rooij and Fine 2018), present at various levels in the company, its structures, its values, and its working practices. The presence of norms that favored rule-breaking made compliance more difficult and delegitimized the authority of the law and the rules that supported it.[31]

(3) *The definition of objectives and the system of regulations.* Volkswagen's goals were too ambitious and did not take into account the resources, budgets, time and potential difficulties people would encounter in accomplishing them. The only way to

---

[31] As Van Rooij and Fine (2018, 43) make clear, toxic culture did not develop with a grand design, with the planning of each action by a specific actor. While CEOs and senior executives certainly play an important role in these processes, they don't plan and control them completely. They instigate some and let others develop without a particular direction. When wrongdoing is endemic in a culture, it is not the fault of a single person or leader, but is traceable to the larger organization itself.

achieve the objectives expected by the management was for the engineers to invent a fraudulent mechanism, otherwise they could have lost their jobs.

To this framework of impossible objectives should be added the system of rules of behavior, both written and unwritten, which should have placed a limit on the behavior of the Volkswagen engineers. These rules were weak, if not non-existent. As Volkswagen itself admitted, there was tolerance for breaking the rules and a culture that tolerated rule-breaking was certainly a key factor in causing the scandal. But a fraud so extensive and concealed for years can only be carried out in an organization within which there is a widespread "toxic culture" that facilitates misconduct. Organizations can develop rules of conduct that are not in line with the law: for example, companies with a long history of violations are more likely to violate again (Baucus and Near 1991; Simpson and Koper 1997). In this way, a "toxic culture" is produced, something also favored by selection and career processes. Clinard and Yeager (1980) show how the recruitment of top executives is often based on seeking "our kind of person" in terms of managerial style and familiarity, and this could interfere with corporate responsibility. The mechanisms of selection and recruitment on the one hand, and organizational socialization on the other, require investigation, in order to understand the propensity or not to accept illegal or criminal practices. It should be remembered that Volkswagen had already been hit by a very serious scandal in 2005, when members of the supervisory board had been rewarded with a trip that included the presence of prostitutes. Of course, criminal sanctions resulted for some of the people involved, but the case testified to behavior that displayed a certain indifference with respect to the legitimacy of the means in order to achieve certain ends.

Returning to the case in question, what was lacking was a system of effective checks and balances. The people who wrote the software were the same who approved it, while in other companies the designers are distinct from those who have to approve the projects (Ewing 2017, 124–125). Volkswagen had a code of conduct that required its employees to follow international laws and regulations. However, the code seemed to apply mostly on paper, as people did not always have the resources to legally pursue their assigned goals (Ewing 2017, 151). This situation created tension between external legitimacy requirements (to follow law and regulations) and internal performance requirements (to become the number one manufacturer in the world) – leaving it to managers and employees to figure out how to do it. The defeat device was certainly a very effective and available solution; an illegal solution in the United States, but not so problematic in Europe, where the use of software to mask emissions was, if anything, merely an infringement, a slight violation without serious consequences in terms of sanctions.

Finally, the metrics for measuring goal achievement were narrow, all focused on financial indicators, excluding other important issues. For example, none of the performance indicators of the "Strategy 2018" plan programmed, or had to do with, environmental or social issues, such as product quality, consumer health and safety, environmental sustainability, or the company's reputation, etc.[32]

Organizational Field Factors

Volkswagen was not the first car company to be involved in this kind of fraud. In 1998, Ford and Honda paid hundreds of millions of dollars in fines and compensation for installing devices that manipulated the measurement of their cars' emissions. The two car manufacturers collaborated with the authorities and settled out of court. Volkswagen itself, years earlier, had been involved in a similar affair, albeit on a much smaller scale. In 1974, the company paid a $120,000 fine for a technical problem regarding the emission control of gasoline cars.[33] What distinguished the 1974 case from that of 2015, and from those of other car manufacturers involved in similar events, was not only the size of the problem, but the aspect of premeditation (McCormick and Smith 2018, 20). Volkswagen was well aware of what it was doing and the consequences it would have on people's health and the environment. When the "Dieselgate" case broke, it became clear that the cars of many other European car manufacturers, virtually all of them, exceeded the emission limits in everyday and road use. However, only Volkswagen had designed a system to actually cheat the tests.

---

[32] The indicators included: (1) deliveries to customers, (2) sales revenue, (3) operating profit, (4) operating return on sales, (5) capital expenditure/sales revenue in the Automotive Division, and (6) net cash flow in the Automotive Division.

[33] Ryan Beene, "VW emissions 'defeat device' isn't the first", *Autoweek*, September 24, 2015.

The problem of car emission tests had already become evident in the early nineties, when the scandal of defeat devices in Cadillac cars emerged, which had made evident the limitations of testing cars only in the laboratory. At the same time, the case brought to light the fact that the increasing computerization of engine controls had paved the way for automotive "cheating". The problem was that the rigid predictability of official tests was an "invitation" for car manufacturers to cheat. In this regard, Kageson, a collaborator with the European Federation for Transport and Environment, stated: "Car manufacturers can use modern electronic equipment to adapt the engine to any type of test cycle" (Ewing 2017, 76). It therefore became important to combine laboratory tests with tests on the road, which were certainly more realistic.

The system of rules on emission limits was not homogeneous and was not always completely clear. There were significant differences in test systems in Europe and the United States and what was illegal in the United States was lawful in Europe. In Europe, the system focused on certification in the pre-production of cars, rather than on post-production verifications. The rules on emissions in the United States were much stricter than those in Europe, due to the difficulty of getting different European countries to agree on a common standard of measures and limits. Each country was free to further restrict the measures adopted at the European level. In this way, given the different standards, a car model that was legal in one country could be illegal to sell in another.

In conclusion, the ways in which the tests were carried out, in the laboratory and not on the road in the context of real use, became an inviting incentive for designers to develop defeat devices as an easy shortcut when they could not find a technical solution to a problem or when the solution was very expensive.

* * *

There are three possible explanations for the "Dieselgate" case.

The first (the "bad-apple" version) is that some engineers resorted to fraudulent behavior out of "individual interest". However, the aspect that distinguishes this case from other cases of corporate deviance, such as some banking scandals, is that those who carried out the violations did not gain anything from having launched a fraud of this size. They would therefore have had to be motivated by something other than money, considering the huge risks they were running.

The second explanation is that the engineers did what they did by "following the orders" of their superiors – even though the latter denied having given these orders and even claimed that they were unaware of what was going on.

The third explanation could be linked to a "failure of leadership" at Volkswagen and of monitoring and control systems.

All three explanations certainly have a foundation of truth. But what seems to be the fundamental question in this case is the relationship between the behavior and actions of the engineers, and the organizational and external environments as formative contexts for human action. A complex dilemma emerges: how to combine the requirements of external legitimacy for an ecological car with the aim of becoming the world's leading car manufacturer and conquering the American market? Pressures relating to external bodies clashed with the competitive pressures of the market and with the internal pressure of leadership in the sector as the number one producer. It is a classic dilemma of neo-institutionalist decoupling: meet the expectations of the environment at the expense of performance, or reject the demands of the environment at the expense of legitimacy (Meyer and Rowan 1977).

The company, in an increasingly competitive environment and with new demands and requirements (such as clean diesel), established objectives that were impossible to achieve in a short time and at a moderate cost. It also turned a deaf ear to the realistic assessments coming from technicians and engineers, so that, to the latter, the deception of using defeat devices seemed the only solution to manage an otherwise unmanageable decoupling.

This case shows how Volkswagen's organizational structure, its governance, its leadership system, and organizational culture, found themselves mediating between the broader regulatory environment and the organizations operating within it. It also shows how particular structural agreements influence the choices of managers and leaders, facilitating flexibility, sometimes deviant, as an organizational response to institutional conflicts in the environment – for example, the conflict between environmental needs (clean diesel) and competitive logic. In such situations, breaking the rules to find a solution can become the norm: something well known to the Volkswagen management, which had given a kind of silent assent until three American doctoral students noticed the problem.

The engineers did what they did, therefore, in full awareness that they were violating the rules regarding emission regulations. But their behavior originated from having to cope with a complex decoupling between external expectations (ecological and environmental needs) and internal expectations (pursuing market leadership). The fact that Volkswagen management pointed the finger mainly at the engineers was an attempt, not an entirely successful one, to shift the blame onto bad apples, onto convenient organizational scapegoats, in order to save, as far as was possible, the chain of command and management from harsher legal consequences.

5 | Organizations and Law: Inquiry Logics and Policies of Blame

5.1 Inquiry Logics: Person vs System

At Rome's Ciampino airport, a small plane crashes at the end of the runway shortly after take-off. The public prosecutor on duty that day and the inspector of the National Flight Safety Agency (ANSV), the Italian state's investigative authority for civil aviation safety, arrive on the spot. The public prosecutor's aim is to ascertain whether there is any responsibility for what happened. The ANSV's aim is to carry out a safety investigation to understand the causes of the accident, in order to prevent it from happening again. Safety investigations therefore have the sole purpose of *prevention*, something that might include the issuance of safety recommendations.

At the risk of simplification, we can say that the prosecutor looks to the past, to what happened, to detect any individual responsibility. The plane wreck is, therefore, a potential body of evidence. The ANSV inspector, on the other hand, looks to the future, to what *could* happen. Therefore, he must immediately understand if there are structural defects in the aircraft, then promptly issue safety recommendations for owners of similar aircraft. In terms of safety, then, the plane wreck is a place of learning. A possible tension clearly emerges between two investigative logics, both legitimate, but with different purposes: the first is aimed at justice for what happened, the second at safety for what could happen.[1] The structure of the two logics, their tensions, and their respective undesired effects are this chapter's subject of analysis.[2]

---

[1] Relations between the two subjects, the public prosecutor and ANSV, improved in part with the issue of EU Regulation no. 996/2010. The regulation in Article 12 provides for the "Coordination of investigations" and following this, ANSV and the Ministry of Justice have signed a preliminary agreement aimed at facilitating mutual cooperation, allowing ANSV to carry out its tasks, even in the event of criminal investigations.

[2] In this chapter, some considerations present in Catino 2006b and 2008 are referred back to and further developed.

When a significant negative event occurs in an organization (accident, misconduct, etc.) criminal judicial proceedings are initiated, aimed at ascertaining causes and accountability and, possibly, imposing sanctions. Considering a negative event primarily as a legal and insurance issue is also the typical response of many organizations when faced with problems of this type. It is a primarily person-based, "accusatory" approach that answers the question: "Whose fault is it?"[3] A second approach, based on the system, provides a different logic of investigation, of an organizational nature. This approach is not intended to determine individual responsibility (excluding cases of willful misconduct and gross negligence), but rather is aimed at understanding and explaining the event so that, through the knowledge acquired, it can be prevented from happening again. These are two ways of considering events, with investigations that arise from different logics, from different processes of framing and cognitive framing, and that generate different consequences. The facts they take into consideration and which they consider relevant are in part different, as the attitude toward the context is different.

The fundamental difference between the two logics is therefore constituted by the objectives they pursue: one, accusatory, is aimed at ascertaining personal responsibility; the other, organizational and functional, is aimed at understanding the causes and organizational factors relating to a particular dangerous event.[4] The two logics use different frames (Goffman 1974) and different sense-making processes (Weick 1995). Consequently, they arrive at different types of accountability. The context in which the investigations are conducted is defined by the different purposes, by the interests at stake, and by the point of view of those who carry them out.[5] Before analyzing the

---

[3] The concept of guilt is present in various ways in all cultures. Only the Sherpas of Nepal have developed peaceful conflict management practices (Douglas 1992). Through reconciliation procedures, the Sherpas try to reduce conflict and, in case of failure, one of the litigators leaves the village. In this way, scapegoats are not required. With regard to this, see C. von Furer-Haimendorf (1964).

[4] The distinction between the two logics has some similarities with the distinction introduced by Philip Zimbardo (2007) between a clinical approach, aimed at treating individual ills and damage, and a public health approach, aimed at treating systemic ills and damage.

[5] The distinction between the two investigative logics has many similarities with the difference between historical truth and procedural truth, or the distinction between judging vs understanding used to distinguish the work of the historian from that of the judge. With regard to this, see Calamandrei 1939; Bloch 1949

different approaches in more detail, it should be noted that when we talk about the accusatory approach, we are not referring only to criminal prosecution. In the case of negative events and organizational failures, also organizations, management, and personnel adopt, out of conviction or convenience, an accusatory approach, mainly based on individual action, or the action of small groups.

Jens Rasmussen, one of the most important scholars in the field of accidents and human error, argues that the problem of investigations into organizational failures has to do with the problem of causality:

In causal explanation of an accident occurrence, its origin will be back-tracked upstream the course of events to find the "cause". No objective stop rule can be devised to terminate this search. It is always possible to go one more step backwards in the search and the decision to stop and to accept an event as "the (root) cause" depends on the discretion of the analyst. (Rasmussen 1993, 3).

Who conducts the analysis and *why*, or with what purpose, are the two fundamental issues to give sense to the analysis itself. Technicians, says Snook (2000, 219), will stop in the analysis when they have found something broken that they can fix; trainers will stop when they have found a criticality in the skills to be trained; magistrates will stop when they have found an individual responsibility to pursue; political leaders will stop when they deem it politically opportune; scientists will stop when they have learned something new. There now follows a more detailed look at the two different logics that can characterize the analysis of an organizational failure.

5.1.1 The Approach to the Person: Accusatory

The approach to the person focuses on the errors and shortcomings of individuals, assuming that people make mistakes because they do not pay enough attention to their task. This approach adopts a linear causal model, leaving the organizational context in the background. It follows that remedial efforts are directed at the people on the front line. The outcome is the attribution of blame and the removal or sanction of the "bad apple", the guilty person.

[1992]; Taruffo 1967; Ginzburg 2002; Fiandaca 2020. On the impossibility of separating the analysis of historical events from judgment on them, and indeed on the need for a moral evaluation of historical facts, see Bloxham (2020).

It should be borne in mind that an accusatory approach is the symptom of strong human motivations aimed at seeking reassurance that the events that occurred have been understood and can be controlled (Kahneman 2011). Furthermore, the accusatory approach is based on some "good reasons" (Boudon 1992), a series of reasons that the agents consider valid for making decisions and motivating the choices made. Nevertheless, the concept of "good reason" has no positive, value-related significance, as the adjective "good" might lead us to believe. Rather, it is indicative of the reasons that the agents believe good, in certain circumstances, for them to act as they did. It is therefore a question of rational choices, even if in this case rationality appears to be the bearer of undesired effects that can conflict in part with the agents' reasons. Basically, the accusatory approach to the person is based on assumptions, such as:

• the voluntary nature of the action. Since human actions are involved in 80–90 percent of accidents and since human actions are perceived as subject to voluntary control, then accidents must be caused by negligence, carelessness, inaccuracy, incompetence, recklessness, etc. The conclusion is that those who make mistakes are negligent;
• individual responsibility. Since the person is responsible for their actions, the approach to the person is aimed at seeking the person responsible for the error. As happens in the criminal justice system, the precise aim is ascertaining personal responsibility.

Furthermore, the approach to the person offers two important advantages:

• it reinforces the sense of justice because it is emotionally satisfying. The identification of the culprit responsible for a serious error, or, even worse, for an accident, even if it is a scapegoat, tends to satisfy the people involved and the general public with respect to the damage suffered;
• it is convenient. Focusing on individual responsibility, on the identification of the bad apple, has undoubted advantages for organizations from a legal, insurance, and economic point of view. It also makes it possible to maintain the organizational structure, the operating rules, and the system of power.

The search for responsibility tends to direct investigation toward the identification of one or more people who have made a mistake and who had "power of control" over their actions, for which they must be sanctioned. The investigation is aimed at identifying who triggered the accident in the final phase. However, it is necessary to consider that the operator's behavior is also conditioned by the previous planning and organizational decisions of managers and designers of the organization and technology. Their power of control has been greater than the operator's, who inherits the results of their work and is therefore also heir to its defects. As Zimbardo has shown, the situations in which people operate are created by systems: these systems provide the institutional support, authority, and resources that make it possible for people to operate in situations (2007, 226).

In an accident analysis aimed at identifying responsibility, the focus is on abnormal unsafe acts and on the actions and omissions that led to the accident, according to the idea of a dynamic flow of events. This tends to exclude from the survey, or in any case to underestimate, those normal, non-dynamic events relating to organizational decision making and design aspects, which could have played a decisive role in preparing the accident conditions. These elements, if not removed, maintain their potential danger. It is certainly easier, for the reasons highlighted above, to identify the person in closest contact with the system (the aircraft pilot, the captain of the ship, the doctor, the nurse, the operator at the control panel, the train driver, etc.) as responsible for the accident. It is undoubtedly more challenging to pinpoint the latent factors of an organizational and managerial nature, the result of collective actions spread over time.

5.1.2 The Approach to the System: Learning

The approach to the system is based on the assumption that fallibility is part of the human condition, and that while the human condition cannot be changed, the conditions in which human beings work can (Reason 1997). While the approach to the person leads to the identification of those responsible for a negative event, the approach to the system aims to increase the system's conditions of safety and reliability, eliminating possible latent factors and the critical issues that gave rise to an organizational failure, to ensure that this cannot be repeated.

The approach to the system traces the causal factors of an event to the entire organization, based on the assumption that if accidents are the result of mistakes made by individuals, these mistakes are socially organized and systematically produced (Vaughan 2016). Organizational failures, such as accidents, result from a linked (usually rare) sequence of failures in the system of defenses, safeguards, barriers, and controls put in place to protect the organization from known risk events. Efforts to remedy and improve are directed both at the specific situations of the error or accident, and at the organizations.

The analysis is also influenced by the knowledge of possible remedies and their applicability. This requires considering other elements normally neglected in the identification of risk factors, such as ordinary activities that may have played a role in triggering the event. This type of analysis results in the adoption of measures that improve the conditions of the system rather than in the identification of a culprit for the incident. The logic of a system-centric investigation is therefore consistent with an organizational approach aimed at identifying the elements that generate an accident.

In this inquiry, the active failures that trigger the accident, committed by the operators closest to the task, are distinguished from organizational and inter-organizational failures, viewed as the organizational criticalities that made it possible. Indeed, sometimes it is the latter that determine a negative event: pressures of time, equivocal technology with ambiguous man–machine interfaces, insufficient education and training, inadequate support tools, a non-safety-oriented work culture, unclear procedures that are not fully usable in concrete situations, communication problems, and more. As already argued, it is obvious that the human factor is the element that frequently triggers the accident, but it is only a first order cause, one piece in the history of the accident. To be comprehensive, the history has to be completed through analysis of the previous sequences and of pre-existing latent and organizational factors.

If the aim is to assign blame, as in the approach to the person, the reconstruction of the causal chain often stops when someone or something is identified as the culprit. The result is superficial and limited analyses, which do not offer useful guidance for reorganizing the system in such a way as to prevent negative events from recurring. In the approach to the system, however, the focus is on learning, with the aim of making the organization safer. The emphasis of the analysis therefore shifts from individual causes to understanding accidents in terms of "reasons" – investigating the reasons why events and errors occurred (Leveson 2011).

The approach to the system consists of a sequence of choices based on the organizational importance of the facts identified which separates causality from moral responsibility, given that they are different categories. The actions carried out by frontline operators cannot be reduced to a dichotomous view of right or wrong with respect to the procedures in use and, therefore, guilty or not guilty. These actions do not take place in an organizational void which is occupied by the free will of the operator. The actions, whether evaluated thereafter as errors or not, are always carried out within a sociotechnical context designed by the organization and its management. In turn, these contexts are influenced by the organizational field in which the organization and people operate. In this sense, it is reductive to talk about linear acts and events that cause an accident since the linear causality model does not incorporate non-linear relationships between events and feedback, such as, for example, the management's commitment to safety and the safety culture present in the system. Moreover, the linear causality model attributes too much importance to the frontline operator involved in the negative event – given that it is this operator who actually inherits the flaws and defects of those who design, organize, and manage the system.

The aim of the approach to the system is, as said before, to make learning possible (Friedberg 1993 [1996]; Argyris and Schön 1996) and to favor organizational change at different levels, thus also introducing a possible clinical aspect. This type of inquiry therefore has a pragmatic value, since its results can help the subjects to review the operating logic of the organizational system, improving the knowledge that the agents have of the system and of their own particular context of action (Friedberg 1993 [1996]).

5.2 The Person Approach: Perverse Effects and Vicious Circle

The two methods of investigation respond to different logics and points of view, and these affect the way in which events are reconstructed, the elements considered significant for the purposes of the analysis, and the consequences and effects. The two logics may regard the same phenomenon differently because different framing processes are implemented. Therefore, it is the type of frame that defines what is relevant to the investigation (see Table 5.1). The two logics differ from a professional, social and institutional point of view.

Table 5.1 *Comparison of investigatory logics*

	Person approach	System approach
Aim	Ascertain responsibility, sanction	Understand, explain, learn, improve
Investigation procedure	Regulated by law, regulations, norms, and procedures	Based on theories, models, and mechanisms
Conception of the cause	Individualizing causal theories	Causal networks; systemic approach; latent factors
Context	In the background, accidental	Fundamental, structuring action
Conception of failure	Individual; negative event caused by human error	Organizationally constructed; human error is a symptom not the cause
Level of result	Individual only; removal of bad apples	Organizational and inter-organizational
Main question	*Who* caused the event?	*What* factors favored the event, so that, if these were removed, the event would not be repeated?
Possible undesired effects	Inertia to change	Individual irresponsibility

The starting point is the different aim, or the different goal to be pursued. Given the alternative of "judging or understanding", the analysis to improve the system tends, as it also does for historians, toward the latter. Croce (1916) pointed out the distinction between historical judgment, pronounced *sub lege*, in the name of established laws, and historical consideration, as a consideration of truth with no intent to keep laws and institutions alive. In this regard, Bloch (1949 [1992]) identifies two types of impartiality: that of the scholar and that of the judge. Both pursue the truth, but there comes a point where their paths diverge. The scholar concludes his work after observing and explaining the results of his research. The judge, having presented and clarified the facts to be judged, still has to issue a verdict.

It is also argued here that *the purpose of the investigation directs the investigation itself*. Which facts are taken into consideration depends in part on the attitude toward the context and in part on the aim of the investigation: one approach is to judge, the other, to understand. The reconstruction of an event can only be selective, as the total knowability of a complex event is impossible: since it cannot be reproduced in its entirety, it cannot be fully relived. The selectivity of the investigation is determined by the perspective adopted and this, in turn, depends on the purpose. In other words, what is examined is only what is considered *significant* with respect to the aims of the investigation, a different way of reconstructing the "truth".[6]

The person (accusatory) approach involves a series of unexpected consequences of the action (Merton 1936), of perverse counter-intuitive effects (Forrester 1970), or effects of composition (Boudon 1992). These are those undesired effects, obtained unintentionally as a result of intentional actions. First of all, as mentioned above, searching for a culprit alone does not improve the organization and does not change the state of things. It is an approach that looks to the past – one that creates a sense of fear of sanctions and litigations, does not foster the reporting of errors by frontline operators, and inhibits organizational learning. The politics of blame is a powerful obstacle to organizational learning from past events. The person approach, therefore, does not make it possible to eliminate the conditions of risk and does not exclude the possibility that the same event may be repeated with other agents.

A further consequence of the person approach regards the creation of scapegoats. Fisse and Braithwaite write: "Scapegoating vilified individuals is endemic in legal systems" (1993, 56). In some cases, management may use the tactic of structuring the organization chart so as to have a "vice-president responsible for going to jail" (40). In this way, given the important role of the sacrificed person, the management team can optimistically expect the prosecutor to be "satisfied"

---

[6] Historical investigation differs from judicial investigation in that it is not designed to identify faults and responsibilities. It also differs from the specific type of organizational investigation referred to here, as it has no intention to improve the system. With reference to the historical method, see Ginzburg 1989 and 2002. On the differences between methods and limits ("exclusionary rule") in the acquisition of evidence in criminal trials, and historical and scientific research, see Dershowitz (1996). For an interesting comparison of the logic of research in science and law, see Latour (2004).

and stop trying to prosecute members of the company's managerial elite. Fisse and Braithwaite (1993) conclude by stating, in relation to this, that "Corporate criminal liability hardly avoids this risk of scapegoating but alleviates it by imposing responsibility on the corporate ruler" (40). Finding a scapegoat can be a very beneficial exchange for management in order to avoid being implicated (Stone 1980).[7] In research carried out several years ago, Drabek and Quarantelli (1967) argued for perfect rationality in identifying scapegoats following disasters and the usefulness to the leadership of attributing blame at an individual level. The indictment of individuals made it possible to avoid costly structural changes, since public opinion was led to believe that an exemplary punishment of the "guilty" figure would serve as a future deterrent to prevent similar events from happening again.

Other effects, as Brändström writes, regard the problem of learning and change (2016, 5):

Sometimes, the logic of "managing accountability" can hinder the learning process; for example, when some of the involved parties just want to "move on" and refrain from lengthy and painful public investigations. Key actors may fear that exposing the facts might put them or the institutions or policies they represent in unfavorable light.

Along the same line of argument, Diane Vaughan (2016) shows that the benefit of an explanation that identifies operators as the immediate cause of an organizational failure is that remedies are possible quickly. Managers can be fired, transferred, or retired. New rules governing operations can be established. With these changes made, the organization can move forward.

Other undesired effects generated by an accusatory approach can be found in the medical sector. The US National Academy of Medicine has set a goal to decrease healthcare errors by 50 percent over five years, but, as the *New England Journal of Medicine* noted, efforts to prevent harm from health treatment are hindered by the "dead weight" of a judicial regime that induces operators to secrecy and silence. This topic will be dealt with in more detail in the next section.

---

[7] A great deal of literature exists highlighting the limits of the effectiveness of punitive control strategies and in particular of deterrence to counter corporate crimes. See: Stone (1975), Braithwaite and Fisse (1987), Clarke (1987), Moore (1987), Coffee (1989), Simpson (2002), to name just a few.

5.2.1 The Phenomenon of Defensive Medicine

One of the most evident consequences of an accusatory approach to the person concerns medicine and healthcare personnel and is known as medical malpractice litigation. The increase in lawsuits in this area has led to three main consequences: (1) the crisis of the malpractice insurance system, due to significant increases in the costs of policies, unsustainable for health facilities, (2) the request for regulatory changes relating to causes for malpractice, (3) the diffusion of so-called defensive medicine.

"Defensive medicine" means a doctor's execution, or omission, of a series of diagnostic or therapeutic practices that are not aimed at the patient's well-being but rather at preventing the doctor from incurring legal responsibility. Clinical practice is therefore guided by the doctor's concern for his own legal protection, rather than by any expectation of benefit for the patient (Kapp 2016). Defensive medicine is divided into "positive" and "negative" (US Congress 1994). Positive defensive medicine results in unnecessary services, such as examinations, procedures, or visits. Negative defensive medicine, on the other hand, manifests itself in a tendency toward abstention on the part of healthcare personnel, such as the failure to perform therapies or surgery because of the high risk of failure, or the decision to avoid high-risk patients or procedures, mainly (but not exclusively) in order to reduce exposure to litigation.

Negative defensive medicine also includes the practice of *replace care* – entrusting the patient to other doctors or other care institutions. This defensive behavior is linked to the increase in medical litigation and requests for compensation from patients. The perception of accusatory and litigation-generating habits often induces doctors to change their professional conduct. Protection of the patient's health can thus, for the healthcare professional, become an objective subordinate to the minimization of legal and punitive risk.

Many doctors believe that getting involved in litigation can damage their professional reputation. The psychological repercussions of litigation, and in particular the loss of self-esteem, are equally important. The state of anxiety caused by being summoned before the court for a petition lasts for a long time even after the verdict is issued (Charles, Wilbert, and Kennedy 1984). The patient is sometimes seen as a real antagonist and the relationship is compromised due to an excess of prudence (Law 1986; Elmore 2005).

In 1978, Tancredi and his collaborators identified a series of problems related to defensive medicine (Tancredi and Barondess 1978), concluding that a significant percentage of doctors (70 percent) practiced defensive medicine for fear of involvement in medico-legal disputes. From other studies on the subject conducted in various countries (the United States, Great Britain, Japan, South Africa, and Canada), it emerges in essence that the percentage of doctors who resort to defensive behavior, whether positive or negative, is around 70 percent, in some cases going up to 98 percent.[8]

The present writer has conducted some research on this phenomenon in Italy.[9] In 2008, the *Società Italiana di Chirurgia*, the Italian Society of Surgery, promoted an inquiry aimed at identifying the most common defensive medicine behavior adopted by surgeons (Forti et al. 2010; Catino 2011).[10] This showed that 77.9 percent of doctors said they had practiced defensive medicine behavior during the last month of work taken into consideration. A second investigation focused on emergency defensive medicine,[11] involving 1,392 doctors of different specialties from all Italian regions (1,327 valid questionnaires): 90.5 percent admitted to having practiced at least one form of defensive medicine behavior during the last month of work. Of these, 77.7 percent requested unnecessary laboratory tests; 72.8 percent made unnecessary annotations in medical records; 67.3 percent requested unnecessary advice from other specialists; 64.1 percent requested unnecessary

---

[8]   See on this point Summerton (1995); Klingman et al. (1996); Passmore and Leung (2002); Studdert et al. (2005); Hiyama et al. (2006); Merenstein, Daumit and Powe (2006); Jackson Healthcare (2009); Bishop, Federman and Keyhani (2010); Sethi et al. (2012); Ortashi et al. (2013); Rothberg et al. (2014); Baicker, Wright and Olson (2015); Yan et al. (2016).

[9]   To address this problem, in the interest of both the patient and public expenditure, the legislator intervened in Italy with two provisions, the Balduzzi Decree (DL n.158/2012) and the Gelli-Bianco Law (L. n. 24/2017). For a critical reading regarding the limits and contradictions of these provisions, see Poggi (2018).

[10]   This research was promoted and directed by the *Centro Studi Federico Stella* (Faculty of Law of the Catholic University of the Sacred Heart of Milan) and conducted with the Department of Sociology and Social Research of the University of Milan-Bicocca, as part of the research directed by professor Gabrio Forti (Forti et al. 2010).

[11]   The research was promoted by the Academy of Emergency Medicine and Care (AcEMC) and by the Management of the Emergency Department of the "U. Parini" hospital in Aosta and financed by the General Management of the Aosta AUSL (Catino, Pesenti Campagnoni, and Locatelli 2011).

invasive examinations; 63.3 percent requested unnecessary hospitalization, only due to pressure from the patient's family members; 61.2 percent required hospitalization for a manageable outpatient patient; finally, 51.8 percent emphasized certain clinical-anamnestic aspects to justify the correctness of their diagnosis. The main reasons stated included: the fear of medical litigation (69 percent); the fear of receiving a request for compensation (50.4 percent); the influence of colleagues' previous litigation experiences (50 percent); previous personal experiences of litigation (34.3 percent); and the concern of incurring disciplinary measures imposed by their own organization (21.2 percent).[12]

It is evident that all this has a significant impact on the costs borne by the health system, and therefore by the community, with important repercussions on the quality of the health services provided.[13] In the United States, in particular, the most recent analyses show costs ranging from \$45.6 (Mello et al. 2010) to 50–65 billion (Giancola 2017; Katz 2019). In Italy, recent surveys have estimated the economic impact of defensive medicine at €9–10 billion, with per capita values of €165, out of a total per capita medical expenditure of €1,847.[14]

In a system with fixed economic and operational resources, such as healthcare, the allocation of resources to unnecessary activities can lead to serious shortcomings in services essential to patient safety. Defensive medicine also contributes to a reduction in the quality of healthcare because unnecessary invasive diagnostic procedures (such as biopsies) represent unnecessary risks for patients. Moreover, ambiguous or false-positive results produce emotional stress and the need for further diagnostic tests, triggering an escalation that is difficult to control.

In conclusion, a rather problematic finding emerged from research published by the *British Medical Journal* in 2015. The research analyzed the malpractice history of a sample of doctors from seven different specialties in Florida hospitals from 2000 to 2009. It was found

[12] Another factor that appears to affect the spread of defensive medicine is the media coverage of any negative outcomes in the treatment of patients and the consequent onset of legal proceedings (Quinn 1998; Madarasz 2012).

[13] On this subject, see the studies carried out by Baldwin et al. (1995); Lewin VHI Inc. (1997); Tillinghast-Towers (2003); Merenstein et al. (2006); PricewaterhouseCoopers' Health Research Institute (2006); Massachusetts Medical Society (2008); Jackson Healthcare (2009); Mello et al. (2010); Giancola (2017); Katz (2019).

[14] www.panoramassicurativo.ania.it/articoli/63785.

that the doctors who made more use of defensive medicine, ordering more unnecessary tests and procedures, were less likely to incur malpractice litigation. Hence, higher costs for the health system made it less likely that doctors would incur litigation from patients or their families.

This could come from the fact that the greater expense on services reduces the likelihood of adverse outcomes, or from the fact that it signals to patients, judges, and juries that, despite an error, the doctor behaved in the best possible way in terms of patient care. These results are certainly not an incentive to reduce unnecessary expense, given the benefits – for doctors – with respect to making litigation less probable.

5.3 From a Person Approach to a System Approach

In conclusion, moving from a person-based, accusatory model to one that is system-based and organizational requires two conditions: (1) a change at all levels of the organizational culture with regard to failure; (2) analysis models appropriate to the complexity of the events.

In relation to the first point, any instrument put in place to improve safety conditions (for example a risk management program, an error reporting system, etc.) will only be effective if it is inserted into a culture based on learning, through the construction of a no-blame culture, among other measures. The experiments will otherwise be unsuccessful, as the powerful and symbolic blaming process is able to stifle any learning attempt. In this regard, the most appropriate concept is that of "just culture" – a culture in which frontline operators or other figures are not sanctioned for actions, omissions, or decisions that they adopted on the basis of their experience and training. A just culture will not, however, tolerate gross negligence, intentional violation, or harmful action (Reason 1997; Dekker 2007).[15] It should be emphasized that an organization based on just culture is not an organization where everything is lawful, as long as it is declared. An organizational culture of this type requires the need to establish boundaries between felonious actions and errors and tolerable actions and errors, so that

---

[15] The publication of the European Union Regulation 691 of 2010, subsequently developed with Regulation 376 of 2014, officially introduced the concept of just culture into the field of continental civil aviation. See also the ICAO Safety Management Manual (SMM), www.icao.int.

the latter category is as broad as possible. An organization that does not implement this distinction, in which any erroneous behavior is tolerated if reported, is an organization that risks losing credibility in the eyes of its members. Above all, it is an organization that does not learn. A just culture is an organizational culture, therefore, that protects people who make mistakes that might be defined as "honest". It is a culture that favors the creation of a climate of trust in which, on the one hand, people are encouraged, even rewarded, for providing essential information relating to safety, while, on the other hand, a dividing line is drawn between acceptable and unacceptable behavior. It constitutes the first step in being able to develop reporting systems for adverse events, errors, and other anomalies, fostering an organizational culture based on trust among operators. If these events are not reported, learning becomes impossible to achieve: reporting is in fact essential for learning, and learning is necessary to improve an organization's conditions of reliability and resilience.

The second condition for an organization's transition to the system-based approach involves the adoption of organizational models of analysis and improvement suited to the complexity of the events. These are systemic and organizational models that consider failures as deriving from the interaction between people, organizational and social structures, design activities, and components of the physical system (Vaughan 2016; Catino 2006a, 2013; Leveson 2011). From a research point of view, it is necessary to move away from questions such as: *Who* caused the accident? toward questions such as: *What* conditions and mechanisms in the organization increased the possibility of the event occurring? *What* circumstances might be involved in producing certain behavior? *How* and *why* did the defenses fail? *What* can we do to prevent the event from happening again?

It should not, therefore, be a matter of limiting things to looking for single causes, but rather of identifying the broad set of conditions that increase the possibility of a negative event occurring.

6 | Conclusions

6.1 Organizational Strategies to Manage Blame: An Analytical Model

In the face of negative events (such as crises, disasters, wrongdoing, business scandals) and organizational failures, there are two different strategies for organizations, both entailing a trade-off between long-term and short-term rationality (see Figure 6.1).

In the first, starting from the acceptance of any eventual responsibility, the organization learns from the event and generates an organizational change of the "double-loop type" (Argyris and Schön 1996). This is aimed at profound changes designed to prevent another similar event from happening. However, this virtuous path can immediately give rise to negative effects, such as serious legal consequences and a reduction in business. In the second scenario, however, the organization tries to shift the blame for what has happened onto an individual or a group of individuals, thus creating a scapegoat. Judge Guido Calabresi argues that scapegoating's core lies in "blaming someone, rather than facing up to the underlying problem" (1994, 86). This second strategy produces undoubted benefits for organizational leadership, ensuring its stability, and allows the organization to survive, without taking significant legal risks and with everything reduced to an insurance problem. No remedial measures have to be implemented and no changes have to be made to the organizational structure.

As Crozier and Friedberg (1977 [1980]) write, no learning can take place within the framework of a gradual and harmonious evolution, rather, every piece of learning requires a rupture; every authentic change implies a crisis and a redefinition of power relations. This strategy, while it is certainly convenient for the organization in the short term, does not generate effective organizational learning in the long term, and therefore does not give rise to any system change. As we will see in more detail below, it is a type of "single-loop" learning (Argyris and

190

Figure 6.1 Scenarios of stigma-management and scapegoating

Schön 1996): by limiting itself to symptoms, it does not prevent these, or similar, events from repeating themselves. Therefore, organizational inertia and limited learning (single-loop) ensure the maintenance of organizational leadership and its system of power and interests.

Based on the empirical evidence analyzed thus far, it is possible to identify some of the factors that play a role in favor of the organizational strategy of scapegoating, rather than that of learning. These factors involve: the type of event, the level of politicization of the event, and the intervention of the judiciary. The three factors are closely interrelated and the media play a significant transversal role with regard to each of them.

Regarding the first factor, *the type of event*, negative events can be divided into "hot" and "cold", based on the reaction they provoke in the wider social system (Bonazzi 1983a). "Hot" negative events are those characterized by an intense emotional reaction and a high level of media attention and can more easily generate scapegoating than "cold" accidents (which have a low level of emotional reaction and media attention). This is due to the media circus that usually accompanies them. "Hot" negative events are in fact reinforced by media representations (Wilkins and Patterson 1990) which transform them into an "explosion of outrage" (Horlick-Jones 1995).

With regard to the second factor, *the politicization of the event*, negative events can be politicized with a certain rapidity, which favors accusatory person-based approaches as well as scapegoating. Processes of accountability arise from questions such as: what happened? Who and what caused this event? Who is responsible for it? Who should be punished? These questions give rise to "blame games" (Brändström and

Kuipers 2003; Roulet and Pichler 2020) – the conflict over the nature of the causes of the event and who should be blamed for what has occurred. The accusatory finger of communities struck by negative events such as disasters zeros in on the figure of a person, effectively transforming a "bolt from the blue" into a "predictable surprise". Here, too, an important role in the production of these dynamics is played by the media and its transformations, especially following the advent of the Internet. These developments have turned crises into television and media events, favoring their politicization through the moral counterpoint between heroes and villains (Wagner-Pacifici 1986). One way to resolve these conflicts, these "blame games" on the part of policy-makers, is to come up with a scapegoat, thus shifting the blame for what happened onto the actions of individuals or groups.

Finally, the third factor concerns *the intervention of the judiciary*, and of criminal law in particular. Based on individual responsibility, this favors the shift of the focus of attention to the person closest to the location of the negative event, such as the frontline operator, pushing organizational and inter-organizational aspects into the background. This also happens due to the need to reconstruct robust causal links – ones that are able to hold up during the trial phase.

These three factors are joined by the mass media, which frequently play a non-neutral role – not, in other words, the simple transmission of information regarding the events that have occurred (Clemente, Durand, and Porac 2016; Roulet and Clemente 2018). Instead, they play a "filter" role that can have significant repercussions in terms of scapegoating. "Media logic" (Altheide and Snow 1979), being its aim to maximize the attention of the public, favors the simplification of communication, speed without in-depth analysis, the emphasization, spectacularization, and personalization of the news. Thus, the mass media selectively focus the attention of the public, mainly zeroing in on the people immediately involved in a negative event and placing less emphasis on the latent factors that may have generated it. In this way they also function as a megaphone for other agents, in particular public prosecutors.

6.2 Implications for Learning of Organizational Strategies to Manage Blame: Vicious and Virtuous Circles

In attributing blame, focus is on a single act, without adequate attention being paid to the context in which the subject has found himself operating. This happens because it is easier to identify the last link in the chain of events, due to both a mechanism of personification of guilt and the difficulty of using and sharing cognitive models that are more complex and appropriate to the situation. This is mainly because this is the way the law normally operates, but also because explanations based on individual error and personal guilt suit the organization involved in the event and its leadership. Some years ago, Perrow (2014) wrote in this regard that, through the retrospective attribution of human error, it is possible to protect organizations that would otherwise be faced with extremely heavy costs for the implementation of concrete system changes. This, Perrow continued, is due to the fact that, if a formal investigation starts from the assumption that it was a single individual who made a mistake, the case is resolved immediately, with no consequences for the organization.

An accusatory approach focused on scapegoating produces a vicious circle. Being aimed mainly at the search for a culprit, it creates a sense of fear of sanctions and litigations. The fear of judicial consequences favors the concealment of errors and inhibits or hinders the reporting of these and other anomalous events – indicators necessary to facilitate system learning and its constant improvement. A punitive organizational culture favors defensive behavior and strategies aimed at avoiding the attribution of blame, rather than identifying the best possible way to carry out the organization's task.

The results of this accusatory approach are organizational inertia and failure to learn from mistakes: if one or more people are responsible for what happened, why change things? From this it follows that the persistence of a culture of guilt, reinforced by a certain type of judicial action, becomes the first obstacle to the creation of greater safety in organizations. For example, a professional system at continuous risk of criminal investigation, such as the medical system, is not more careful and diligent. Rather, it is one that reduces the risks of those who act through seeking greater formal safeguards – even, as we have seen in section 5.3., to the detriment of the patient.

A "double-loop" approach to the system, aimed at organizational change, focuses on the search for the organizational conditions that give rise to incidents and favors the reporting of errors aimed at removing latent critical factors. The outcomes are organizational learning from mistakes and failures, and the progressive reduction of risks in organizations. The approach to the system therefore fosters greater awareness and, on the basis of the lesson learnt from the event, the attempt to generate a greater predictive ability in the organization's operations (Toft and Reynolds 1994). This approach is typical of the "generative organization" (Westrum 1995), a type of organization that is constantly alert and that continuously learns and reviews its own procedures. A generative organization is a highly reliable organization, which never considers safety as a condition that has been definitively achieved, but as a goal to be perpetually pursued (LaPorte and Consolini 1994; Weick, Sutcliffe, and Obstfeld 1999; Weick and Sutcliffe 2015).

In the light of what has been said so far – without prejudice to the requirements of justice, which are not called into question here – we can conclude that, in the face of organizational failures, accidents, and other negative events, it is necessary to think of other ways that can produce changes, improvements and, above all, organizational and institutional learning which go beyond mere individual sanction.

6.2.1 Single-Loop and Double-Loop Learning

As already mentioned, Argyris (1993, 2004; Argyris and Schön 1996) describes two forms of organizational learning: single-loop and double-loop.[1] With single-loop learning, procedures are corrected based on results obtained. Errors are seen and avoided, but without calling the logic of the system into question. For example, a company's marketing managers, finding that monthly sales are below expectations, can investigate the reasons for the decrease, looking for a new interpretation that allows them to implement remedial actions aimed at raising the sales performance back to a higher level (Argyris and Schön 1996). The single-loop model is essentially based on a form of analysis and intervention that begins with (a) detecting an error, a result that does not match expectations, (b) linking that error to underlying

---

[1] We have already seen this model, albeit briefly, in section 3.5. In relation to these types of change, Boin (et al. 2008, 16) identifies three types of reaction that can follow a crisis: (1) "fine-tuning", involving limited adaptations of policies and practices, without affecting assumptions and background values; (2) "policy reform", involving greater change, but limited to the formal aspect, such as guidelines, standards, procedures, etc.; and (3) "paradigm shift", involving a real and radical change in policies, organizational models, and basic cultural assumptions.

strategies and assumptions, and (c) modifying these strategies and assumptions in order to maintain the performance of the organization within existing organizational values and norms. In other words, the values and norms remain unchanged.

A second type of learning, known as turnaround (Hedberg 1981, 10) or double-loop (Argyris and Schön 1996) makes it possible to see that the process from which the error originated, the organizational failure, is defective and that it is therefore necessary to change the logic of the system. It is a type of learning that modifies the underlying theories-in-use (strategies, basic assumptions, values, and norms), as well as the way data is interpreted, and problems identified and addressed.

The double-loop learning investigation process is, therefore, more complex than the single-loop model, requiring the organization to take note at all levels of conflicts and problems that have neither a simple nor univocal solution. With respect to dilemmas, to conflicting needs, it is necessary, for example, to decide between production and safety, between growth and predictability.

Applying the distinction between the two types of learning to cases presented in this book, it can be said that, with single-loop learning, the organization is limited to removing the person involved in the event and making some changes to procedure, without calling into question or changing the theories-in-use. With double-loop learning, organizational and institutional change is initiated. This process is characterized by a fundamental question, which is not whether the organization has learned everything it could learn from a specific event or organizational failure but, rather, whether the organization is convinced that it should manage things better in the future (Turner and Pidgeon 1997).

For example, with reference to the Tangentopoli/"Bribesville" case, the discovery of numerous cases of corruption that had been going on for some time highlights the limits of a merely punitive response, even though this should certainly be ensured. As David Nelken (2002) argued, this case did not prompt useful discussion regarding what changes were necessary to avoid the repetition of corrupt practices, such as consociativism, the sharing out of executive offices, and patronage. According to Nelken, it was a missed opportunity: the Tangentopoli investigation did not come out of nowhere, but was inserted in a context characterized by corrupt practices that were low-level and widespread. Culprits were eliminated with no changes made to the context that fostered their behavior, leaving the door wide open for the recurrence of the same practices with other actors.

The presence of so-called systemic corruption (Vannucci 2012) is an indicator, a signal of a problem that has social, political, and administrative origins and therefore also requires another type of treatment, another type of solution. In other words, sanctions alone do not seem to reduce the phenomenon – if anything, the risk is that they increase the degree of awareness of those who commit the violations. In this regard, the distinction introduced by D'Alberti between subjective and objective corruption is useful, where the former concerns the behavior of individuals, while the latter has to do with the deterioration and decay of institutional systems (2020, 23). Objective corruption is the corruption of the system that creates the field of action for the subjective corruption of people. The greater the objective corruption, the greater the subjective corruption. In a double-loop logic of change, therefore, it is necessary to modify the objective aspect, as well as to repress the subjective aspect. Of course, changing conditions that favor objective corruption are certainly more complex than actions aimed at limiting subjective corruption. This involves changing administrative systems, the simplification of procedures and bureaucracy, selection and recruitment based on merit-based criteria, adequate incentive systems, and other measures – all things that are complicated, but not impossible, to plan and implement.

6.2.2 Some "Virtuous" Examples in which Scapegoating is Not Used

The previous chapters have described some cases regarding a vicious circle of learning and scapegoating (*Costa Concordia*, Abu Ghraib and "Dieselgate"). A few virtuous examples do exist, however.

One of these is the investigation conducted by NASA following the space shuttle *Columbia* disaster. Seventeen years after the *Challenger* disaster and after eighty-eight launches, the *Columbia* shuttle disintegrated on February 1, 2003, as it was re-entering Earth's atmosphere at the end of the mission. Seven astronauts lost their lives. Eighty-one seconds after the launch, when the shuttle was at approximately 65,000 feet and travelling at a speed of approximately 2,500 kilometers/hour, a fragment of insulating foam broke off the spacecraft's bipod ramp and hit a heat shield tile on the left wing, causing a small breach in the thermal protection system. On re-entry, the breach allowed burning air to penetrate the insulating shield and progressively melt the aluminum structure, causing the structure to weaken, the shuttle to lose control, the wing to break, and eventually the orbiter to collapse.

Immediately after the accident, NASA formed CAIB, the Columbia Accident Investigation Board, made up of members of NASA itself, aviation experts, a former astronaut, some civilian investigators, and two professors of engineering. The CAIB collaborated with experts in human factors, social sciences, and organization and seven months later, on August 26, made the report on the accident public. It emerged that NASA had continued with the shuttle launches despite being aware of the problems relating to the possible detachment of the foam. There had been numerous missed learning opportunities to avoid such a tragedy. In addition, it was found that some engineers who had noticed problems during the launch were reprimanded for asking for more images of the launch without respecting the hierarchical chain.

It is worth underlining the investigation logic that characterized the board and the inquiry, with an approach that went beyond human error and individual blame and was aimed at producing recommendations for greater safety.

Many accident investigations do not go far enough. They identify the technical cause of the accident, and then connect it to a variant of "operator error" – the line worker who forgot to insert the bolt, the engineer who miscalculated the stress, or the manager who made the wrong decision. But this is seldom the entire issue. When the determinations of the causal chain are limited to the technical flaw and individual failure, typically the actions taken to prevent a similar event in the future are also limited: fix the technical problem and replace or retrain the individual responsible. Putting these corrections in place leads to another mistake – the belief that the problem is solved. The Board did not want to make these errors. (CAIB 2003, 97)

Too often, accident investigations blame a failure only on the last step in a complex process, when a more comprehensive understanding of that process could reveal that earlier steps might be equally or even more culpable. In this Board's opinion, unless the technical, organizational, and cultural recommendations made in this report are implemented, little will have been accomplished to lessen the chance that another accident will follow ... The loss of *Columbia* and her crew represents a turning point, calling for a renewed public policy debate and commitment regarding human space exploration. One of our goals has been to set forth the terms for this debate. (CAIB 2003, 6)

According to the CAIB, NASA's organizational culture and structure had as much to do with the origin of the accident as the actual detachment of the insulating foam. The central element of the investigation on the causal model of the event involved the entire organization. For the CAIB, the loss of *Columbia* and its crew represented a turning point, requiring a renewed political debate regarding space exploration. One of the board's objectives was to establish the terms of this debate, providing elements for a "double-loop" form of learning.

Another positive example is the investigation into an accident that took place in March 1989 in Dreyden, Ontario. This plane crash, at first glance, had all the characteristics of a simple accident caused by pilot error. A Fokker airliner, after having accumulated a significant delay at departure due to a series of problems, had taken off in adverse weather conditions, without carrying out the de-icing procedure necessary to remove ice and snow from the wings. Due to this accumulation of ice, it crashed a kilometer after take-off. A commission was set up chaired by Supreme Court Judge Virgil P. Moshansky who, from the very start, rejected simplistic explanations that attributed any blame to the pilot (as had been the case up to then for 80 percent of aircraft accidents) and wanted to supplement the commission with a multidisciplinary team composed of pilots, human factor experts, and engineers, to identify the causes of the accident. Judge Moshansky gave a wide-ranging interpretation to his mandate:

The mandate of this Commission was to investigate a specific air crash and to make recommendations in the interests of aviation safety. In carrying out this mandate, it was necessary to conduct a critical analysis of the aircraft crew, of Air Ontario Inc., of Transport Canada, and of the environment in which these elements interacted ... I have adopted a system-analysis approach, with emphasis on an examination of human performance. (Moshansky 1992, xxv)

After twenty months of work, the accident was interpreted in terms very different from the original hypotheses: organizational criticalities were identified at every level, together with latent factors that had made it possible. Moshansky, considering the concrete possibility of identifying and correcting these latent factors before they became significant, describes the accident as a failure of the air transport system in its entirety, at a systemic level (1992, 5–6).

Multiple deficiencies were identified, in government regulation, airline management, personnel management, education and training, communication methods, and more. The report showed that competitive pressures, permitted by commercial deregulation, had led to lower safety standards and that many equivocal practices and questionable procedures in the industry had placed the pilot in a very difficult operational situation. The plane should not have been scheduled to refuel at an airport that did not have adequate equipment, and neither training nor manuals had sufficiently warned the pilot of the dangers of ice on the Fokker F-28's wings. Incorrect decisions and behavior had therefore depended on organizational failures: individuals had inherited these defects from the system. Moshansky concluded the report by stating that, while the pilot had certainly made a wrong decision, this was in the context of an integrated air transport system which, had it worked properly, could have prevented the decision to take-off (Moshansky 1992, 1102). A total of 191 recommendations were then formulated to improve air traffic safety, starting with de-icing procedures. Moshansky's analysis represents the first institutional application of a systemic and organizational approach to the investigation of air accidents.

The investigation of the accident was innovative because it did not limit itself to analyzing only the final phases of the event and the role of the frontline operator. It also adopted a systemic and organizational approach, with improvement as an objective, and involved experts from different disciplines. It stands as an example of an inquiry that went beyond the search for a scapegoat (single-loop) to pursue organizational learning outcomes aimed at modifying the factors that contributed to the accident at all levels (double-loop). It was, in other words, a completely different thing from the inquiry into the *Costa Concordia* accident.

Positive examples like those illustrated above, as well as the negative ones described previously, highlight the need to find institutional design solutions that form an alternative to criminal law alone and/or processes of individual blaming in order to address complex organizational and social problems. Otherwise, we are left with the creation of scapegoats and organizational inertia.

6.3 Reckonings: On the Limits of Criminal Law (Alone) in Dealing with Wrongdoing in Organizations

The events and cases analyzed so far, some of them dramatic, certainly require a response – a response that in some cases should be legal. There is certainly no intention here to support open decriminalization or dispensing with criminal law. Analysis of the situational, organizational, and systemic elements of an event does not in itself, justify, nor absolve, the figures involved. At the same time, however, the need emerges for what Mary Fulbrook (2018), with reference to Nazi crimes, calls "reckonings", in order to come to terms with what happened, while looking to the future, and to learn from these events so that they can never happen again. A strategy is required, therefore, that goes both beyond the scapegoat and beyond a generalized attribution of guilt.

The previous chapters highlighted the limits of a merely punitive response to the problem of organizational failures, for two types of reason: on the one hand, this response is sometimes *simplistic* and tends to reduce complex organizational problems that have developed over time into individual errors; and, on the other, it hinders organizational and institutional *learning processes*.

With regard to the former reason, and in relation to the matter of criminality, it should be emphasized that systemic considerations and organizational learning do not take place in a trial because there is a lack of tools to do so and the magistrate's work has a different purpose.[2] Sometimes, especially if it is necessary to ascertain complex facts that involve multiple organizations, sophisticated technologies and multifaceted professional systems, and over long periods of time, it becomes very difficult for the magistrate to find the necessary cohesion to establish the concept of guilt. The search for a culprit can then be reduced to identifying an available scapegoat, as the simplest solution.

For example in a company, the absence of clear standards in relation to what constitutes a danger influences management decisions, while creating pressure for those who are further down in the hierarchy.

---

[2] With reference to the *Costa Concordia* case, the president of the panel of judges himself stated: "I am not interested in the history of previous navigation, nor am I interested in the future of navigation [...] it is certainly not the business of this trial" (Court of Grosseto, 2014h, part II, 46–47).

Without clear sharing of what a significant risk is, the burden of proof to determine what constitutes a danger falls on the professionals who are most directly in contact with the front line. The latter, however, may not have the authority by themselves to declare an emergency when necessary. It becomes difficult, therefore, for the legal system to assign responsibility when organizations give rise to harmful results.

The merely punitive response demonstrates numerous limitations, from the point of view of analysis and diagnosis, and of intervention. Where analysis-diagnosis is concerned, criminal law frequently, though not always, focuses on the "short history" and the paradigm of the individual actor. In this way, the organizational context and the field of action within which the actions of the individual actor take shape remain in the background, as do the procedural and longitudinal dimensions that foster this type of action and behavior. Instead, as already stated, many forms of behavior can be adequately understood and explained only within the context in which they were shaped and on the basis of their long history. It is therefore essential to analyze the toxic role of bad systems and bad situations in inducing normal people to behave pathologically within organizations.[3] Furthermore, from the point of view of intervention, the punitive response is late and limited. It arrives when events have already occurred and at most affects the visible part of the iceberg – visible organizational action and behavior, the cases discovered and actually prosecuted, leaving unchanged the numerous similar actions and forms of behavior that are not discovered.[4]

To sum up, the risk is that the criminal law perspective is based on a vision that is too narrow and inadequate to tackle certain organizational problems, thus contributing to unintentionally producing scapegoats. According to Forti, the concept of the scapegoat is essential in terms of understanding what connects justice, criminal justice in particular, with broader and deeper social, psychological, and anthropological dynamics. Blaming other subjects for negative events exempts us from blame, blaming a person rather than the system leaves the system unchanged and makes it possible for similar events to recur. "The

---

[3] On this point, see Zimbardo (2007), who says that systems provide the institutional support, authority, and resources that allow people to operate in situations.

[4] In his book *The Limits of Criminal Sanction* (1968), Herbert Packer states that sanctions are an expensive way of regulating human behavior.

price of such a punitive and sanctioning distortion", writes Forti, "is the loss of that transformative force that is most effective for our societies, which could and should emanate from the right treatment for the victims, which is ultimately also the best treatment for the norms themselves" (2018, 140).

Criminal prosecutions, argues Garland (1990), do not allow the causes of a crime to be dealt with objectively, favoring instead an uncritical attitude and concentrating energies on identifying a scapegoat rather than toward the reconstruction of social conditions. The scapegoat, a typical target of moral panic, as the scholar states, is not chosen by chance. Rather, we tend to select those subjects whose wrongdoing frightens spectators, precisely because it refers to personal fears and unconscious desires (Garland 2008, 15). For this reason, we speak of a "cultural" scapegoat.

With regard to the second aspect relating to the consequences of a merely punitive response, it emerged in the study that this hinders organizational and institutional learning processes. With the intervention of the judicial investigation by itself, in fact, the system does not improve: sometimes "composition effects" are also generated (Boudon 1992), which further hinder organizational learning and system improvement.

As Turner and Pidgeon (1997) wrote, the impact of the legal system has the power to stifle any attempt at learning from errors, as it is impossible to completely isolate an otherwise well-functioning, intra-organizational learning system from the formidable and symbolic process of lawsuits that every disaster gives rise to. For example, in the course of a judicial investigation, improvements to an organization could be omitted since they might demonstrate that the organization could have managed to prevent the incident. Therefore, improvements constitute an implicit admission of foregoing negligence. After a conviction leading to the removal of individuals, management interested in maintaining the status quo could well argue that, with the managers removed from their posts, there is no reason to change the structure of the system. There is a difference between being motivated by external conditions to seek alternatives and being forced by external subjects or circumstances to adopt specific changes. Pursuing an approach based on the amoral calculator, bad apple or bad employee is a scapegoating strategy that distracts from more important processes and problems that, if left unchanged, increase the likelihood of negative events occurring again (Geis 1967; Lee and Ermann 1999; Perrow 1999).

There therefore emerges the need to find other institutional answers to these problems, both in terms of their analysis and their solution. Resorting to criminal prosecution to understand how things went certainly demonstrates a limit, but also the need of awareness for action – an awareness that could, indeed should, be developed by other agents and institutional contexts. It is therefore necessary to think of institutional experimentation in order to identify places, practices, and mechanisms aimed at promoting organizational and institutional learning. This learning must be based on the analysis of the sources of failure, defining inferences regarding causes and effects in order to find and implement remedial measures. These are learning logics that are not always followed, as the cases dealt with in this book demonstrate.

6.4 Civic Epistemology: Imperfect Learning and Problems of Change

One of the main difficulties hindering organizational change is the tendency to rush forward to a solution without first of all worrying about the problem (Crozier 1995). There are many limits to organizational and collective learning from failures. Above all, the real world provides *ambiguous feedback* about the possible causes of an organizational failure.

Second, organizational learning takes place in *highly politicized environments* in which efforts to determine the causes of failures are not designed to promote learning, but rather to protect the interests of organizational leadership. Within organizations, interpretations of the causes of failures are politicized: the power and interests of the leadership frequently direct internal investigations to locate these causes in the errors of operators.

Third, the *difficulties in reporting* events, based on data that are often inaccurate and incomplete, and the *secrecy* due to compartmentalization and disincentives to share information, render the learning process very complex and problematic.

By pondering the problem of learning by human societies and the ways in which it occurs, Sheila Jasanoff introduced the concept of "civic epistemology", describing the way in which a nation produces public knowledge about a certain event, such as a disaster, a terrorist attack, or some other phenomenon that generates significant consequences (Jasanoff 2005a). Civic epistemology is defined as how "Public ways of knowing ... are constituted, displayed, and reaffirmed within the decision-making processes of states, including those aimed at the management of risk and prevention of harm" (Jasanoff 2005b, 211).

Jasanoff studied the reaction to three disasters by three quite different nations: India with the 1984 Bhopal chemical disaster, Great Britain with "mad cow disease" (Bovine Spongiform Encephalopathy – BSE) in 1986, and the United States with the 9/11 terrorist attack in 2001. Extending the analytical tool developed in her previous book (2005a), Jasanoff compares the forms of investigation into the disasters, the styles of public investigation, the issue of public responsibility, the strategies used to achieve objectivity in the analysis, and the bases of the expertise used. All these elements constitute civic epistemology, a form, it might be said, of the micropolitics of guilt. India's response to Bhopal was marked by public distrust of the government and social protests. Although now officially closed, the case continues to generate protest, with the participation of people from the successive generation. Britain's response to mad cow disease was primarily judicial in nature, based on the assumption of the reliability of the civil servants involved. The civic epistemology of the United States in the wake of 9/11 was characterized by the establishment of a bipartisan commission, with analytical tools and techniques based on formal analytical methods, avoiding the participation of ordinary citizens and expert civil servants.

Indian citizens tried to blame Union Carbide and the Indian government, but their protests, though persistent over time, proved irrelevant. Both the British and the Americans shied away from adopting a blaming approach of the individual kind, particularly in relation to their political leaders in Downing Street and the White House. The British dissolved the offending government agency and distributed its functions. The Americans also resorted to organizational restructuring, but, in contrast, opted for centralization rather than decentralization.

An important point that emerges from these comparisons is that the particular nature of the civic epistemologies of nations lies, in part, in the boundary between moral and factual causes of events or, in other words, between responsibility and guilt. The important lesson is to understand how the different organizations and the states within which they operate are shaped by a specific civic epistemology – for example, in the case of the Covid-19 pandemic caused by the new coronavirus designated as SARS-CoV-2. Sheila Jasanoff has provided an important metaframework to be able to do this.

In *Upheaval* (2019), Jared Diamond explains how some nations successfully recover from situations of severe crisis by adopting selective change mechanisms. By comparing seven nations, Diamond draws some lessons for change, including: "Accept responsibility, avoid victimization, self-pity and blaming others" (426). Accepting, rather than denying, responsibility for what happened, avoiding focusing only on yourself as victim, without recognizing the need for change, are also some of the cornerstones for successful learning in organizations.

At the University of Michigan graduation ceremony at Ann Arbor in 1988, Joseph Brodsky, winner of the 1987 Nobel Prize for Literature, urged people to keep their "blame-thirsty" index finger in check: "Of all the parts of your body, be most vigilant over your index finger, for it is blame-thirsty … The moment that you place blame somewhere, you undermine your resolve to change anything; it could be argued even that that blame-thirsty finger oscillates as wildly as it does because the resolve was never great enough in the first place".

6.4.1 Some Proactive Indications

At this point, it might be useful to introduce and briefly discuss some proactive matters touching on how to avoid the conditions that favor the genesis of scapegoats.

(1) *Recognize trade-offs, make them explicit and manage them.* If trade-offs remain dormant, they escape organizational control. Organizations frequently develop conflicting systems of norms – between safety rules and those concerning the pursuit of objectives, for example. This creates uncertainty in people's behavior because they are forced to decide whether to follow one system of rules or another, in both cases violating one of the two systems. In these situations, compliance becomes quite difficult. The dilemmas need to be made explicit so that they can be managed and regulated. As Monahan and Quinn claim, "when organizational leaders set financial goals for subunits and set their workers loose to pursue those goals, they encourage norm-violating behavior while simultaneously buffering themselves from accountability for the actions of lower-level participants" (2006, 365). When

a situation of decoupling is created in the organization (Meyer and Rowan 1977) – in other words, separation between organizational structures and requests for compliance, on the one hand, and the action and pursuit of organizational objectives, on the other – the doors are opened for deviance in the organization.

(2) *Monitor the processes of normalization of deviance and drift to danger.* It is important that every organization monitors behavior and work practices that tend to be located at the boundaries of the rules in use, and at the boundaries of the formal organization. Such behavior, not yet illegal or violations, can undermine the conditions of safety and legality in the organization – this can also happen through processes of *escalation of commitment.* In this way, deviance, which has become normal, progressively extends the boundaries of what is acceptable and accepted within a work group, or management, or the entire organization. A possible countermeasure to this process consists of relying on external parties who, not being co-opted by other members of the system, can introduce signals that are different from the other team members, challenging established concepts within the organization (Vaughan 2016, 417).

(3) *Recognize and eliminate toxic culture.* Toxic culture (Van Rooij and Fine 2018, 43) does not originate from a design, with each action planned, by specific agents. While CEOs and senior executives certainly play an important role in the processes in which it develops, they do not plan and control them completely. They instigate some (e.g., goal setting, or blame avoidance), while simply letting others develop with no particular direction. When wrongdoing is endemic in a culture, it is not the fault of a single leader, but part of the broader organization. To "detox" an organizational culture, therefore, it is not enough to punish those who are found guilty of certain actions by replacing them with other people. The latter would risk being subject to the same constraints and incentives and therefore to conform to the same behavior as those that went before them, while possibly being a little more careful. A "detox" operation consistent with the double-loop change first implies a broad and open discussion about what happened and what went wrong, then a radical change of mechanisms, work practices, incentives, internal rules, and other aspects that established the context for wrongdoing. Simply removing the bad apples is not enough.

(4) *Encourage paths of learning from failure that are not based on blame.* If, every time an organizational failure occurs the focus is on identifying a culprit, political processes tend to promote the avoidance of blame rather than critical sense and honesty (Turner and Pidgeon 1997). If an organization really intends to consider and solve problems, if it really wants to redefine the policies that have not worked, then its members, at all levels, must be able to learn from mistakes in a non-punitive way and to promote shared investigations regarding what went wrong. The solution is not a "blame free" organization, but an organization which distinguishes between guilty errors and tolerable errors, so that this latter category is as broad as possible. This is because it is impossible to isolate an organization's learning system from the blaming process that follows any organizational failure, or from the lawsuits generated by accidents and disasters. Blaming processes prevent any attempt at learning.

References

Abbot, A. (2001), *Time Matters: On Theory and Method*, Chicago: Chicago University Press.

Abdushkour, H., Turan, O., Boulougouris, E., and Kurt, R.E. (2018), "Comparative Review of Collision Avoidance System in Maritime and Aviation", *The 3rd International Symposium on Naval Architecture and Maritime*, February 8, pp. 1–13.

Adut, A. (2005), "A theory of scandal: Victorians, homosexuality, and the fall of Oscar Wilde", *American Journal of Sociology*, 111 (1), pp. 213–248.

Alexander, D.A. (2005), "An interpretation of disaster in terms of changes in culture, society and international relations". In R.W. Perry and E.L. Quarantelli, eds., *What is a Disaster: New Answers to Old Questions* (pp. 25–38), Philadelphia: Xlibris.

Alexander, J.C. (1988), "Culture and political crisis: 'Watergate' and Durkheimian sociology". In J.C. Alexander, ed., *Durkheimian Sociology: Cultural Studies* (pp. 187–224), Cambridge: Cambridge University Press.

Allport, G. (1954 [1979]), *The Nature of Prejudice*, New York: Doubleday Anchor.

Altheide, D. and Snow R.P. (1979), *Media Logic*, Beverly Hills: Sage Publications.

Anderson, C.A., Lepper, M.R., and Ross, L. (1980), "Perseverance of social theories: The role of explanation in the persistence of discredited information", *Journal of Personality and Social Psychology*, 39 (6), pp. 1037–1049.

Arendt, H. (1964), *Eichmann in Jerusalem: A Report on the Banality of Evil*, New York: The Viking Press.

Argyris, C. (2004), *Reasons and Rationalizations: The Limits to Organizational Knowledge*, Oxford: Oxford University Press.

Argyris, C. (1993), *Knowledge of Action: A Guide to Overcoming Barriers to Organizational Change*, San Francisco: Jossey-Bass Inc.

Argyris, C. and Schön, D. (1996), *Organizational Learning II: Theory, Method, and Practice*, London: Addison-Wesley Publishing Company.

Arthaud-Day, M.L., Certo, S.T., Dalton, C.M., and Dalton, D.R. (2006), "A changing of the guard: Executive and director turnover following corporate financial restatements", *Academy of Management Journal*, 49 (6), pp. 1119–1136.

Asch, S.E. (1952), *Social Psychology*, New Jersey: Prentice Hall Inc.

Asch, S.E. (1946), "Forming impressions of personality", *Journal of Abnormal and Social Psychology*, 41 (3), pp. 1230–1240.

Ashforth, B.E. and Humphrey, R.H. (1997), "The ubiquity and potency of labeling in organizations", *Organization Science*, 8 (1), pp. 43–58.

Ashforth, B.E. and Humphrey, R.H. (1995), "Labeling processes in the organization: Constructing the individual", *Research in Organizational Behavior*, 17, pp. 413–461.

Baicker, K., Wright, B.J., and Olson, N.A. (2015), "Reevaluating reports of defensive medicine", *Journal of Health Politics, Policy and Law*, 40 (6), pp. 1157–1177.

Bailey, J.J. (1997), "Individual scapetribing and responsibility ascriptions", *Journal of Business Ethics*, 16 (1), pp. 47–53.

Bailey, J.J. and Alexander, R.A. (1993), "Organizational social cues, framing, and justice: Effects on management's ethical decisions", *The International Journal of Organizational Analysis*, 1 (2), pp. 133–160.

Baldwin, L.M., Hart, L.G., Lloyd, M., Fordyce, M., and Rosenblatt, R.A. (1995), "Defensive medicine and obstetrics", *Journal of the American Medical Association*, 274 (20), pp. 1606–1610.

Balfour, D.L., Adams, G.B., and Nickels, A.E. (2020), *Unmasking Administrative Evil*, New York: Routledge.

Bandura, A. (2016), *Moral Disengagement: How People Do Harm and Live with Themselves*, New York: Macmillan.

Barnett, M.L. and King, A.A. (2008), "Good fences make good neighbors: A longitudinal analysis of an industry self-regulatory institution", *Academy of Management Journal*, 51 (6), pp.1150–1170.

Baron, J. and Hershey, J.C. (1988), "Outcome bias in decision evaluation", *Journal of Personality and Social Psychology*, 54 (4), pp. 569–579.

Bartollas, C., Miller, S.J., and Dinitz, S. (1974), "Becoming a scapegoat: Study of a deviant career", *Sociological Symposium*, 11, pp. 84–97.

Battisti, F.M. (1982), *La sociologia dello scandalo*, Bari: Laterza.

Baucus, M.S. and Near, J.P. (1991), "Can illegal corporate behavior be predicted? An event history analysis", *Academy of Management Journal*, 34 (1), pp. 9–36.

Bazerman, M.H. and Watkins, M. (2004), *Predictable Surprises*, Boston: Harvard Business School.

Beale, S.S. (2006), "The new media's influence on Criminal Justice Policy: How market-driven news promotes punitiveness", *William and Mary Law Review*, 48 (2), pp. 397–481.

Beck, U. (1986), *Risikogesellschaft. Auf dem Weg in eine andere Moderne*, Frankfurt am Main: Suhrkamp Verlag (Eng. transl. *Risk Society: Towards a New Modernity*, London: SAGE Publications Ltd, 1992).

Becker, H.S. (1963), *Outsiders: Studies in the Sociology of Deviance*, New York: The Free Press.

Benoit, W.L. (2015), *Accounts, Excuses, and Apologies: Image Repair Theory and Research*, Albany: SUNY Press (2nd ed.).

Berger, J. and Zelditch, M. (1968), "Reviewed Work(s), 'Sociological theory and modern society,' by T. Parsons", *American Sociological Review*, 33 (3), pp. 446–450.

Berger, P.L. and Luckmann, T. (1966), *The Social Construction of Reality: A Treatise in the Sociology of Knowledge*, New York: Doubleday.

Bettauer, H. (1922 [1929]), *The City without Jews: A Novel of our Time*, Jacksonville, Florida: Bloch Publishing Company.

Bishop, T.F., Federman, A.D., and Keyhani, S. (2010), "Physician's views on defensive medicine: A national survey", *Archives for Internal Medicine*, 170 (12), pp. 1081–1083.

Blaney, J.R., Benoit, W.L., and Brazeal, L.M. (2002), "Blowout!: Firestone's image restoration campaign", *Public Relations Review*, 28 (4), pp. 379–392.

Bloch, M. (1949 [1992]), *The Historian's Craft*, Manchester: Manchester University Press.

Bloxham, D. (2020), *History and Morality*, Oxford: Oxford University Press.

Boeker, W. (1992), "Power and managerial exit: Scapegoating at the top", *Administrative Science Quarterly*, 27 (3), pp. 538–547.

Boin, A., McConnell, A., and 't Hart, P., eds. (2008), *Governing after Crises: The Politics of Investigation Accountability and Learning*, Cambridge: Cambridge University Press.

Boin, A., 't Hart, P., McConnell, A., and Preston, T. (2010), "Leadership style, crisis response and blame management: The case of Hurricane Katrina", *Public Administration*, 88 (3), pp. 706–723.

Boin, A., 't Hart, P., Stern, E., and Sundelius, B., eds. (2017), *The Politics of Crisis Management: Public Leadership under Pressure*, Cambridge: Cambridge University Press.

Bolino, M., Kacmar, M., Turnley, W., and Gilstrap, J.B. (2008), "A multilevel review of impression management motives and behaviors", *Journal of Management*, 34 (6), pp. 1080–1109.

Bonazzi, G. (1983a), *Colpa e potere: Sull'uso politico del capro espiatorio*, Bologna: il Mulino.

Bonazzi, G. (1983b), "Scapegoating in complex organizations: The results of a comparative study of symbolic blame-giving in Italian and French public administration", *Organization Studies*, 4 (1), pp. 1–18.

Boudon, R., ed. (1992), *Traité de Sociologie*, Paris: Presses Universitaires de France.

Bovens, M. and 't Hart, P. (1996), *Understanding Policy Fiascos*, New Jersey: Transaction Publishers.

Bovens, M., 't Hart, P., Dekker, S., and Verheuvel, G. (1999), "The politics of blame avoidance. Defensive tactics in a Dutch crime-fighting fiasco". In K.A. Helmut, ed., *When Things Go Wrong: Organizational Failures and Breakdowns* (pp. 123–142), Thousand Oaks, CA: SAGE Publications.

Bower, J.A. (2007), "Thereby become a monster: Complex organizations and the torture at Abu Ghraib", Dissertation, https://scholarworks .wmich.edu/cgi/viewcontent.cgi?article=1836&context=dissertations.

Boxenbaum, E. and Jonsson, S. (2008), "Isomorphism, diffusion and decoupling". In R. Greenwood, C. Oliver, K. Sahlin, and R. Suddaby, eds., *The SAGE Handbook of Organizational Institutionalism* (pp. 78–98), Thousand Oaks, CA: SAGE Publications.

Braithwaite, J. and Fisse, M. (1987), "Self-regulation and the control of corporate crime". In C.D. Shearing and P.C. Stenning, eds., *Private Policing* (pp. 194–220), Beverly Hills, CA: Sage.

Brambilla, M., Carraro, L., Castelli, L., and Sacchi, S. (2019), "Changing impressions: Moral character dominates impression updating", *Journal of Experimental Social Psychology*, 82, pp. 64–73.

Brändström, A. (2016), "Accountability and blame management. Strategies and survival of political office-holders", Doctoral thesis, Swedish Defence University, Department of Security, Strategy and Leadership (ISSL), CRISMART (National Center for Crisis Management Research and Training).

Brändström, A. and Kuipers, S. (2003), "From 'normal incidents' to political crisis: Understanding the selective politicization of policy failures", *Government and Opposition*, 38 (3), pp. 279–305.

Bremmer, J. (1983), "Scapegoat rituals in ancient Greece", *Harvard Studies in Classical Philology*, 87, pp. 299–320.

Brereton, P. (2020), *Inspector-General of the Australian Defence Force Afghanistan Inquiry Report*, IGADAF, www.defence.gov.au/about/ reviews-inquiries/afghanistan-inquiry.

Brinson, S.L. and Benoit, W.L. (1999), "The tarnished star: Restoring Texaco's damaged public image", *Management Communication Quarterly*, 12 (4), pp. 483–510.

Bromley, P. and Powell, W.W. (2012), "From smoke and mirrors to walking the talk: Decoupling in the contemporary world", *The Academy of Management Annals*, 6 (1), pp. 483–530.

Brown, J. (1986), *Social Psychology*, New York: Free Press (2nd ed.).

Browning, C.R. (1992), *Ordinary Men: Reserve Police Battalion 101 and the Final Solution in Poland*, New York: Harper Collins Publishers, Inc.

Bucher, R. (1957), "Blame and hostility in disaster", *The American Journal of Sociology*, 62 (5), pp. 467–475.

Bundy, J. and Pfarrer, M.D. (2015), "A burden of responsibility: The role of social approval at the onset of a crisis", *Academy of Management Review*, 40 (3), pp. 345–369.

Bundy, J., Pfarrer, M.D., Short, C.E., and Coombs, W.T. (2017), "Crises and crisis management: Integration, interpretation, and research development", *Journal of Management*, 43 (6), pp. 1661–1692.

Burke, K. (1969), *A Grammar of Motives*, Berkeley: University of California Press.

Burke, K. (1941), *The Philosophy of Literary Form: Studies in Symbolic Action*, Baton Rouge: Louisiana State University Press.

Burkert, W. (1979), *Structure and History in Greek Mythology and Ritual*, Los Angeles-London: University of California Press.

Butler, J.V., Serra, D., and Spagnolo, G. (2020), "Motivating whistleblowers", *Management Science*, 66 (2), pp. 605–621.

Calabresi, G. (1994), "Speech. Scapegoats", *Quinnipiac Law Review*, 14 (1), pp. 83–90.

Calamandrei, P. (1939), "Il giudice e lo storico", *Rivista di Diritto Processuale Civile*, Volume XVI – Parte 1, pp. 105–128.

Campbell, C. (2013), *Scapegoat: A History of Blaming Other People*, New York: Overlook Duckworth.

Canosa, R. (1985), *Tempo di peste: Magistrati ed untori nel 1630 a Milano*, Milano: Sapere Edizioni.

Carberry, E.J. and King, B.G. (2012), "Defensive practice adoption in the face of organizational stigma: Impression management and the diffusion of stock option expensing", *Journal of Management Studies*, 49 (7), pp. 1137–1167.

Carra, E. (1999), *Il caso Citaristi*, Palermo: Sellerio.

Casanova, R. (2014), "Bouc émissaire", *Les Cahiers Dynamiques*, 60 (2), pp. 37–43.

Catino, M. (2011), "Why doctors practice defensive medicine? The side-effects of medical litigation", *Safety Science Monitor*, 15 (1), pp. 1–12.

Catino, M. (2010a), "The Linate disaster: A multilevel model of accident analysis". In P. Alvintzi and H. Eder, eds., *Crisis Management* (pp. 187–210), Hauppauge, New York: Nova Science Publishers, Inc.

Catino, M. (2010b), "Gatekeepers miopi? Aspetti organizzativi nel fallimento dei controlli", *Stato e Mercato*, 2, pp. 219–253.

Catino, M. (2009a), *Miopia organizzativa: Problemi di razionalità e previsione nelle organizzazioni*, Bologna: il Mulino.

Catino, M. (2009b), "Blame culture and defensive medicine", *Cognition, Technology and Work*, 11(4), pp. 245–253.

Catino, M. (2008), "A review of literature: Individual blame vs. organizational function logics in accident analysis", *Journal of Contingencies and Crisis Management*, 16 (1), pp. 53–62.

Catino, M. (2006a), *Da Chernobyl a Linate: Incidenti tecnologici o errori organizzativi?*, Milano: Bruno Mondadori (2nd ed.).

Catino, M. (2006b), "Logiche dell'indagine: Oltre la cultura della colpa", *Rassegna Italiana di Sociologia*, 1, pp. 7–36.

Catino, M. (2005), "Incidenti tecnologici nel trasporto ferroviario", *Ergonomia*, N. 1, pp. 36–51.

Catino, M. (2003), "4 minuti e 38 secondi. Il disastro di Linate come incidente organizzativo", *Studi Organizzativi*, 3, pp. 129–157.

Catino, M., Patriotta, G. (2013), "Learning from errors: Cognition, emotions and safety culture in the Italian air force", *Organization Studies*, 34 (4), pp. 437–467.

Catino, M., Pesenti Campagnoni, M., and Locatelli, C. (2011), "La medicina difensiva: Una ricerca sul pronto soccorso in Italia", *Pratica Medica & Aspetti Legali*, 5 (1), pp. 35–43.

Cerulo, K.A. (2006), *Never Saw It Coming: Cultural Challenges to Envisioning the Worst*, Chicago: The Chicago University Press.

Cesarani, D. (2004), *Eichmann: His life and Crimes*, London: Heinemann.

Chancellor, L. (2019), "Public contempt and compassion: Media biases and their effects on Juror impartiality and wrongful convictions", *Manitoba Law Journal*, 42 (3), pp. 427–444.

Chapman, D. (1968), *Sociology and the Stereotype of the Criminal*, London: Tavistock Press.

Charles, S., Wilbert, J.R., and Kennedy, E.C. (1984), "Physicians' self-reports of reactions to malpractice litigation", *American Journal of Psychiatry*, 141 (4), pp. 563–565.

Christie, N. (1986), "Suitable enemies". In H. Bianchi and R. Van Swaaningen, eds., *Abolitionism: Towards a Non-Repressive Approach to Crime* (pp. 42–54), Amsterdam: Free University Press.

Clarke, M. (1987), "Prosecutorial and administrative strategy to control business crimes". In C.D. Shearing and P.C. Stenning, eds., *Private Policing* (pp. 247–265), Beverly Hills, CA: Sage.

Clemente, M., Durand, R., and Porac, J. (2016), "Organizational wrongdoing and media bias". In D. Palmer, R. Greenwood, and K. Smith-Crowe, eds., *Organizational Wrongdoing: Key Perspectives and New Directions* (pp. 435–473), Cambridge: Cambridge University Press.

Clinard, M.B. and Yeager, P.C. (1980), *Corporate Crime*, New York: Free Press.

Clini, P. (1967), *Il processo degli untori nella peste del 1630*, Milano: Giordano Editore.

Coen, F. (1994), *Dreyfus*, Milano: Mondadori.

Coffee, J.C. Jr. (1989), "Corporate crime and punishment: A non-Chicago view of the economics of criminal sanctions", *American Criminal Law Review*, 17 (4), pp. 419–476.

Coffee, J.C. Jr. (1981), "'No soul to damn: No body to kick': An unscandalized inquiry into the problem of corporate punishment", *Michigan Law Review*, 79 (3), pp. 386–459.

Coleman, J.S. (1990), *Foundations of Social Theory*, Cambridge, MA: Harvard University Press.

Coleman, J.S. (1982), *The Asymmetric Society*, Syracuse, New York: Syracuse University Press.

Coleman, J.S. (1974), *Power and the Structure of Society*, New York: Norton & Company, Inc.

Coleman, J.W. (1987), "Toward an integrated theory of white-collar crime", *American Journal of Sociology*, 93 (2), pp. 406–439.

Coletti, V. (2020), *Genova 2011: Analisi di un processo*, Genova: De Ferrari.

Collins, D., Reitenga, A.L., and Sanchez, J.M. (2008), "The impact of accounting restatements on CFO turnover and bonus compensation: Does securities litigation matter?", *Advances in Accounting*, 24 (2), pp. 162–171.

Columbia Accident Investigation Board (CAIB)(2003), *Report, Volume One*, Washington (DC), National Aeronautics and Space Administration and the Government Printing Office.

Connelly, B.L., Trevis Certo, S., Duane Ireland, R., and Reutzel, C.R. (2011), "Signaling theory: A review and assessment", *Journal of Management*, 37 (1), pp. 39–67.

Coombs, W.T. (2007), "Protecting organization reputations during a crisis: The development and application of situational crisis communication theory", *Corporate Reputation Review*, 10 (3), pp. 163–176.

Coombs, W.T. and Holladay, S.J. (2006), "Halo or reputational capital: Reputation and crisis management", *Journal of Communication Management*, 10 (2), pp. 123–137.

Coombs, W.T. and Holladay, S.J. (2002), "Helping crisis managers protect reputational assets: Initial tests of the situational crisis communication theory", *Management Communication Quarterly*, 16 (2), pp. 165–186.

Cordero, F. (2007), "Introduzione". In A. Manzoni, *Storia della colonna infame* (pp. 5–30), Milano: Bur.

Cordero, F. (1985), *La fabbrica della peste*, Roma-Bari: Laterza.

Cornelissen, J.P. and Werner, M.D. (2014), "Putting framing in perspective: A review of framing and frame analysis across the management and organizational literature", *Academy of Management Annals*, 8 (1), pp. 181–235.

Crant, J.M. and Bateman, T.S. (1993), "Assignment of credit and blame for performance outcomes", *Academy of Management Journal*, 36 (1), pp. 7–27.

Crelinsten, R.D. (2003) "The world of torture: A constructed reality", *Theoretical Criminology*, 7 (3), pp. 293–318.

Croce, B. (1916), "Il Manzoni storiografo". In B. Croce (1969), *Alessandro Manzoni: Saggi e discussioni* (pp. 33–52), Bari: Laterza.

Crocker, K.M. (2021), "A scapegoat theory of bivens", *William & Mary Law School Scholarship Repository*, 96 (5), pp. 1943–1969.

Crocker, J., Voelkl, K., Testa, M., and Major, B. (1991), "Social stigma: The affective consequences of attributional ambiguity", *Journal of Personality and Social Psychology*, 60 (2), pp. 218–228.

Crozier, M. (1995), *La crise de l'intelligence: Essai sur l'impuissance des élites à se réformer*, Paris: InterEditions.

Crozier, M. and Friedberg, E. (1977 [1980]), *Actors and Systems : The Politics of Collective Action*, Chicago: The University of Chicago Press.

Cyert, R.M. and March, J.G. (1963), *A Behavioral Theory of the Firm*, Upper Saddle River, NJ: Prentice-Hall.

D'Alberti, M. (2020), *Corruzione*, Rome: Treccani.

De Tocqueville, A. (1848–1849 [2000]), *Souvenirs*, Paris: Gallimard, Folio Histoire.

Danniau, S. and Meynckens-Fourez, M. (2015), "Bouc émissaire dans les institutions: Pistes pour sortir de ce positionnement", *Thérapie Familiale*, 36 (4), pp. 409–422.

Daudigeos, T., Pasquier, V., and Valiorgue, B. (2014), "Bouc-émissaires, lynchages médiatiques et contestation des pratiques irresponsables des firmes multinationals", *Revue de l'Organisation Responsable*, 9 (2), pp. 46–59.

Debord, G. (1970), *The Society of the Spectacle*, London: Black and Red.

Dekker, S. (2007), *Just Culture: Balancing Safety and Accountability*, Aldershot: Ashgate.

Delumeau, J. (2011), *La peur en occident*, Paris: Librairie Arthème Fayard.

Denzin, N.K. (1978), *The Research Act*, New York: McGraw-Hill.

Dershowitz, A.M. (1996), *Reasonable Doubts: The Criminal Justice System and the O.J. Simpson Case*, New York: Simon & Schuster.

Desai, H., Hogan, C.E., and Wilkins, M.S. (2006), "The reputational penalty for aggressive accounting: Earnings restatements and management turnover", *Accounting Review*, 81 (1), pp. 83–112.

Desmond, J. and Kavanagh, D. (2003), "Organization as containment of acquisitive mimetic rivalry: The contribution of René Girard", *Culture & Organization*, 9 (4), pp. 239–251.

Devers, C.E., Dewett, T., Mishina, Y., and Belsito, C.A. (2009), "A general theory of organizational stigma", *Organization Science*, 20 (1), pp. 154–171.

Di Lieto, A. (2015), *Bridge Resource Management: From the Costa Concordia to Navigation in the Digital Age*, Brisbane QLD Australia: Hydeas Pty Ltd.

Diamond, J. (2019), *Upheaval: Turning Points for Nations in Crisis*, New York: Back Bay Books.

Diestre, L. and Santaló, J. (2020), "Why do firms suffer differently from input stigmatization? The costs of removing stigmatized inputs", *Organization Science*, 31 (1), pp. 47–66.

Dillon, R.L. and Tinsley, C.H. (2008), "How near-misses influence decision making under risk: A missed opportunity for learning", *Management Science*, 54 (8), pp. 1425–1440.

DiMaggio, P.J. and Powell, W.W. (1983), "The iron cage revisited. Institutional isomorphism and collective rationality in organizational fields", *American Sociological Review*, 48 (2), pp. 147–60.

Dingwall, G. and Hillier, T. (2016), *Blamestorming, Blamemongers and Scapegoats*, Bristol: Policy Press.

Djabi, M. and Sitte de Longueval, O. (2020), "Scapegoating in the organization: Which regulation modes?", *M@n@gement*, 23 (2), pp. 1–19.

Douglas, M. (1992), *Risk and Blame*, London and New York: Routledge.

Douglas, T. (1995), *Scapegoats: Transferring Blame*, London and New York: Routledge.

Drabek, T.E. (1968), *Disaster in Aisle 13*, Disaster Research Centre series, College of Administrative Science, The Ohio State University.

Drabek, T.E. and Quarantelli, E. (1967), "Scapegoats, villains and disasters", *Transaction*, 4 (4), pp. 7–12.

Drumheller, T. (2006), *On the Brink: An Insider's Account of How the White House Compromised American Intelligence*, New York: Carrol and Graf.

Eagle, J. and Newton, P.M. (1981), "Scapegoating in small groups: An organizational approach", *Human Relations*, 34 (4), pp. 283–301.

Edelman, L.B. and Stryker, R. (2005), "A Sociological approach to law and the economy". In N.J. Smelser and R. Swedberg, eds., *The Handbook of Economic Sociology* (pp. 527–551), Princeton: Princeton University Press.

Eisenhardt, K.M. (1989), "Building theories from case study research", *Academy of Management Review*, 14 (4), pp. 532–550.

Eisenhardt, K.M. and Graebner, M.E. (2007), "Theory building from cases: Opportunities and challenges", *The Academy of Management Journal*, 50 (1), pp. 25–32.

Ellis, R. (1994), *Presidential Lightning Rods: The Politics of Blame Avoidance*, Lawrence: University Press of Kansas.

Elmore, J. (2005), "Does litigation influence medical practice?", *Radiology*, 236 (1), pp. 37–46.

Elsbach, K.D. (1994), "Managing organizational legitimacy in the California cattle industry: The construction and effectiveness of verbal accounts", *Administrative Science Quarterly*, 39 (1), pp. 57–88.

Elsbach, K.D. and Sutton, R.I. (1992), "Acquiring organizational legitimacy through illegitimate actions: A marriage of institutional and impression management theories", *Academy Management Journal*, 35 (4), pp. 699–738.

Ermann, M.D. and Lundman, R.J., eds. (2002), *Corporate and Governmental Deviance: Problems and Organizational Behavior in Contemporary Society*, New York: Oxford University Press (2nd ed.).

Eusebi, L. (2011), "La prevenzione dell'evento non voluto: Elementi per una rivisitazione dogmatica dell'illecito colposo e del dolo eventuale". In *Studi in onore di Mario Romano, II* (pp. 963–1003), Napoli: Jovene Editore.

Ewing, J. (2017), *Faster, Higher, Farther: How one of the World's Largest Automakers Committed a Massive and Stunning Fraud*, New York: W.W. Norton & Company.

Farinelli, G. and Paccagnini, E., eds. (1988), *Processo agli untori: Milano 1630, Cronaca e atti giudiziari*, Milano: Garzanti.

Faulkner, R. (2011), *Corporate Wrongdoing and the Art of the Accusation*, London: Anthem Press.

Fay, G.R. and Jones, A.R. (2004), "Investigation of the Abu Ghraib prison", August 23, www.thetorturedatabase.org/document/fay-report-investigation-205th-military-intelligence-brigades-activites-abu-ghraib.

Fazio, R.H., Eiser J.R., and Shook, N.J. (2004), "Attitude formation through exploration: Valence asymmetries", *Journal of Personality and Social Psychology*, 87 (3), pp. 293–311.

Feeley, M. and Simon, J. (1992), "The new penology. Notes on the emerging strategy of corrections and its implications", *Criminology*, 30 (4), pp. 449–474.

Ferrajoli, L. (2000), *Diritto e ragione: Teoria del garantismo penale*, Bari-Roma: Laterza (6th ed.).

Ferretti, N. (2019), *Il capro espiatorio: Israele e la crisi dell'Europa*, Torino: Lindau.

Fiandaca, G. (2020), "Giustizia penale e storia: Spunti di riflessione", *Meridiana*, 97, pp. 23–33.

Findley, K.A. and Scott, M.S. (2006), "The multiple dimensions of tunnel vision in criminal cases", *Wisconsin Law Review*, 2 (1023), pp. 291–397.

Fine, G.A. (1997), "Scandal, social conditions, and the creation of public attention: Fatty Arbuckle and the 'problem of Hollywood,'" *Social Problems*, 44 (3), pp. 297–323.

Fine, G.A. (1996), "Reputational entrepreneurs and the memory of incompetence: Melting supporters, partisan warriors, and images of President Harding", *American Journal of Sociology*, 101 (5), pp. 1159–1193.

Finney, H.C. and Lesieur, H.R. (1982), "A contingency theory of organizational crime". In S. Bacharach, ed., *Research in the Sociology of Organizations* (pp. 255–259), Greenwich CT: JAI Press.

Fiske, S.T. and Neuberg, S. (1990), "A continuum of impression formation, from category-based to individuating processes: Influences of information and motivation on attention and interpretation", *Advances in Experimental Social Psychology*, 23, pp. 1–74.

Fiske, S.T., Harris L.T., and Cuddy, A.J. (2004), "Why ordinary people torture enemy prisoners", *Science*, 306 (5701), pp. 1482–1483.

Fisse, B. and Braithwaite, J. (1993), *Corporations, Crime and Accountability*, Cambridge: Cambridge University Press.

Fligstein, N. (1990), *The Transformation of Corporate Control*, Cambridge, MA: Harvard University Press.

Fligstein, N. (1987), "The interorganizational power struggle: Rise of finance personnel to top leadership in large corporations, 1919–79", *American Sociological Review*, 52 (1), pp. 44–58.

Forman, J. Jr. (2012), "Racial critiques of mass incarceration: Beyond the new Jim Crow", *New York University Law Review*, 87 (1), pp. 21–69.

Forrester, J. (1970), *Urban Dynamics*, Cambridge, MA: MIT Press.

Forti, G. (2018), *La cura delle norme: Oltre la corruzione delle regole e dei saperi*, Milano: Vita e Pensiero.

Forti, G. and Bertolino, M., eds. (2005), *La televisione del crimine*, Milano: Vita e Pensiero.

Forti, G., Catino, M., D'Alessandro, F., Mazzuccato, C., and Varraso, G. (2010), *Il problema della medicina difensiva*, Pisa: Edizioni ETS.

Frazer, J. (1915 [2009]), *The Golden Bough: A Study in Magic and Religion*, II Vol., Oxford: Oxford University Press.

Free, R. (1994), *The role of procedural violations in railways accidents*, PhD Thesis, University of Manchester.

Freud, S. (1905 [2003]), *The Joke and Its Relation to the Unconscious*, London: Penguin Classics.

Friedberg, E. (1993 [1996]), *Power and Rules: The Organizational Dynamics of Collective Action*, Farnham, UK: Ashgate Publishing.

Frugoni, C. (2020), *Paure medievali: Epidemie, prodigi, fine del tempo*, Bologna: il Mulino.

Fulbrook, M. (2018), *Reckonings*, Oxford: Oxford University Press.

Gaeta, A. (2012), *Il capitano e la Concordia: Inchiesta sul naufragio all'isola del Giglio*, Villorba: Edizioni a Nordest.

Gamson, W.A. and Scotch, N.A. (1964), "Scapegoating in baseball", *American Journal of Sociology*, 70 (1), pp. 69–72.

Gangloff, K.A., Connelly, B.L., and Shook, C.L. (2016), "Of scapegoats and signals: Investor reactions to CEO succession in the aftermath of wrongdoing", *Journal of Management*, 42 (6), pp. 1614–1634.

Garapon, A. (2001), *Bien juger: Essai sur le ritual judiciaire*, Paris: Éditions Odile Jacob.

Garapon, A. (1996), *Le gardien des promesses : Justice et démocratie*, Paris: Éditions Odile Jacob.

Garapon, A. and Salas, D. (1996), *La République pénalisée*, Paris: Hachette Livre.

Garfinkel, H. (1956), "Conditions of successful degradation ceremonies", *American Journal of Sociology*, 61 (5), pp. 420–424.

Garland, D.W. (2008), "On the concept of moral panic", *Crime, Media, Culture*, 4 (1), pp. 9–30.

Garland, D.W. (1990), *Punishment and Modern Society: A Study in Social Theory*, Oxford: Oxford University Press.

Garrett, B.L. (2014), *Too Big to Jail: How Prosecutors Compromise With Corporations*, Cambridge, MA: Harvard University Press.

Geis, G. (1967), "White-collar crime: The heavy electrical equipment and antitrust cases of 1961". In M. Clinard and R. Quinney, eds., *Criminal Behavior Systems: A Typology* (pp. 139–150), New York: Holt, Rinehart and Winston.

Gemmill, G. (1989), "The dynamics of scapegoating in small groups", *Small Group Research*, 20 (4), pp. 406–418.

Giancola, P. (2017), "Does defensive medicine impact the cost of healthcare?", www.swlaw.com/blog/health-law-checkup/2017/04/05/does-defensive-medicine-impact-the-cost-of-healthcare/.

Giglioli, P.P. (1997), "Processi di delegittimazione e cerimonie di degradazione". In P.P. Giglioli, S. Cavicchioli, and G. Fele, *Rituali di degradazione: Anatomia del processo Cusani* (pp. 15–73), Bologna: il Mulino.

Ginzburg, C. (2017), *Storia notturna: Una decifrazione del sabba*, Milano: Adelphi.

Ginzburg, C. (2002), *The Judge and The Historian: Marginal Notes on a Late-Twentieth-Century Miscarriage of Justice*, London and New York: Verso Books.

Ginzburg, C. (1989), *Clues, Myths, and the Historical Method*, Baltimore: The Johns Hopkins University Press.

Girard, R. (1999 [2001]), *I see Satan Fall Like Lightning*, Ossining, NY: Orbis.

Girard, R. (1987), "Generative scapegoating". In W. Burkert, R. Girard, J., and Z. Smith, eds., *Violent Origins: Ritual Killing and Cultural Formation* (pp. 73–105), Stanford, CA: Stanford University Press.

Girard, R. (1985), *La route antique des hommes pervers*, Paris: Grasset.

Girard, R. (1982 [1989]), *The Scapegoat*, Baltimore: Johns Hopkins University Press.

Girard, R. (1974), "The plague in literature and myth author(s)", *Texas Studies in Literature and Language*, 15 (5), pp. 833–850.

Girard, R. (1972 [1979]), *Violence and the Sacred*, Baltimore: Johns Hopkins University Press.

Glasberg, D.S. and Skidmore, D. (1998) "The dialectics of white-collar crime: The anatomy of the savings and loan crisis and the case of the Silverado Banking, Savings and Loan Association", *American Journal of Economics and Sociology*, 57 (4), pp. 423–449.

Glassman, R.B. (1973), "Persistence and loose coupling in living systems", *Behavioral Science*, 18 (2), pp. 83–98.

Gleason, C.A., Jenkins, N.T., and Johnson, W.B. (2008), "The stigma effects of accounting restatements", *Accounting Review*, 83 (1), pp. 83–110.

Goffman, E. (1974), *Frame Analysis: An Essay on the Organization of Experience*, New York: Harper & Row.

Goffman, E. (1963), *Stigma: Notes on the Management of Spoiled Identity*, Englewood Cliffs, NJ: Prentice Hall.

Gourevitch, P. and Morris, E. (2008), *Standard Operating Procedure: A War Story*, London: Pan Macmillan.

Greenstein, F.I. (1982), *The Hidden-Hand Presidency: Eisenhower as Leader*, New York: Basic Books.

Greenwood, R., Oliver, C., Sahlin, K., and Suddaby, R., eds. (2008), *The SAGE Handbook of Organizational Institutionalism*, Thousand Oaks, CA: SAGE Publications.

Greer, C. and McLaughlin, E. (2011), "Trial by media: Policing, the 24/7 news mediasphere and the politics of outrage", *Theoretical Criminology*, 15 (1), pp. 23–44.

Grey, C. (2012), *Decoding Organizations. Bletchley Park, Codebreaking and Organization Studies*, Cambridge: Cambridge University Press.

Guthrie, C., Rachlinsky, J.J., and Wistricliff, A.J. (2001), "Inside the judicial mind", *Cornell Law Faculty Publications*, 86 (4), pp. 777–830.

Haslam, S.A. and Reicher, S. (2007), "Beyond the banality of evil: Three dynamics of an interactionist social psychology of tyranny", *Personality and Social Psychology Bulletin*, 33 (5), pp. 615–622.

Hedberg, B. (1981), "How organizations learn and unlearn". In P.C. Nystrom and W.H. Starbuck, eds., *Handbook of Organizational Design, vol 1: Adapting Organizations to Their Environments* (pp. 3–27), New York: Oxford University Press.

Helms, W.S. and Patterson, K.D. (2014), "Eliciting acceptance for 'illicit' organizations: The positive implications of stigma for MMA organizations", *Academy of Management Journal*, 57 (5), pp. 1453–1484.

Hersh, S.M. (2004a), "The gray zone. How a secret Pentagon program came to Abu Ghraib", *The New Yorker*, 80 (13), pp. 38–43.

Hersh, S.M. (2004b), *Chain of Command: The Road from 9/11 to Abu Ghraib*, New York: Harper Collins Publishers, Inc.

Hilberg, R. (1996), *The Politics of Memory: A Journey of a Historian*, Chicago: Ivan R. Dee, Publisher.

Hiyama, T., Yoshihara, M., Tanaka, S., et al. (2006), "Defensive medicine practices among gastroenterologists in Japan", *World Journal of Gastroenterology*, 12 (47), pp. 7671–7675.

Hochstetler, A. and Copes, H. (2001) "Organizational culture and organizational crime". In N. Shover and J.P. Wright, eds., *Crimes of Privilege* (pp. 210–22), New York: Oxford University Press.

Hood, C. (2002), "The risk game and the blame game", *Government and Opposition*, 37 (1), pp. 15–37.

Hood, C., Jennings, W., Dixon, R., Hogwood, B., and Beeston C. (2009), "Testing times: Exploring staged responses and the impact", *European Journal of Political Research*, 48 (6), pp. 695–722.

Horlick-Jones, T. (1995), "Modern disasters as outrage and betrayal", *International Journal of Mass Emergencies and Disasters*, 13 (3), pp. 305–315.

Hudson, B.A. (2008), "Against all odds: A consideration of core-stigmatized organizations", *Academy of Management Review*, 33 (1), pp. 252–266.

Hudson, B.A. and Okhuysen, G.A. (2009), "Not with a ten-foot pole: Core stigma, stigma transfer, and improbable persistence of men's bathhouses", *Organization Science*, 20 (1), pp. 134–153.

Human Rights Watch (2004), *The Road to Abu Ghraib*, www.hrw.org/sites/default/files/reports/usa0604.pdf.

Hutter, M.B. and Lloyd-Bostock, S.M. (2017), *Regulatory Crisis: Negotiating the Consequences of Risk, Disasters and Crises*, Cambridge: Cambridge University Press.

Jackall, R. (1988), *Moral Mazes: The World of Corporate Managers*, New York: Oxford University Press.

Jackson Healthcare (2009), *Defensive medicine: Impacts beyond costs*. The report can be downloaded from the site, www.jacksonhealthcare.com.

Jacquart, P. and Antonakis, J. (2015), "When does charisma matter for top-level leaders? Effect of attributional ambiguity", *Academy of Management Journal*, 58 (4), pp. 1051–1074.

Jasanoff, S. (2005a), *Designs on Nature: Science and Democracy in Europe and United States*, Princeton: Princeton University Press.

Jasanoff, S. (2005b), "Restoring reason: Causal narratives and political culture". In B. Hutter and M. Power, eds., *Organizational Encounter with Risk* (pp. 209–232), Cambridge: Cambridge University Press.

Jensen, M. (2006), "Should we stay or should we go? Accountability, status anxiety, and client defections", *Administrative Science Quarterly*, 51 (1), pp. 97–128.

Joffe, J. (2004), "The demons of Europe", *Commentary*, January, www
.commentary.org/articles/josef-joffe/the-demons-of-europe/.

Johansen, W., Aggerholm, H. K., and Frandsen, F. (2012), "Entering new
territory: A study of internal crisis management and crisis communication
in organizations", *Public Relations Review*, 38 (2), pp. 270–279.

Jonsson, S., Greve, H.R., and Fujiwara-Greve, T. (2009), "Undeserved loss:
The spread of legitimacy loss to innocent organizations in response to
reported corporate deviance", *Administrative Science Quarterly*, 54 (2),
pp. 195–228.

Kahneman, D. (2011), *Thinking Fast and Slow*, London: Penguin Books.

Kahneman, D. and Tversky, A. (1979), "Prospect Theory: An analysis of
decision under risk", *Econometrica*, 47 (2), pp. 263–291.

Kapp, M.B. (2016), "Defensive medicine: No wonder policymakers are confused", *International Journal of Risk & Safety in Medicine*, 28 (4), pp.
213–219.

Kassin, S.M., Dror, I.E., and Kukucka, J. (2013), "The forensic confirmation bias: Problems, perspectives, and proposed solutions", *Journal of
Applied Research in Memory and Cognition*, 2 (1), pp. 42–52.

Katz, E.D. (2019), "Defensive medicine: A case and review of its status and
possible solutions", *Clinical Practice and Cases in Emergency Medicine*,
3 (4), pp. 329–332.

Keane, C. (1995), "Loosely coupled systems and unlawful behaviour: Organization theory and corporate crime". In F. Pearce and L. Snider, eds.,
Corporate Crime: Contemporary Debates (pp. 168–178), Toronto: University of Toronto Press.

Keenan, M. (2011), *Child Sexual Abuse and the Catholic Church: Gender,
Power, and Organizational Culture*, Oxford: Oxford University Press.

Kelman, H. and Hamilton, V.L. (1989), *Crimes of Obedience*, New Haven,
CT: Yale University Press.

Kennedy, J.E. (2000), "Monstrous offenders and the search for solidarity
through modern punishment", *Hasting Law Journal*, 51(5), pp. 829–908.

Klingman, D., Localio, A.R., Sugarman, J., et al. (1996), "Measuring defensive medicine using clinical scenario surveys", *Journal of Health Politics,
Policy and Law*, 21 (2), pp. 185–210.

Kramer, R.C. (1982) "Corporate crime: An organizational perspective". In
P. Wickman and T. Dailey, eds., *White-Collar and Economic Crime* (pp.
75–94), Lexington, MA: Lexington Books.

Lagadec, P. (1993), *Preventing Chaos in a Crisis: Strategies for Prevention,
Control and Damage Limitation*, New York: McGraw Hill Education.

Lamin, A. and Zaheer, S. (2012), "Wall Street vs. Main Street: Firm strategies for defending legitimacy and their impact on different stakeholders",
Organization Science, 23 (1), pp. 47–66.

Langer, E.J. (1975), "The illusion of control", *Journal of Personality and Social Psychology*, 32, pp. 311–328.

Lanzara, G.F. (2016), *Shifting Practices: Reflections on Technology, Practice, and Innovation*, Cambridge, MA: The MIT Press.

LaPorte, T. and Consolini, P. (1994), "Working in practice but not in theory: Theoretical challenges of high reliability organizations", *Journal of Public Administration Research and Theory*, 1 (1), pp. 19–47.

Latané, B. and Darley, J.M. (1970), *The Unresponsive Bystander: Why Doesn't He Help?*, New York: Appleton-Century-Crofts.

Latour, B. (2004), *La fabrique du droit: Une ethnographie du Conseil d'État*, Paris: Éd. La Découverte, Poche.

Laufer, W.S. (2008), *Corporate Bodies and Guilty Minds: The Failure of Corporate Criminal Liability*, Chicago: The University of Chicago Press.

Laufer, W.S., (2002), "Corporate prosecution, cooperation, and the trading of favors", *Iowa Law Review*, 87 (2), pp. 643–667.

Law, S. (1986), "A consumer perspective on medical malpractice", *Law & Contemporary Problems*, 49 (2), pp. 305–320.

Lee, M.T. and Ermann, M.D. (1999), "Pinto 'madness' as a flawed landmark narrative: An organizational and network analysis", *Social Problems*, 46 (1), pp. 30–50.

Leeson, P.T. and Russ, J.W. (2018), "Witch trials", *The Economic Journal*, 128 (613), pp. 2066–2105.

Leplat, J. (1987), "Occupational accident research and system approach". In J. Rasmussen, K. Duncan and J. Leplat, eds., *New Technology and Human Error* (pp. 181–191), New York: John Wiley & Sons.

Levack, B.P. (2016), *The Witch-Hunt in Early Modern Europe*, New York: Routledge (4th ed.).

Leveson, N.G. (2011), *Engineering a Safer World. Systems Thinking Applied to Safety*, Cambridge, MA: MIT Press.

Levi, P. (1986 [2015]), "The drowned and the saved". In A. Goldstein, ed., *The Complete Works of Primo Levi, Vol. III* (pp. 2405–2570), New York: Liveright.

Levine, A.G. (1982), *Love Canal: Science, Politics, and People*, Lexington, Massachusetts: Lexington Books.

Lewin VHI Inc. (1997) "Estimating the costs of defensive medicine". In *Report prepared for the MMI Companies*, Fairfax, VA: Lewin VHI Inc.

Liska, A.E. (1987), *Perspectives on Deviance*, Englewood Cliffs, NJ: Prentice-Hall (2nd ed.).

Locatelli, A. (1930), *L'affare Dreyfus: La più grande infamia del secolo scorso*, Milano: Corbaccio.

Lopez, D. (2008), *Il desiderio, il sacrificio, il capro espiatorio*, Vicenza: Angelo Colla Editore.

Lord, C.G., Ross, L., and Lepper, M.R. (1979), "Biased assimilation and attitude polarization: The effects of prior theories on subsequently considered evidence", *Journal of Personality and Social Psychology*, 37 (11), pp. 2098–2109.

Luban, D. (1993), "Are criminal defenders different?", *Michigan Law Review*, 91 (7), pp. 1729–1766.

Luhmann, N. (1991), *Soziologie des Risikos*, Berlin: Walter de Gruyter (Eng. transl. *Risk. A Sociological Theory*, London: Routledge, 2002).

Machiavelli, N. (1513 [2015]), *The Prince*, London: Penguin Classics.

Madarasz, K. (2012), "Information projection: Model and applications", *Review of Economic Studies*, 79 (3), pp. 961–985.

Mann, T. (2021 [1918]), *Reflections of a Non-political Man*, New York: NYRB Classics.

Manzoni, A. (1840 [1964]), *The Column of Infamy*, Oxford: Oxford University Press.

March, J.G. and Olsen, J.P. (1975), "The uncertainty of the past: Organizational learning under ambiguity", *European Journal of Political Research*, 3 (2), pp. 147–171.

March, J.G. and Simon, H.A. (1958), *Organizations*, New York: John Wiley and Sons.

Marcus, A.A. and Goodman, R.S. (1991), "Victims and shareholders: The dilemmas of presenting corporate policy during a crisis", *Academy of Management Journal*, 34 (2), pp. 281–305.

Markovits, A.S. and Silverstein, M., eds. (1988), *The Politics of Scandal. Power and Process in Liberal Democracies*, New York: Holmes & Meier Publisher, Inc.

Marrus, M.R. (1990), "Antisemitismo popolare". In N.L. Kleeblat, ed., *L'affare Dreyfus: La storia, l'opinione, l'immagine* (pp. 95–107), Torino: Bollati Boringhieri.

Martinazzoli, M. (2020), "*Per una requisitoria manzoniana*". In Manzoni, A., *La peste a Milano*, Brescia: Morcelliana Scholé (pp. 229–272).

Massachusetts Medical Society (2008), "Investigation of defensive medicine in Massachusetts", www.macrmi.info/application/files/6715/9379/9330/MMS_Defensive_Medicine_Report_2008.pdf.

Mayer, J. (2008), *The Dark Side: The Inside Story of How the War on Terror Turned into a War on American Ideals*, New York: Doubleday.

McCormick, E. and Smith, N.C. (2018), "Volkswagen's emissions scandal: How could it happen", *Harvard Business Publishing education*, https://hbsp.harvard.edu/product/IN1465-PDF-ENG.

McGraw, K.M. (1991), "Managing blame: An experimental test of the effects of political accounts", *American Political Science Review*, n. 85 (4), pp. 1133–1157.

McGraw, K.M. (1990), "Avoiding blame: An experimental investigation of political excuses and justifications", *British Journal of Political Science*, 20 (2), pp. 119–132.

Mello, M.M., Chandra, A., Gawande, A.A., and Studdert, D.M. (2010), "National costs of the medical liability system", *Health Affairs*, 29 (9), pp. 1569–1577.

Merenstein, D., Daumit, G.L., and Powe, N.R. (2006), "Use and costs of non-recommended tests during routine preventive health exams", *American Journal of Preventive Medicine*, 30 (6), pp. 521–527.

Merton, R.K. (1936) "The unanticipated consequences of purposive social action", *American Sociological Review*, 1 (6), pp. 894–904.

Meyer, J.W. (1977), "The effect of education as an institution", *American Journal of Sociology*, 83 (1), pp. 55–77.

Meyer, J.W. and Rowan, B. (1977), "Institutionalized Organizations. Formal structure as myth and ceremony", *American Journal of Sociology*, 83 (2), pp. 340–363.

Milgram, S. (1974), *Obedience to Authority: An Experimental View*, London: Tavistock.

Mishina, Y. and Devers, C.A. (2011), "On being bad: Why stigma is not the same as bad reputation". In M. Barnett and T. Pollock, eds., *The Oxford Handbook of Corporate Reputation* (pp. 202–220), Oxford: Oxford University Press.

Mohliver, A. (2019), "How misconduct spreads: Auditors' role in the diffusion of stock-option backdating", *Administrative Science Quarterly*, 64 (2), pp. 310–336.

Monahan, S.C. and Quinn, B.A. (2006), "Beyond 'bad apples' and 'weak leaders'. Toward a neo-institutional explanation of organizational deviance", *Theoretical Criminology*, 10 (3), pp. 361–385.

Moore, C.A. (1987), "Taming the giant corporation? Some cautionary remarks on the deterrability of corporate crime", *Crime and Delinquency*, 33 (3), pp. 379–402.

Moore, D.A. and Healy, P.J. (2008), "The trouble with overconfidence", *Psychological Review*, 115 (2), pp. 502–517.

Moore, D.A. and Schatz, D. (2017), "The three faces of overconfidence", *Social and Personality Psychology Compass*, 11 (8), pp. 1–12.

Moscovici, S. (1985), "Social influence and conformity". In G. Lindzey and E. Aronson, eds., *Handbook of Social Psychology*, Vol. 2 (pp. 347–412), New York: Random House.

Moshansky, V.P., Commissioner (1992), *Commission of Inquiry into the Air Ontario Crash at Dryden, Ontario, Final Report*, Ottawa: Ministry of Supply and Service.

Naumovska, I. and Lavie, D. (2021), "When an industry peer is accused of financial misconduct: Stigma versus competition effects on non-accused firms", *Administrative Science Quarterly*, 66 (4), pp. 1130–1172.

Neal, D.M. (1984), "Blame assignment in a diffuse disaster situation: A case example of the role of an emergent citizen group", *International Journal of Mass Emergencies and Disasters*, 2 (2), pp. 251–266.

Neal, D.M. and Perry, J.B. Jr. (1980), "A note on blame and disaster: A case of the winter of 1976–1977", paper presented at the *North Central Association meetings* in Dayton, Ohio.

Nelken, D. (2002), "Tangentopoli". In M. Barbagli and U. Gatti, eds., *La criminalità in Italia* (pp. 55–65), Bologna: il Mulino.

Nicolini, F. (1937), *Peste e untori nei 'Promessi sposi' e nella realtà storica*, Bari-Roma: Laterza.

Nisbett, R.E. and Ross, L. (1980), *Human Inference: Strategies and Short-comings of Social Judgement*, Englewood Cliffs, NJ: Prentice-Hall.

Noelle-Neumann, E. (1974), "The spiral of silence: A theory of public opinion", *Journal of Communication*, 24 (2), pp. 43–51.

Ortashi, O., Virdee, J., Hassan, R., Mutrynowsky, T., and Abu-Zidan, F. (2013), "The practice of defensive medicine among hospital doctors in the United Kingdom", *BMC Medical Ethics*, 14, pp. 42 ss.

Orton, D.J. and Weick, K.E. (1990), "Loosely coupled systems: A reconceptualization", *Academy of Management. The Academy of Management Review*, (15) 2, pp. 203–223.

Owens, L.A. (2011), "Confidence in banks, financial institutions, and Wall Street, 1971–2011", *Public Opinion Quarterly*, 76 (1), pp. 142–162.

Packer, H.L. (1968), *The Limits of the Criminal Sanction*, Stanford: Stanford University Press.

Palmer, D. (2014), "Robert R. Faulkner: Corporate wrongdoing and the art of the accusation", *Administrative Science Quarterly*, 59 (2), pp. 370–373.

Palmer, D. (2013), "The new perspective on organizational wrongdoing", *California Management Review*, 56 (1), pp. 5–23.

Palmer, D. (2012), *Normal Organizational Wrongdoing: A Critical Analysis of Theories of Misconduct in and by Organizations*, Oxford: Oxford University Press.

Palmer, D., Smith-Crowe, K., and Greenwood, R., eds. (2016), *Organizational Wrongdoing: Key Perspectives and New Directions*, Cambridge: Cambridge University Press.

Palombo, T. (2008), *La mia vita da uomo di mare: Da Camogli all'Isola del Giglio, dalle navi da carico ai prestigiosi comandi di navi passeggeri*, Grosseto: Editrice Innocenti.

Parker, R. (1983), *Miasma: Pollution and Purification in Early Greek Religion*, Oxford: Clarendon Press.

Paruchuri, S. and Misangyi, V.F. (2015), "Investor perceptions of financial misconduct: The heterogeneous contamination of bystander firms", *Academy of Management Journal*, 58 (1), pp. 169–194.

Passmore, K. and Leung, W.C. (2002), "Defensive practice among psychiatrists: A questionnaire survey", *Postgraduate Medical Journal*, 78, pp. 671–673.

Patton, M.Q. (1987), *How to Use Qualitative Methods in Evaluation*, Newbury Park: Sage Publications Inc.

Perera, S.B. (1986), *The Scapegoat Complex: Toward a Mythology of Shadow and Guilt*, Toronto: Inner City Books.

Perrow, C. (2014), *Complex Organizations: A Critical Essay*, Brattleboro, Vermont: Echo Point Books & Media.

Perrow, C. (1999), *Normal Accidents: Living with High-Risk Technologies*, New York: Basic Books (2nd ed.).

Perrow, C. (1991), "A society of organizations", *Theory and Society*, 20 (6), pp. 725–62.

Pestalozza, U. (1930), "Capro espiatorio". In *Enciclopedia Italiana*, www.treccani.it.

Piazza, A. and Jourdan, J. (2018), "When the dust settles: The consequences of scandals for organizational competition", *Academy of Management Journal*, 61 (1), pp. 165–190.

Pierson, P. (1994), *Dismantling the Welfare State?*, Cambridge, UK: Cambridge University Press.

Poggi, F. (2018), *La medicina difensiva*, Modena: Mucchi Editore.

Pontikes, E., Negro, G., and Rao, H. (2010), "Stained Red: A study of stigma by association with blacklisted artists during the 'Red Scare' in Hollywood, 1945–1960", *American Sociological Review*, 75 (3), pp. 456–478.

Pozner, J.E. and Harris, D.J. (2016), "Who bears the brunt? A review and research agenda for the consequences of organizational wrongdoing for individuals". In D. Palmer, R. Greenwood, and K. Smith-Crowe, eds., *Organizational Wrongdoing: Key Perspectives and New Directions* (pp. 404–434), Cambridge: Cambridge University Press.

Powell, W.W. and DiMaggio, P.J., eds. (1991), *The New Institutionalism in Organizational Analysis*, Chicago: University of Chicago Press.

Prendergast, C. (1993), "A theory of 'yes men,'" *American Economic Review*, 83 (4), pp. 757–770.

Presthus, R. (1962), *The Organizational Society: An Analysis and a Theory*, New York: Knopf.

Preston, T. (2011), *Pandora's Trap: Presidential Decision Making and Blame Avoidance in Vietnam and Iraq*, Lanham: Rowman & Littlefield Publishers.

Preto, P. (1987), *Epidemia, paura e politica nell'Italia moderna*, Roma-Bari: Laterza.

PricewaterhouseCoopers' Health Research Institute, *The price of excess: Identifying waste in healthcare spending*, USA, http://medecon.pbworks .com/f/Price+of+Waste.pdf.

Quinn, R. (1998), "Medical malpractice insurance: The reputation effect and defensive medicine", *Journal of Risk Insurance*, 65 (3), pp. 467–484.

Rasmussen, J. (1993), "What can be learned from disasters in other endeavors? Perspectives on the concept of human error", Manuscript for invited contributions to *Human Performance and Anesthesia Technology*, Society for Technology in Anesthesia Conference, New Orleans, February.

Rasmussen, J. (1990), "Human error and the problem of causality in analysis of accidents", *Philosophical Transactions of the Royal Society*, 327 (1241), pp. 449–462.

Rasmussen, J. and Svedung, I. (2000), *Proactive Risk Management in a Dynamic Society*, Karlstad: Swedish Rescue Services Agency.

Reason, J. (1997), *Managing the Risks of Organizational Accidents*, Aldershot: Ashgate.

Revel, B. (1936), *L'affare Dreyfus (1984–1906)*, Milano: Bruno Mondadori.

Ripamonti, G. (1641 [2009]), *La peste di Milano del 1630*, Milano: Mediolanensia.

Radoynovska, N. and King, B.G. (2019), "To whom are you true? Audience perceptions of authenticity in nascent crowdfunding ventures", *Organization Science*, 30 (4), pp. 781–802.

Rose, R. and Davies, P.L. (1994), *Inheritance in Public Policy: Change Without Choice in Britain*, New Haven, CT: Yale University Press.

Ross, L. (1977), "The intuitive psychologist and his shortcomings distortions in the attribution process". In L. Berckowitz, ed., *Advances on Experimental Social Psychology*, vol. 10 (pp. 173–220), New York: Academic Press.

Ross, L. and Nisbett, R.E. (2011), *The Person and the Situation: Perspectives of Social Psychology*, London: Pinter & Martin Ltd.

Rossmo, D.K. and Pollock, J.M. (2019), "Confirmation bias and other systemic causes of wrongful convictions: A sentinel events perspective", *Northeastern University Law Review*, 11 (2), pp. 792–835.

Rothbart, M. and Park, B. (1986), "On the confirmability and disconfirmability of trait concepts", *Journal of Personality and Social Psychology*, 50 (1), pp.131–142.

Rothberg, M.B., Class, J., Bishop, T.F., Friderici, J., Kleppel, R., and Lindenauer, P.K. (2014), "The cost of defensive medicine", *Journal of American Medical Association*, 174 (11), pp. 1867–1868.

Roulet, T.J. (2020), *The Power of Being Divisive: Understanding Negative Social Evaluations*, Stanford: Stanford Business Books.

Roulet, T.J. (2015), "'What good is Wall Street?' Institutional contradiction and the diffusion of the stigma over the finance industry", *Journal of Business Ethics*, 130 (2), pp. 389–402.

Roulet, T. J. and Clemente, M. (2018), "Let's open the media's black box: The media as a set of heterogeneous actors and not only as a homogenous ensemble", *Academy of Management Review*, 43 (2), pp. 327–329.

Roulet, T.J. and Pichler, R. (2020), "Blame game theory: Scapegoating, whistleblowing and discursive struggles following accusations of organizational misconduct", *Organization theory*, 1 (4), pp. 1–30.

Rowe, W.G., Cannella, A.A., Rankin, D., and Gorman, D. (2005), "Leader succession and organizational performance: Integrating the commonsense, ritual scapegoating, and vicious-circle succession theories", *Leadership Quarterly*, 16 (2), pp. 197–219.

Rozad, K. (2013), *Critical champions or careless condemners? Exploring news media constructions in cases of wrongful conviction*, MA Thesis, Wilfrid Laurier University, https://scholars.wlu.ca/etd/1764/.

Russo, C. (2011), "VTS, AIS e altri sistemi di monitoraggio del traffico marittimo", *GIURETA. Rivista di Diritto dell'Economia, dei Trasporti e dell'Ambiente*, vol. IX, pp. 415–437.

Sanvitale, F. and Palmegiani, A. (2011), *Un mostro chiamato Girolimoni*, Roma: Sovera Edizioni.

Sartori, G. (2011), *Logica, metodo e linguaggio nelle scienze sociali*, Bologna: il Mulino.

Schettino, F. and Abate, V. (2015), *Le verità sommerse*, Napoli, Graus Edizioni.

Schlesinger, J.R. (2004), *Final Report of the Independent Panel to Review DoD Detention Operations*, Arlington, VA: Independent Panel to Review DoD Detention Operations.

Schröder-Hinrichs, J.U., Hollnagel, E., and Baldauf, M. (2012), "From Titanic to Costa Concordia – a century of lessons not learned", *WMU Journal of Maritime Affairs*, 11, pp. 151–167.

Sciascia, L. (1981), "Nota". In A. Manzoni (1840 [1981]), *Storia della colonna infame* (pp. 169–190), Palermo: Sellerio editore.

Selznick, P. (1949), *TVA and Grass Roots*, Berkeley, CA: University of California Press.

Seneca, L.A. (1998), *L'ira*, Milan: Rizzoli.

Sethi, M.K., Obremskey, W.T., Natividad, H., Mir, H.R., and Jahangir, A.A. (2012), "Incidence and costs of defensive medicine among orthopedic surgeons in United States: A national survey study", *Sport Medicine*, 41, pp. 69–73.

Siegel, P.A. and Brockner, J. (2005), "Individual and organizational consequences of CEO claimed handicapping: What's good for the CEO may not be so good for the firm", *Organizational Behavior and Human Decision Processes*, 96 (1), pp. 1–2.

Silvestri, A. (2012), *Il caso Dreyfus e la nascita dell'intellettuale moderno*, Milano: FrancoAngeli.

Simmons, J.L. (1965), "Public stereotypes of deviants", *Social Problems*, 13 (2), pp. 223–232.

Simon, H.A. (1957), *Models of Man: Social and Rational*, New York: John Wiley and Sons.

Simon, J. (2007), *Governing Through Crime*, Oxford: Oxford University Press.

Simonetti, L. (2020), *La scienza in tribunale vol. 2*, Roma: Fandango Libri.

Simonetti, L. (2018), *La scienza in tribunale*, Roma: Fandango Libri.

Simpson, S.S. (2002), *Corporate Crime, Law, and Social Control*, Cambridge: Cambridge University Press.

Simpson, S.S. and Koper, C.S. (1997), "The changing of the guard: Top management characteristics, organizational strain, and antitrust offending", *Journal of Quantitative Criminology*, 13 (4), pp. 373–404.

Skolnick, J.H. and Fyfe, J.J. (1993), *Above the Law: Police and the Excessive Use of Force*, New York: Free Press.

Slovic, P., Fischhoff, B., and Lichtenstein, S. (1985), "Characterizing perceived risk". In R.W. Kates, C. Hohenemser, and J.X. Kasperson, eds., *Perilous Progress: Managing the Hazards of Technology* (pp. 91–125), Boulder, CO: Westview Press.

Smelser, N.J. (1962), *Theory of Collective Behavior*, New York: Free Press.

Snook, S.A. (2000), *Friendly Fire: The Accidental Shootdown of U.S. Black Hawks Over Northern of Iraq*, Princeton: Princeton University Press.

Stangneth, B. (2014), *Eichmann before Jerusalem: The Unexamined Life of a Mass Murderer*, New York: Alfred A. Knopf.

Stern, E.K. (1997), "Crises and learning: A balance sheet", *Journal of Contingencies and Crisis Management*, 5 (2), pp. 69–86.

Stone, C.D. (1980), "The place of enterprise liability in the control of corporate conduct", *Yale Law Journal*, 90 (1), pp. 1–77.

Stone, C.D. (1975), *When the Law Ends*, New York: Harper and Row.

Strasser, S. (2004), *The Abu Ghraib Investigations: The Official Reports of the Independent Panel and Pentagon on the Shocking Prisoner Abuse in Iraq*, New York: Public Affairs.

Stuchlik, J. (2021), *Intention and Wrongdoing: In Defense of Double Effect*, Cambridge: Cambridge University Press.

Studdert, D.M., Mello, M.M., Sage, W.M., et al. (2005), "Defensive medicine among high-risk specialist physicians in a volatile malpractice environment", *Journal of the American Medical Association*, 239, pp. 2609–2617.

Summerton, N. (1995), "Positive and negative factors in defensive medicine: A questionnaire study of general practitioners", *British Medical Journal*, 310 (6971), pp 27–29.

Surette, R. (2003), "The media, the public and criminal justice policy", *Journal of the Institute of Justice and International Studies*, 2, pp. 39–51.

Sutton, R.I. and Callahan, A.L. (1987), "The stigma of bankruptcy: Spoiled organizational image and its management", *Academy of Management Journal*, 30 (3), pp. 405–436.

Taguba, A.M. (2004), "AR 15–6 Investigation of the 800th Military Police Brigade", www.thetorturedatabase.org/document/cia-copy-taguba-report-ar-15-6-investigation-800th-military-police-brigade-0?search_url=search/apachesolr_search/taguba%20Investigation%20of%20the%20800th%20Military%20Police%20Brigade.

Tancredi, L.R. and Barondess, J.A. (1978), "The problem of defensive medicine", *Science*, 200 (4344), pp. 879–82.

Taruffo, M. (1967), "Il giudice e lo storico: Considerazioni metodologiche", *Rivista di Diritto Processuale*, XXII, pp. 438–465.

't Hart, P. (1993), "Symbols, rituals and power: The lost dimensions of crisis management", *Journal of Contingencies and Crisis Management*, 1 (1), pp. 29–43.

Thiel, P. (2014), *Zero to One: Notes on Startups, or How to Build the Future*, New York: Crown Business.

Thompson, J. (2000), *Political Scandal: Power and Visibility in the Media Age*, Cambridge: Polity Press.

Thompson, J. (1967), *Organizations in Action*, New York: McGraw.

Thorndike, L. (1936), "Magic, Witchcraft, Astrology and Alchemy". In C.W. Previte-Orton and Z.N. Brooke, eds., *The Close of the Middle Ages: The Cambridge Medieval History* (pp. 660–687), Cambridge: Cambridge University Press.

Tillinghast-Towers, P. (2003), *U.S. Tort Costs: 2003 Update, Trends and Findings on the Cost of the U.S. Tort System* 17, www.omm.com/omm_distribution/newsletters/client_alert_class_action/pdf/tort_costs_trends_2003_update.pdf.

Toft, B. and Reynolds, S. (1994), *Learning from Disasters: A Management Approach*, Oxford: Butterworth-Heinemann.

Trope, Y. and Liberman, A. (1996), "Social hypothesis testing: Cognitive and motivational mechanisms". In E.T. Higgins and A.W. Kruglanski, eds., *Social Psychology: Handbook of Basic Principles* (pp. 239–270). New York: Guilford Press.

Tucidide (1979), *La guerra del Peloponneso*, 2 vols, Parma: Collana Classici della Fenice.

Turner, B.A. (1978), *Man-Made Disasters*, London: Wykeham Publications.

Turner, B. and Pidgeon, N. (1997), *Man-Made Disasters*, Oxford: Butterworth Heinemann (2nd ed.).

Uhalde, M. (2016), *Crise sociale et transformation des entreprises*, Paris: L'Harmattan.

US Congress, Office of Technology Assessment (1994), *Defensive Medicine and Medical Malpractice*, Washington, DC: US Government Printing Office.

Van Erp, J., ed. (2018), "The organizational aspects of corporate and organizational crime", *Administrative Science*, Special Issue, February.

Van Maanen, J. (2011), *Tales of the Field: On Writing Ethnography*, Chicago: The Chicago University Press.

Van Ours, J.C. and Van Tuijl, M. (2016), "In-season head-coach dismissals and the performance of professional football teams", *Economic Inquiry*, 54 (1), pp. 591–604.

Van Rooij, B. and Fine, A. (2018), "Toxic corporate culture: Assessing organizational processes of deviancy". In J. Van Erp, ed., *The Organizational Aspects of Corporate and Organizational Crime* (pp. 13–50), *Administrative Science*, Special Issue, February.

Vannucci, A. (2012), *Atlante della corruzione*, Torino: Edizioni Gruppo Abele.

Vaughan, D. (2021), *Dead Reckoning: Air Traffic Control, System Effects, and Risks*, Chicago: The University of Chicago Press.

Vaughan, D. (2016), *The Challenger Launch Decision: Risk Technology, Culture, and Deviance at Nasa*, Chicago: The University of Chicago Press.

Vaughan, D. (1999), "The dark side of organizations: Mistake, misconduct, and disaster". *Annual Review of Sociology*, 25 (1), pp. 271–305.

Vaughan, D. (1983), *Controlling Unlawful Organizational Behavior: Social Structure and Corporate Misconduct*, Chicago: The University of Chicago Press.

Veltford, H. and Lee, G.F. (1943), "The Cocoanut Grove fire: A study in scapegoating", *The Journal of Abnormal and Social Psychology*, 38 (2), pp. 138–154.

Vergès, J. (2011), *Les erreurs judiciaires*, Paris: Presses Universitaires de France.

Vergne, J.P. (2012), "Stigmatized categories and public disapproval of organizations: A mixed methods study of the global arms industry (1996–2007)", *Academy of Management Journal*, 55 (5), pp. 1027–1052.

Vernant, J.P. (1972), "Ambiguité et renversement. Sur la structure énigmatique d'Edipe-Roi". In J.P. Vernant and P.V. Naquet, eds., *Mythe et tragédie en Grèce ancienne –I* (pp. 88–120), Paris: Librairie François Maspero.

Verri, P. (1804 [2006]), *Osservazioni sulla tortura*, Milano: Bur Rizzoli.

Vitiello, G. (2008), *La commedia dell'innocenza: Una congettura sulla detective story*, Roma: Luca Sossella Editore.

Von Furer-Haimendorf, C. (1964), *The Sherpas of Nepal*, Berkeley: University of California Press.

Wagner-Pacifici, R.E. (1986), *The Moro Morality Play: Terrorism and Social Drama*, Chicago: University of Chicago Press.

Warren, D.E. (2007), "Corporate scandals and spoiled identities: How organizations shift stigma to employees", *Business Ethics Quarterly*, 17 (3), pp. 477–496.

Warren, D.E. (2006), "Ethics initiatives: The problem of ethical subgroups". In E.B. Mannix, M. Neale, and A. Tenbrunsel, eds., *Research on Managing Groups and Teams: Ethics* (pp. 83–100), London: Elsevier Science Press.

Watzlawick, P., Beavin J.J., and Jackson D.D. (1967), *The Pragmatic of Human Communication*, New York: Norton.

Weaver, K.R. (1986), "The politics of blame avoidance", *Journal of Public Policy*, 6 (4), pp. 371–398.

Weeber, S.C. (2008), *An International Perspective on Political Scandals* (July), https://ssrn.com/abstract=2294030.

Weick, K.E. (1995), *Sensemaking in Organizations*, Thousand Oaks, CA: SAGE Publications.

Weick, K.E. (1990), "The vulnerable system: Analysis of the Tenerife air disaster", *Journal of Management*, 16 (3), pp. 571–593.

Weick, K.E. (1987), "Organizational culture as a source of high reliability", *California Management Review*, 29 (2), pp. 112–127.

Weick, K.E. (1985), "A stress analysis of future battlefields". In J.G. Hunt and J.D. Blair, eds., *Leadership on the Future Battlefield* (pp. 32–46), Washington, DC: Pergamon-Brassey's.

Weick, K.E. (1976), "Educational organization as loosely coupled systems", *Administrative Science Quarterly*, 21 (1), pp. 1–19.

Weick, K.E. and Sutcliffe, K.M. (2015), *Managing the Unexpected: Sustained Performance in a Complex World*, Hoboken: Wiley (3rd ed.).

Weick, K.E., Sutcliffe, K.M., and Obstfeld, D. (1999), "Organizing for high reliability: Processes of collective mindfulness". In B. Staw and R. Sutton, eds., *Organizational Behavior* (pp. 81–123), Stamford, CT: Jai Press Inc.

Weiner, B. (1986), *An Attributional Theory of Motivation and Emotion*, New York: Springer Verlag.

Westrum, R. (1995), "Organizational dynamics and safety". In N. McDonald, N.A. Johnston, and R. Fuller, eds., *Application of Psychology to the Aviation System* (pp. 75–80), Aldershot: Averbury Aviation.

Wiesenfeld, B.M., Wurthmann, K., and Hambrick, D.C. (2008), "The stigmatization and devaluation of elites associated with corporate failures: A process model", *Academy of Management Review*, 33 (1), pp. 231–251.

Wilkins, L. and Patterson, P. (1990), "The political amplification of risk: Media coverage of disasters and hazards". In J. Handmer and E. Penning-Roswell, eds., *Hazards and the Communication of Risk* (pp. 79–94), Aldershot: Gower Technical.

Wilson, P.E. (1993), "The fiction of corporate scapegoating", *Journal of Business Ethics*, 12 (10), pp. 779–784.

Woods, D.D., Dekker, S., Cook, R., Johannesen, L., and Sarter, N. (2010), *Behind Human Error*, Farnham: Ashgate.

Woodward, B. (2008), *The War Within: A Secret White House History, 2006–2008*, New York: Simon and Schuster.

Woodward, B. (2006), *State of Denial: Bush at War, Part III*, New York: Simon and Schuster.

Yan, S.C., Hulou, M.M., Cote, D.J., et al. (2016), "International defensive medicine in neurosurgery: Comparison of Canada, South Africa and United States", *World Neurosurgery*, 95, pp. 53–61.

Yin, T.K. (2018), *Case Study Research and Applications*, Thousand Oaks, CA: SAGE Publications.

Zald, M.N. (1990), "History, sociology and theories of organization". In J.E. Jackson, ed., *Institution in American Society. Essays in Market, Political, and Social Organizations* (pp. 81–106), Ann Arbor: The University of Michigan Press.

Zavyalova, A., Pfarrer, M.D., Reger, R.K., and Shapiro, D.L. (2012), "Managing the message: The effects of firm actions and industry spillovers on media coverage following wrongdoing", *Academy of Management Journal*, 55 (5), pp. 1079–1101.

Zhang, R., Wong, M.S., Toubiana, M., and Greenwood, R. (2021), "Stigma beyond levels: Advancing research on stigmatization", *Academy of Management Annals*, 15 (1), pp. 188–222.

Zimbardo, P. (2007), *The Lucifer Effect: How Good People Turn Evil*, New York: Random House.

Sources

The documents and materials used for the analysis of the *Costa Concordia* case are listed below.

Judicial Documents

Preliminary Investigation

Court of Grosseto (Tribunale di Grosseto) (2012), *Verbale dell'interrogatorio di Francesco Schettino*, Ufficio del GIP, January 17 (pp. 151).

Port Captaincy of Livorno (Capitaneria di porto di Livorno) (2012), *Inchiesta sommaria relativa al sinistro marittimo. Naufragio della nave da crociera Costa Concordia*, October 4 (pp. 134).

Public Prosecutor's Office, Court of Grosseto (Procura della Repubblica presso il Tribunale di Grosseto) (2012), *Processo verbale di presentazione e deposito di consulenza tecnica*, October 18 (pp. 63).

Public Prosecutor's Office, Court of Grosseto (Procura della Repubblica presso il Tribunale di Grosseto) (2013a), *Fascicolo del Pubblico Ministero, Procedimento penale n. 12/285* (pp. 451).

Public Prosecutor's Office, Court of Grosseto (Procura della Repubblica presso il Tribunale di Grosseto) (2013b), *Richiesta di rinvio a giudizio*, February 25 (pp. 707).

Special Evidence Pretrial Hearing

Court of Grosseto (Tribunale di Grosseto), (2012a), *Consulenza tecnica di parte nell'interesse delle persone offese*, Ufficio del GIP, January 31 (pp. 10).

Court of Grosseto (Tribunale di Grosseto) (2012b), *Memoria ex art. 393 c.p.p. datata 28.02.2012 – Atti per la richiesta di estensione dell'incidente probatorio* (2 files, pp. 1716).

Court of Grosseto (Tribunale di Grosseto) (2012c), *Verbale di udienza di incidente probatorio*, March 3 (pp. 18).

Court of Grosseto (Tribunale di Grosseto) (2012d), *Relazione tecnica dei consulenti nominati dal GIP*, Ufficio del GIP, September 11 (pp. 270).

Court of Grosseto (Tribunale di Grosseto) (2012e), *Verbale di udienza di incidente probatorio*, Ufficio del GIP, October 15 (pp. 62).

Court of Grosseto (Tribunale di Grosseto) (2012f), *Verbale di udienza di incidente probatorio*, Ufficio del GIP, October 16 (pp. 145).

Court of Grosseto (Tribunale di Grosseto) (2012g), *Verbale di udienza di incidente probatorio*, Ufficio del GIP, October 17 (pp. 156).

First Instance Judgement

Court of Grosseto (Tribunale di Grosseto) (2013), *Sentenza di patteggiamento*, Ufficio del GIP, July 20 (pp. 23).

Court of Grosseto (Tribunale di Grosseto) (2013a), *Relazione Perizia tecnico-fonica*, 24 September (pp. 45).

Court of Grosseto (Tribunale di Grosseto) (2013b), *Trascrizione Perizia tecnico-fonica*, (pp. 207).

Court of Grosseto (Tribunale di Grosseto) (2014), *Verbale di udienza*, Corte d'Assise, June 30 (pp. 97).

Court of Grosseto (Tribunale di Grosseto) (2014a), *Verbale di udienza*, Corte d'Assise, July 1 (pp. 150).

Court of Grosseto (Tribunale di Grosseto) (2014b), *Verbale di udienza*, Corte d'Assise, July 2 (pp. 138).

Court of Grosseto (Tribunale di Grosseto) (2014c), *Verbale di udienza*, Corte d'Assise, July 3 (pp. 351).

Court of Grosseto (Tribunale di Grosseto) (2014d), *Verbale di udienza*, Corte d'Assise, July 4 (pp. 60).

Court of Grosseto (Tribunale di Grosseto) (2014e), *Verbale di udienza*, Corte d'Assise, October 8 (pp. 59).

Court of Grosseto (Tribunale di Grosseto) (2014f), *Verbale di udienza*, Corte d'Assise, December 2 (pp. 211).

Court of Grosseto (Tribunale di Grosseto) (2014g), *Verbale di udienza*, Corte d'Assise, December 3 (pp. 238).

Court of Grosseto (Tribunale di Grosseto) (2014h), *Verbale di udienza*, Corte d'Assise, December 11 (pp. 252).

Court of Grosseto (Tribunale di Grosseto) (2014i), *Verbale di udienza*, Corte d'Assise, December 12 (pp. 177).

Court of Grosseto (Tribunale di Grosseto) (2014l), *Verbale di udienza*, Corte d'Assise, December 13 (pp. 129).

Court of Grosseto (Tribunale di Grosseto) (2014m), *Verbale di udienza*, Corte d'Assise, December 17 (pp. 137).

Court of Grosseto (Tribunale di Grosseto) (2015), *Sentenza di primo grado del disastro Costa Concordia – Francesco Schettino*, July 10 (pp. 553).

Second Instance Judgement

Florence Court of Appeal (Corte d'Appello di Firenze) (2016), *Sentenza – Francesco Schettino*, May 31 (pp. 686).

Court of Cassation Appeals

Supreme Court of Cassation (Corte Suprema di Cassazione) (2017), *Sentenza – Francesco Schettino*, May 12 (pp. 151).

Other Materials

Court of Grosseto (Tribunale di Grosseto) (2015), *Audio della Requisitoria del P.M. Leopizzi*, Corte d'Assise, January 22 (duration 2.44.54).

Florence Court of Appeal (Corte d'Appello di Firenze) (2016), *Audio della Requisitoria del P.G. Ferrucci*, May 20 (duration 41.09).

Florence Court of Appeal (Corte d'Appello di Firenze) (2016), *Audio dell'Arringa dell'Avv. Senese*, May 20 (duration 3.58.22).

Florence Court of Appeal (Corte d'Appello di Firenze) (2016), *Audio delle Repliche del Avv. Senese*, May 27 (duration 1.50.05).

Florence Court of Appeal (Corte d'Appello di Firenze) (2016), *Audio delle Repliche del Avv. Senese*, May 27 (duration 54.01).

Videos

Costa Concordia AIS video a few minutes before the accident until the ship is stopped.

AIS video of the sail-by salute carried out on the island of Giglio on August 14, 2011 with the *Costa Concordia* by a different captain.

Voyage Data Recorder (VDR) recordings, complete with all relevant voyage data of the ship.

Technical and Administrative Investigations and Other Documents

Civil Protection (Protezione Civile) (2012), *The Costa Concordia Shipwreck Summary of Emergency Response Management*, Report a cura del Dipartimento della Protezione civile – Ufficio gestione delle emergenze (pp. 51).

European Union Civil Protection Team (2012), *Report: Observation Mission Giglio Island*, January 26–29 (pp. 17).

Italian Maritime Investigative Body on Marine Accidents (2012), *Marine Accident Investigation C/S Costa Concordia 13th January 2012*, May 18, London (pp. 61).

Ministry of Infrastructure and Transports (2012), *Report on the Safety Technical Investigation, Marine Casualties Investigative Body: Cruise Ship Costa Concordia* (pp. 181).

Senate of the Republic (Senato della Repubblica) (2012), *Indagine conoscitiva sulla sicurezza della navigazione marittima, con riferimento al tragico incidente che si è verificato al largo dell'isola del Giglio nella notte del gennaio 13 2012*, 6 sessions from January 25 to February 9, 2012.

Senate of the Republic (Senato della Repubblica) (2012), *Resoconto stenografico, 8° commissione permanente, 356ᵃ seduta*, January 26 (pp. 28).

World Maritime University (2013), *From Titanic to Costa Concordia a century of lessons not learnt*, December 4, Nottingham (pp. 31).

Videos

Videos Provided by Captain Schettino

- L'onore del marinaio ("Sailor's Honor"): https://video.ilmattino.it/primopiano/francescoschettinoonoremarinaio-2311182.html
- Scomode verità ("Inconvenient truths"): www.youtube.com/watch?v=P7LEz3WlBwg
- La norma e la coscienza ("The norm and conscience"): www.youtube.com/watch?v=5007zVcw4b4

Other Videos

Interview with Captain Francesco Schettino, edited by Codacons:
First part: www.youtube.com/watch?v=vitfdF0dBWk (34:56)
Second part: www.youtube.com/watch?v=L6Sy_4u7STA (28:15)
Third part: www.youtube.com/watch?v=Xr7503yRjjA (32.47)

Norms and Regulations

Directive 2002/59/EC of the European Parliament and of the Council of June 27, 2002 establishing a community vessel traffic monitoring and information system and repealing Council Directive 93/75/EEC.

Guidelines for Vessel Traffic Services, IMO Resolution A.857(20), adopted on November 27, 1997.

International Maritime Organization (2010), *International Safety Management Code (ISM)*, London.

International Maritime Organization (1974, 1980), *International Convention for the Safety of Life at Sea (SOLAS)*, www.imo.org/en/About/Conventions/Pages/International-Convention-for-the-Safety-of-Life-at-Sea-(SOLAS),-1974.aspx, concluded in London on November 1, 1974.

Italian Law n. 51, March 7, 2001 containing Provisions for prevention of pollution deriving from the maritime transport of hydrocarbons and for maritime traffic control.

Italian Ministerial Decree n. 56, March 7, 2012, containing General provisions to limit or prohibit the transit of merchant ships for the protection of sensitive areas in the territorial sea.

Interviews, Conversations and Email Correspondence

Lawyers for several people indicted for trial: 5; Captain Francesco Schettino: numerous email communications and video conversations; Investigative journalists who followed the investigation: 3; Experts in navigation law: 1; Ship designers: 3; Experts in transport safety: 1; Helicopter pilot, member of the accident rescue team: 1; Inhabitants of the islands of Giglio and Elba: 3.

Index

Printed in the United States
by Baker & Taylor Publisher Services